Work-Based Learning

Level 3
NVQ

MANAGEMENT

Bethan Bithell

Nigel Parton

Bernadette Watkins

ALWAYS LEARNING

PEARSON

Published by Pearson Education Limited, Edinburgh Gate, Harlow, Essex, CM20 2JE.

Heinemann is a registered trademark of Pearson Education Limited

www.pearsonschoolsandfecolleges.co.uk

Text © Pearson Education Limited 2012

Edited by Julia Bruce
Designed by Tek-Art
Typeset by Phoenix Photosetting, Chatham, Kent
Index by Indexing Specialists (UK) Ltd
Original illustrations © Pearson Education Ltd
Cover design by Pearson Education Ltd
Cover photo/illustration © **Alamy Images**: Gary Wainwright

The rights of Bethan Bithell, Nigel Parton and Bernadette Watkins to be identified as authors of this work has been asserted by them in accordance with the Copyright, Designs and Patents Act 1988.

First published 2012

15 14 13
10 9 8 7 6 5 4 3 2

British Library Cataloguing in Publication Data
A catalogue record for this book is available from the British Library

ISBN 978 0 435 07786 0

Printed in Great Britain by Ashford Colour Press Ltd

Acknowledgements
The authors and publisher would like to thank the following individuals and organisations for permission to reproduce photographs:

Alamy Images: ableimages 122, Adam Parker 276, Bernd Tschakert 42, Fancy 35, Jeff Morgan 09, 222, Juice Images 48, 157, Laura Doss/Fancy 255; **Corbis:** Chicasso/Blend Images 62, Ira L. Black 124, Jetta Productions/Blend Images 202, Joel Rogers 170, Randy Faris 74; **Getty Images:** Assembly/The Image Bank 2, Chris Parker/Axiom Photographic Agency 260, Gary John Norman/Stone 192, Kirby Lee 216, Simon Roberts 238, thenakedsnail 10, Tom Pidgeon 98; **Press Association Images:** Ng Han Guan/AP 26; **Shutterstock.com:** abd 214, AJP 236, Andresr 134, baranq 56, IKO 96, Joe Gough 88, Mehmet Dilsiz 190, Michal Kowalski 198, Tamara Kulikova 146, Warren Goldswain 24, Wong Yu Liang 258, Yuri Arcurs 45; **Workplace Products:** 89

All other images © Pearson Education

We are grateful to the following for permission to reproduce copyright material:

Figures
Figures A2 and D13 'Honey and Mumford's Learning Cycle' in *The Manual of Learning Styles*, Peter Honey Publications (Honey, P., and Mumford, A. 1986). Reproduced with permission of Pearson Education Ltd; Figures A2, D5, and D10 from Motivation and Personality, 3rd edition (Maslow, A.H., and eds Frager, R.D., Fadiman, J.) copyright © 1987. Printed and electronically reproduced by permission of Pearson Education, Inc., Upper Saddle River, New Jersey; Figure B5 from 'Team Roles' by Meredith Belbin, www.belbin.com. Reproduced with kind permission of Belbin Associates; Figures B5 and E10 from "How to Choose a Leadership Pattern", Harvard Business Review, Vol 36, pp.95–101 (Robert Tannenbaum and Warren H. Schmidt 1958), copyright © 1958 by the President and Fellows of Harvard College. All Rights Reserved; Figure B6 from John Adair's model on working with others http://www.johnadair.co.uk/, copyright © John Adair; Figure B6 from 'The managerial grid', Advanced Management Office Executive, Vol 1 (9) (Blake, R.R. and Moulton, J.S. (adapted by James R Martin) 1962), copyright © Society for Advancement of Management. Reproduced by permission of Society for Advancement of Management and Professor James R. Martin; Figure B10b from "HSG65, Successful Health and Safety Management", www.hse.gov.uk, Contains public sector information published by the Health and Safety Executive and licensed under the Open Government Licence v1.0; Figure C6 from 'PDSA cycle' in The New Economics for Industry, Government, Education, Second Edition, The MIT Press (Deming, W.E.) Figure 13, p.132, copyright © 2000 Massachusetts Institute of Technology, by permission of The MIT Press and The W.Edwards Deming Institute; Figure C6 and F1 from Defining the "Field at a Given Time", Psychological Review, Vol 50, pp.292–310 (Lewin, K. 1943), copyright © American Psychological Association; and Figure D10 adapted from 'Conflict and Negotiation Process in Organizations' in Handbook of Industrial and Organizational Psychology, 2nd edition, Consulting Psychologists Press, Palo Alto, CA (, K. Eds Dunnette, M.D., and Hough, L.H. 1992) Vol 3, p.660, copyright © 1992 by L. M. Hough. Adapted by permission.

Logos
Logo C6 from RNLI, www.rnli.org.uk. Reproduced with kind permission from RNLI.

Screenshots
Screenshot D5 from MS Project screenshot. Microsoft product screenshot reprinted with permission from Microsoft Corporation.

Tables
Table B5 from "Developmental sequence in small groups", Psychological Bulletin, Vol 63 (6), pp.384-399 (Bruce Tuckman 1965), Group Facilitation, Spring 2001. Source: American Psychological Association.

Text
Extract B6 from "Finding the missing spark!" by Anthony Landale, 26 September 2011, www.futureengagedeliver.com/09/2011/finding-the-missing-spark/. Reproduced by permission of Anthony Landale.

Every effort has been made to contact copyright holders of material reproduced in this book. Any omissions will be rectified in subsequent printings if notice is given to the publishers.

Websites
Pearson Education Limited is not responsible for the content of any external internet sites. It is essential for tutors to preview each website before using it in class so as to ensure that the URL is still accurate, relevant and appropriate. We suggest that tutors bookmark useful websites and consider enabling students to access them through the school/college intranet.

Contents

NVQ Unit numbers

The unit numbers used in this book are those used by the Council for Administration (CfA), the Sector Skills Body for Management. However, awarding organisations use different unit numbering within their specifications. The table below maps the unit numbers of the most popular awarding organisations to the CfA numbering.

	Edexcel	EDI	ILM	OCR
A2: Manage own professional development within an organisation	1	CU868	L/600/958	A02
B5: Set objectives and provide support for team members	2	CU761	M/600/9600	B05
D5: Plan, allocate and monitor work of a team	3	CU858	Y/600/9669	D05
B6: Provide leadership and direction for own area of responsibility	5	CU762	T/600/9601	B06
B10b: Manage risk in own area of responsibility	7	CU870	L/600/9619	B10b
C6: Implement change in own area of responsibility	12	CU873	M/600/9659	C06
D2a: Develop working relationships with colleagues and stakeholders	13	CU856	H/600/9660	D02a
D10: Manage conflict in a team	20	CU861	R/600/9685	D10
D11: Lead and manage meetings	21	CU862	Y/600/9686	D11
D13: Support individuals to develop and take responsibility for their performance	23	CU874	D/600/9690	D13
E10: Make effective decisions	30	CU864	F/600/9715	E10
F1: Plan and manage a project	35	CU883	J/600/9750	F01

How to use this book

This book has been written to help you achieve your NVQ Level 3 qualification. It covers the mandatory units and a range of optional units from the 2010 standards, giving you a broad choice of content to match your needs.

Throughout you will find the following learning features.

Key Terms

Essential terminology and phrases are explained in clear and accessible language. Where these appear in the book, the first instance of the word appears in **bold** so you know there is a definition nearby.

Activity · 30 minutes

Use these tasks to apply your knowledge, understanding and skills. These activities will help you to develop your understanding of the underpinning theory and key techniques you will need in your day-to-day working life.

Each activity includes a suggested time for completion, which will help you to keep track of your learning.

Portfolio Task · 45 minutes

These are tasks that cover grading criteria from the NVQ standards. You can use these tasks to generate evidence for your portfolio. You should discuss the activities with your assessor to agree what types of evidence can be gathered.

Functional Skills

You may be taking Functional Skills alongside your NVQ – if so, these are opportunities for you to apply your English or mathematics skills in a team leading role.

Checklist

These features help you to identify important information or steps in a task that need to be completed.

Team talk

See how the unit applies to the real world of work, and receive best-practice hints and tips for making the most of your time in the workplace.

Links to Technical Certificate

If you are taking your NVQ as part of an Apprenticeship, you will need to complete a Technical Certificate qualification. Key topics from the Technical Certificate are covered in more detail within units of the NVQ, as identified through this feature. There is a range of different qualifications that can be used as the Technical Certificate, so check with your assessor which qualification you will be completing.

www.contentextra.com/management

The accompanying website holds a grid to map topics from the Technical Certificate to the NVQ qualifications. The website can be accessed using the following details:

Username: Management
Password: Handbook

Unit A2 Manage own professional development within an organisation

This unit looks at the importance of identifying and evaluating the skills and knowledge needed to be an effective manager and leader. The main purpose of this unit is to explore the ways in which you can identify and assess your career and personal goals and ways of realising those goals.

In your workplace, you are likely to have appraisal meetings with your manager to discuss your future development. During these meetings you will put in place objectives that will help you to monitor the achievement of your goals.

Staff appraisal meetings can be used to:

- identify your strengths and weaknesses
- assist you in assessing your current level of job performance
- assist you in improving your performance
- motivate you to develop yourself
- identify your potential performance problems
- identify your skills and knowledge gaps.

All of the above will be discussed to some extent during this unit.

What you will learn:

- Be able to assess own career goals and personal development
- Be able to set personal work objectives
- Be able to produce a personal development plan
- Be able to implement and monitor own personal development plan

Links to Technical Certificate

If you are completing your NVQ as part of an Apprenticeship Framework, you will find the following topics are also covered in your Technical Certificate:

- Improving own management and leadership performance
- Understanding how to assess career and personal goals

Be able to assess own career goals and personal development

It is likely that your personality traits and characteristics will have driven you to pursue your particular choice of career. You may have had some idea of what career path you would like to follow from a young age and perhaps advice from careers advisers will have helped you to reach a final decision.

Identify own career and personal goals

Knowing where you would like your career path to take you helps you to set your personal goals and objectives to assist with realising your ambitions. Consider the simple but effective three-part personal action plan in Figure A2.1.

Your personal action plan can help you to plan your career path in detail. You can set objectives for yourself (Where do I want to be?) and put strategies in place to help you to achieve your personal objectives (How will I get there?).

Having completed your personal action plan and having devised your personal objectives, your next step is to develop strategies that will help you to achieve your objectives. A useful tool to help with this process is a traditional action plan. A suggested template that you can use is shown in Figure A2.2.

An action plan similar to this will enable you and your managers to identify clear actions that will help you to achieve your personal objectives and career goals.

To make sure you identify a career that you will enjoy and will be comfortable pursuing, you should consider your:

- likes and dislikes
- **characteristics** and **attributes**
- work-related experience to date
- strengths and weaknesses
- skills, competencies and knowledge
- ability to work well as part of a team or as an individual.

Name: Beth Greene	
Period from: August 2012	**To:** Sept 2012

1. Where am I now?
I currently work as a First Line manager overseeing the work of 11 operatives on Red shift.

2. Where do I want to be?
  a. In one year: enrol on a middle managers' course as an aspiring middle manager
  b. In two years: shadow and receive coaching from an experienced production manager
  c. In five years: work as a production manager at middle management level

3. How will I get there?
  a. Select most appropriate course for aspiring middle managers and discuss cost, location etc. with line manager and HR manager
  b. Through negotiation with line manager and HR manager organise shadowing of an experienced production manager and organise coaching sessions from an experienced production manager
  c. Apply for internal vacancies for production manager or related middle management positions

Date for review: 30th September 2012

Employee signature: **Date:**

Manager signature: **Date:**

Figure A2.1 An example of a personal action plan.

Name:						
Job Title:						
Date:						
Action/Task	**By whom**	**By when**	**Resources needed**	**Completion date**	**Review date**	**Manager signature**
Obtain information and enrol upon a middle management level training course	Myself	30 May 2012	Time/Fees Materials Information	31 July 2012	28 Nov 2012	
Organise shadowing of an experienced production manager	Myself HR Line manager	30 June 2012	Time	30 June 2012	30 Sept 2012	
Implement coaching sessions from experienced production manager	Myself Line manager HR Production manager	30 June 2012	Learning style Inventory Training plan Time Review sheets	30 June 2012	30 Nov 2012	

Figure A2.2 Sample action plan template.

Key Terms

Characteristics – your character e.g. good humoured.
Attributes – the qualities you have e.g. hard working.

Activity ⏱ 30 minutes

Using the bullet point list on page 4 as a guide, identify a career that you believe you would enjoy and be comfortable with. Write down your responses and show them to your assessor.

SWOT Analysis

A SWOT analysis is a tool that will help you to analyse your own strengths, weaknesses, opportunities and threats. SWOT stands for:

- Strengths
- Weaknesses
- Opportunities
- Threats

In terms of meeting your own personal objectives and career goals, you can draw up a SWOT analysis to identify your strengths and any areas that might need some improvement. Examine the example in Figure A2.3.

Strengths	Weaknesses
• Good communication skills • Approachable • Knowledgeable • Technically minded • Good time keeping	• Unassertive nature • Poor negotiation skills • Not good dealing with conflict
Opportunities	**Threats**
• Middle management training course • Assertiveness training • Conflict resolution training	• Nervous at interviews • Not willing to relocate • No time to attend training sessions due to family commitments

Figure A2.3 SWOT analysis – personal career goals.

Personality traits and career choice

The theorist John Holland carried out research on the links between a person's type of personality and their likely career choice.

The chart below is based upon Holland's work and illustrates how career goals might be influenced by someone's personality.

Personality trait	Typical choice of career
Realistic A person who likes physical work or being outdoors. A person who likes to be hands on and mechanically minded.	Forestry, farming, building work, cooks, auto mechanics
Investigative A person who likes to work with data and enjoys organising and understanding it. This person tends to be a problem solver and uses technical ability to complete tasks.	Statistician, engineering, computer analysts
Social A caring person who likes to work closely with others. Helpful and caring person who tends to co-operate.	Social work, teaching, religion, nurses
Conventional A person who is well-organised, methodical and likes to have rules in place. This person is a loyal follower and has traditional views.	Accounting, military, administration, book keeping
Artistic A person who likes to express ideas, feelings and is imaginative. Rewards creativity.	Design, entertainment, advertising, musical directors
Enterprising A person who likes conversation and persuading others. Likes to gain power and status and enjoy a lot of activities. Enjoys leading a project and is entrepreneurial.	Publishing, sales, employee relations, sales representatives

Table A2.1 How career goals might be influenced by someone's personality.

Portfolio Task 1 — 45 minutes

Links to LO1: Assessment criterion 1.1
Make a list of your personal objectives and career goals. Consider your achievements to date and the opportunities available to you. Discuss your list with your assessor.

PLTS

By completing this activity, you will assess your current performance, identify opportunities and achievements and set future goals (RL1, 2, 3).

Assess how own career goals affect work role and professional development

Your managers may already encourage you to continuously develop yourself, for instance by offering you opportunities to acquire new skills through attending training courses. This process is often referred to as **continuous professional development (CPD)**. Your professional development will help you to become more effective and efficient in your work, which in turn, means that you will be helping your organisation to meet its targets. Your development opportunities are likely to be identified, agreed and reviewed in your staff appraisal meetings.

Key Term

Continuous professional development (CPD) – when employees are given opportunity to gain new skills and knowledge through work-related training.

Remember

Your staff appraisals give you the opportunity to discuss your identified career goals with your manager and to work out how your professional development activity can help you to achieve them.

It is important to assess how your identified career goals might affect your current work role. You should therefore evaluate your work activities so you can reflect upon:

- what you do well
- what areas might need improvement
- how what you do now can help you to further your career.

Being aware of both your current workplace activities and your personal career goals will help you to identify gaps in the skills and knowledge you possess and to identify where professional development activity will be needed. You can then discuss your findings with your manager to agree how you can progress with your career plans.

Expectations

When assessing your current work role and how your skills, competencies and attributes might help you to achieve your career goals, you may find it useful to reflect upon what your organisation expects of a good manager. Some of these expectations may include:

- being an effective communicator
- being effective at dealing with relationship difficulties, such as conflict situations
- managing time effectively
- being approachable
- being a good decision maker and involving others in the process
- managing resources effectively (including managing budgets)
- understanding the needs of your stakeholders
- having good knowledge of the product or service you provide
- supporting others – especially those you manage
- acting within the limits of the authority given to you
- identifying your development needs, the needs of those you manage and the needs of your organisation.

Being aware of your career goals and ambitions may encourage you to examine your current role in more detail.

Portfolio Task 2 ⏲ 60 minutes

Links to LO1: Assessment criterion 1.2
Examine how the skills, knowledge and competencies that you currently possess can help you to work towards your identified career goals.

1. Make a list of your current skills and competencies.

2. Make a list of the skills and competencies you think you will need to fulfil your career ambitions.

3. Assess the gap between the skills and competencies you have now and those you will need in the future.

4. List typical training activities that will help you to build on those skills and competencies you think you need to improve upon.

Discuss your responses with your assessor.

PLTS

By completing this task you will be engaging with issues that affect your job role. You will provide a persuasive case to your assessor and propose practical ways forward to deal with the issues you face (EP 1, 2, 3).

An assessment of your future career goals might affect your current work role in the following ways.

- You could become more committed to your organisation's business **objectives**.
- You could be willing to take your organisation's **policies** and **procedures** more seriously and develop a deeper understanding of them.
- You could become focused on what other managers are doing in the organisation and how well they do it.

> **Key Terms**
>
> **Policies** – written statements set by managers that everybody must follow e.g. no smoking policy.
>
> **Procedures** – ways of doing something e.g. a filing procedure will outline how to store and organise documents correctly.
>
> **Objective** – what you want to achieve.

All of the above can help you to think about ways you can build upon what you do now in work, to help you to achieve your career goals and ambitions in the future.

When assessing how your career goals affect your work role and professional development, you must remain positive at all times. If you feel that your current role doesn't help you to achieve your career goals then you could easily become demotivated, which may affect your performance and prevent you from meeting your targets.

Be able to set personal work objectives

Ideally, your personal objectives should be SMART, this means that they should be:

- Specific
- Measurable
- Achievable
- Realistic
- Timebound.

For example, if one of your objectives is 'To work towards becoming a middle manager', this is not SMART as it doesn't state how you

intend to achieve this, or by when. If you rewrite your objective as 'To enrol on an ILM Level 4 Management course to help me to work towards middle management status by 30 November 2012' then you have some idea of how you intend to achieve your objective and by when. Of course, while this makes your objective more specific, to make it completely SMART you would also need to reflect upon how *realistic* and *achievable* it is, for instance in terms of your time, your organisation's training budget and so on.

Agree SMART personal work objectives in line with organisational objectives

The SMART personal work objectives that you agree with your manager should be in line with your organisation's SMART business objectives. This means that wherever possible your personal work objectives should, in some way, assist your organisation to achieve its own business objectives. Base your personal SMART objectives on:

- what your current main responsibilities are
- what you have done over the last six months
- what knowledge and skills you have learnt over the last six months
- how your new knowledge and skills can be put to good use.

Your objectives should also consider:

- what you haven't done well over the last six months
- what further professional development is needed to improve what you do.

> **Remember**
>
> To achieve your ambitions and career goals, you have to be honest about what you are not doing well currently. It is only by finding ways to improve that you can work towards your career goals with confidence.

It is important to examine how achieving your personal work objectives will also help your organisation to achieve its overall business objectives. If one of your organisation's objectives is to increase sales volume by ten per cent by

30 March next year, for instance, then your department or team will have specific targets to meet (as will other departments) to help the organisation achieve this objective. In turn, each team member and their managers will have personal objectives set for them and these are likely to be agreed during staff appraisal interviews.

Figure A2.4 How objectives are achieved within an organisation.

Figure A2.4 illustrates how every individual and every department or team helps the organisation to achieve its overall objectives. Without everyone knowing what their own objectives are, and how these link to the organisation's objectives, it is unlikely that the organisation will be successful.

Management by objectives

Many years ago, management theorist Peter Drucker devised a method of dividing the business objectives of an organisation into smaller departmental or team objectives. He believed that

each individual's personal development would be enhanced if they have a good understanding of:

- what their line manager's own objectives for the department or team are
- how their line manager intends to achieve their department's or team's objectives.

Peter Drucker called this process 'management by objectives' (MBO) and suggested that if managers are to be responsible for achieving their department's/team's objectives, then each of their team members must, in turn, understand how their own personal work objectives link to the achievement of these.

Drucker identified a six stage process of management by objective:

- Stage 1: At senior level, clearly define the corporate objectives.
- Stage 2: Analyse and evaluate the management tasks and set out clear formal job specifications which identify allocated responsibilities and decisions to specific managers.
- Stage 3: Discuss and set out performance standards.
- Stage 4: Agree and set out specific objectives to individuals.
- Stage 5: Devise and set individual targets with the corporate objectives identified above.
- Stage 6: Monitor achievement of the objectives by establishing a management information system.

By agreeing SMART personal work objectives, you and your manager can assess how well these will help you – and the team you manage – to work towards your organisation's business objectives. This means that you and your line manager will discuss and explore opportunities for you to:

- develop yourself professionally within the organisation
- have one-to-one discussions to review your progress with your manager on a regular basis
- monitor how well you are working towards the achievement of your personal objectives by measuring outcomes periodically.

Activity 🕐 45 minutes

Write a brief description of how you think your personal work objectives link to your organisation's business objectives.

Discuss your responses with your assessor.

Remember

If everyone works together to ensure that your organisation meets its business objectives, jobs are more likely to remain secure. This highlights the importance of everyone achieving their personal work objectives – and why personal development is so important.

An example of a modern company that puts these principles into practice is Vodafone. The company believes that through developing its managers, who each have identified personal objectives, it will improve its business performance, helping it to meet its organisational objectives. Following from this, in 2007, as part of their Leadership and Development Strategy Vodafone introduced a scheme to develop its managers.

Training activities

Once your development opportunities have been agreed, your training activities must be identified and could take a number of forms.

- On the job training – to develop your existing skills and enhance your working knowledge you might shadow a more experienced member of staff. Alternatively, you may receive coaching or mentoring or attend in-house training courses.

- Off the job training – to enhance your existing knowledge and learn new skills, you may attend

Completing a distance learning course could be just one type of training activity you undertake.

a college or a private training provider for training sessions.

- Distance learning – to learn new skills and competencies by studying selected topic areas you might enrol on a correspondence course, where you receive learning materials to study independently and send work off to be marked. You will then receive feedback from your tutor. Alternatively, you might enrol on an e-learning course where you are tutored online.

Through further discussion with your line manager, you should develop a plan that will take into account your training and development needs. It is often useful to draw up a plan similar to the one below.

Identified opportunities for development	Skills/knowledge gap	SMART objective	Resources needed and/or support from others	Training opportunities
To be more assertive when dealing with conflict situations in my team	How to manage conflict	To successfully complete a conflict management course by 31 March	Staff time, training material, training budget	Two-day course at a local training provider's premises

Figure A2.5 An example development plan.

If you use a plan similar to Table A2.5 on page 10, not only does it identify your personal SMART objectives, but it also enables you and your manager to be clear about what you have agreed.

Remember

When agreeing your personal work objectives, it is a good idea not to set too many at the same time. Often, being faced with too many objectives can be overwhelming, resulting in loss of confidence and feelings of insecurity.

Portfolio Task 3 ⏱ 45 minutes

Links to LO2: Assessment criterion 2.1

In order to help your organisation meet its business objectives it is necessary to set SMART personal work objectives. You will have discussed and agreed your SMART objectives with your manager during your last appraisal meeting and you will have completed a personal development plan. Prepare a 500-word document identifying:

- how you agreed your SMART objectives with your manager
- how you made sure these objectives were in line with the organisation's objectives and the importance of doing so.

Discuss your personal development plan and your 500-word document with your assessor.

PLTS

By completing this task you will be reflecting upon what you have learnt in the past. You will communicate your learning to your assessor (RL6).

Functional Skills

By completing this portfolio task, it will give you the opportunity to practise your Functional Skills in ICT at Level 2. By preparing your 500-word document on a computer, you will be developing, presenting and communicating information. In addition, you will be practising your Level 2 Functional Skills in English.

Be able to produce a personal development plan

Your personal work objectives will have been set to reflect your future personal development needs and your SWOT analysis will have identified your current strengths along with any areas that may need improving.

Identify gaps between objectives set, own current knowledge and skills

You may now find it useful to compare the knowledge and skills needed for your current work role with the knowledge and skills you will need for your future identified work roles. Managers often refer to this process as a **skills audit**.

Key Term

Skills audit – reviewing of existing skills against the skills needed to complete a task.

Audit your skills

Skills audits are conducted by organisations to identify the existing skills of their staff and to help to identify any skills gaps. Steps can then be taken to train existing staff in order to fill those gaps or, alternatively, new members of staff can be recruited who already possess the missing skills.

Similarly, you can conduct a personal skills audit, which will enable you to identify:

- the knowledge and skills you have now
- the knowledge and skills you will need to meet your smart objectives and further your career
- the training, learning and development you will need to undertake to fill your identified skills gaps.

Remember

The mix of skills and knowledge that you – and every other employee – possess will collectively contribute to the achievement of your organisation's business objectives.

11

Identifying skill gaps

There are many ways you can identify your skill gaps including:

- Staff appraisals – a discussion between you and your line manager, which should take place every six or twelve months. Your current and previous performance will be reviewed and your future development needs identified. These development needs can be translated into personal work objectives enabling you to plan how you wish to progress in your organisation. A personal development plan is often agreed and drawn up during this process.

- Monthly supervision meetings – these will enable you and your manager to examine the progress you are making towards the achievement of your objectives and whether you are closing the gaps between your current skills and knowledge and those you need to achieve your and the organisation's ambitions.

- Continuous Professional Development (CPD) – a process whereby employees are encouraged to keep up-to-date with the latest ideas and changes taking place in their industry. If your organisation promotes CPD, you will be encouraged to attend training courses and update sessions to help you gain additional skills and knowledge.

Remember

In some organisations a staff appraisal is referred to as a professional development review (PDR).

Some of the ways you can assess your current skills, knowledge and competencies include:

- an examination of your job description and **person specification** to assess how well you carry out your work tasks and meet your essential requirements

Key Term

Person specification – a document that identifies the essential and desirable skills and knowledge to complete a job role.

- an examination of your workplace policies to assess how well you adhere to them and how often you refer to them

- an examination of your department's or team's procedures to assess how they impact upon your current job role – and how well you adhere to them.

Person specification

To help you to identify the knowledge and skills you will need to meet your personal objectives, you should ask your line manager or your human resources manager for examples of person specifications. For example, if your objective is to work towards becoming a middle manager, then you should examine a person specification that your human resources department has issued to applicants for a middle management position in the past. This document will outline the desirable and essential skills and knowledge required to be a middle manager. It will give you some idea of the skill gaps you may need to fill.

Activity 🕐 30 minutes

Think back to your identified SMART personal objectives and identify which of the skills listed below you currently possess and which you will need to meet your personal objectives. This will help you to decide which areas you need to improve upon:

- organisational
- interpersonal
- leadership and management
- IT
- technical
- numerical
- communication
- problem solving.

Remember

Some of the skills you currently possess will be transferable. This means you will be able to use them in a variety of jobs and settings. An example would be your communication skills.

Job Title:	**Payroll supervisor**	
Department:	**Finance**	
Location:	**Southport**	
Requirements	**Essential**	**Desirable**
Personal attributes	Good communication skills Well organised Good timekeeping Meeting deadlines	Work as part of a team Work on own initiative

Knowledge/ qualification	GCSE English Grade C or above
	GCSE Maths Grade C or above
	RSA Word and Text Processing
	Knowledge of:
	    employment law
	    SAGE accounts
	    payroll systems
		Management NVQ Level 3

Experience	Controlling payroll Maintaining financial documentation e.g. ledgers, profit and loss etc.	Some payroll management experience

Figure A2.6 An example of a person specification.

The format of a person specification may look similar to the example in Figure A2.6.

> **Remember**
>
> A copy of a person specification will give you some idea of the generic skills and knowledge required, but some of the skills listed will be specific to particular roles, such as those required for someone working in finance.

To recap, you need to be fully aware of the SMART personal objectives you have agreed with your line manager and of your current skills, knowledge and competencies. You probably will have identified a gap between your existing skills and knowledge and the skills and knowledge you need to be able to achieve your personal objectives.

You can learn a lot about yourself and your current skills set through self-analysis. It is useful to be honest with yourself about how well you put your knowledge and skills to good use and you can consider this by responding to the following statements as honestly as you can.

- I am quick to resolve any problems my team members have.
- I encourage the team I manage to raise standards continuously.

- I am an effective communicator.
- I am approachable and have good interpersonal skills.
- I am very supportive and protect the team I manage.

You could develop this process further and produce a self-appraisal form, to keep as a record of your own skills and competencies.

Date of self assessment:
My views on my skills and competencies: **1.** The quality of my work **2.** My ability to manage and lead my team effectively **3.** My ability to plan work with my team to meet targets **4.** My technical skills **5.** My ability to communicate effectively **6.** My ability to empathise with my team members
How valuable has any training I have received been? (over the last 6 months)
What training would I like over the next 6 months?

Figure A2.7 An example of a self assessment form.

Remember

It is a good idea to use a reflective journal. You could record, weekly, what you have done well, what you have not done well and what areas can be improved upon. Because each entry will be dated, you can use the journal as a reference document to monitor your improvement.

Using feedback to improve performance

Collecting feedback from others is valuable as it enables you to reflect on the way you use your current knowledge and skills within your own workplace. The feedback you receive can help you to assess development needs both for your current and future workplace roles. You can collect feedback from:

- peer managers (those who work at the same level as you)
- your line manager
- the team members you manage
- any other staff members you liaise with regularly
- your customers or other stakeholders.

Sometimes the feedback you receive will be verbal rather than written, for instance when your line manager praises you or a team member thanks you for being supportive. You should always make notes of such feedback, so that you can make reference to it in the future – during your staff appraisal for example. Your reflective journal would be a good place to do this.

Capturing feedback in writing, as below, provides you with a document that you can use to help update your skills audit, SWOT analysis, reflective journal or other important development tools.

Remember

Some organisations use a process called 360-degree feedback. This means that employees working at any level in the organisation receive feedback on their performance from anyone they have daily contact with, including subordinates, external customers and suppliers.

My name is .... and I would be grateful if you would complete this form to enable me to analyse my performance and behaviour in my workplace

Area to be assessed	Always	Sometimes	Never	Please add any comments
Do I complete my work on time and meet deadlines?				
Does the quality of my work meet the standards expected of me by the organisation/my team?				
Do I communicate effectively?				
Do I demonstrate effective interpersonal skills?				
Do I approach my work with enthusiasm?				
Do I support my team well?				

Name of person completing form:

Position Held:

Date:

Thank you for taking the time to complete this form.

Please return it to .... by ....

Figure A2.8 An example of a feedback questionnaire.

Produce a development plan

Producing a development plan will give you the opportunity to consider in greater detail how you will meet your workplace objectives and personal goals. In particular, it will help you to assess:

- your current position (where you are now)
- your future desires (where you want to be)
- your plans to achieve your desires (how you will get there).

> **Remember**
>
> Your objectives and goals are likely to be of a short, medium and long-term nature.

A personal development plan (PDP), as shown below, should outline the skills that you need to develop and the actions you will need to take to enable you to develop those skills. Your plan should be agreed between you and your line manager and will usually be drawn up as part of your staff appraisal process. Other tools, such as a SWOT analysis, skills audits and feedback sheets can also be used to inform and feed into your plan.

Ideally, your plan should encourage you to decide:

- what you want to learn
- what skills you want to develop
- what actions you need to take
- what resources you will need
- what support you will need
- the date you want to complete your actions by
- the date you will review your progress with your manager.

> **Remember**
>
> Your SWOT analysis, action plans, skills audit and other tools you may have used should be considered alongside your personal development plan and, in some cases, feed into it.

Your plan will help you to increase your knowledge and skills set, which means you will:

- become more confident
- become more flexible
- increase your opportunity for career progression
- increase your self esteem

Name of post holder: Date of today's review: Date of last review:			Name of Manager:	
What skills/knowledge I need/want to develop?	**What actions must I take to achieve this?**	**What resources and/or support will I need?**	**Target date for completion**	**Target date for review with manager**
Development objective 1: *Managing Conflict in the workplace*	*Attend an in-house training session*	*Time to attend and training materials*	*30th July*	*30th August*
Development objective 2:				
Development objective 3:				
Post holder's signature:			**Manager's signature:**	

Figure A2.9 An example personal development plan.

- be open to more challenging tasks
- build upon your transferable skills.

A well-produced plan will also help you to break down your goals, objectives, ambitions and desires into smaller tasks and activities that will be easier to achieve. Trying to achieve everything all at once can be stressful, unsuccessful and demotivating.

Portfolio Task 4 45 minutes

Links to LO3: Assessment criteria 3.1, 3.2
Produce and complete a development plan using the personal development plan document in Figure A2.9 as a template.

Discuss this document with your assessor.

PLTS

By completing this activity you will assess your current achievement and identify any opportunities that may be available. You will look for new challenges and/or responsibilities and set goals to help you realise the opportunities identified (SM1; CT1, 3; RL1, 2).

Functional Skills

You may be able to use your findings from the above task to help develop your Level 2 Functional Skills in ICT: Developing, presenting and communicating information if you reproduce your PDP on a computer.

Learning styles

Identifying skills gaps is one thing, filling them is another. In order to maximise your chance of success it is useful to identify how you learn and apply that knowledge to your learning process. A useful tool for identifying your learning style is Kolb's Experiential Learning Cycle.

Kolb's Experiential Learning Cycle

David Kolb created a learning cycle in 1979 to identify the way people learn. He looked at four points:

- Learning and what was felt during a period of learning. An example of this could be using a

particular computer program for the first time, and assessing it.

- Thinking about how useful the period of learning was.
- Looking at ideas and theories related to the learning experience. In terms of using a new computer program, this stage would be to understand how it functions.
- Testing the learning. In our example, this would mean using the new program to try out what has been learned.

Activity ⏱ 30 minutes

Spend some time researching David Kolb's learning cycle. From your research, create your own diagram of the cycle. Discuss with your manager how you could use this cycle in practice.

Remember

It can be helpful to identify your own learning style. For example, some people learn more by visual means whereas other people learn more from 'doing' something (a 'hands on' approach).

Honey and Mumford's Learning Cycle

Theorists Peter Honey and Alan Mumford created an approach to learning as follows:

- Activists (do something) – people who actively enjoy the challenges that new learning experiences offer.
- Reflectors (think about it) – people who like to stand back and review a learning experience in a thoughtful way.
- Theorists (make sense of it) – people who like to think the learning experience through in logical steps.
- Pragmatists (test it out) – people who like to try out new ideas and enjoy problem solving and decision making as part of a learning experience.

Activity ⏱ 45 minutes

Spend some time researching into the work of Honey and Mumford (1986) and identify your own preferred learning style. Discuss your findings with your manager and assessor.

Unit A2 Manage own professional development within an organisation

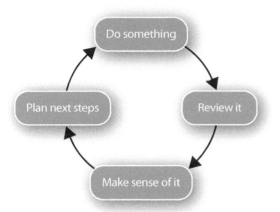

Figure A2.10 Honey and Mumford's Learning Cycle.

Checklist

When evaluating the skills and knowledge gaps you have, remember to look at your:

- communication skills
- listening skills
- time management skills
- stress management
- leadership skills.

Be able to implement and monitor own personal development plan

Your PDP, in agreement with your line manager, will have helped you to identify the activities you need to undertake to develop yourself to meet your personal goals and objectives. Common areas for development are:

- chairing meetings effectively
- time management skills
- delegation skills
- leadership and management skills
- conflict resolution skills
- planning, controlling and coordinating skills.

Plan activities identified in own development plan

Your next step must be to decide how you will organise and arrange your training and development activities. Think back to the format you used for your action plan – you could use a similar template to help you work out how you will organise your development activities. Alternatively, you could devise a document similar to the one shown in Figure A2.11.

Proposed develop-ment activity	SMART objective	Resources needed	Training/ development method	Location	Dates	Approved by	Cost	Comple-tion	Review date
Chairing team meetings effectively	To complete training on 'Effective chairing of meetings' by 31 March	Staff time, training budget, training material, travelling expenses	Two off-the-job training sessions at HND Training Ltd	Wrexham	2 March 3 March	DR	£450		
Trainee name:				Signature:			Date:		
Line Manager name:				Signature:			Date:		
HR Manager name:				Signature:			Date:		

Figure A2.11 An example training plan.

Training plans, regardless of their format and content, should clearly outline:

- what the proposed training/development activity is
- when the training is to be provided
- the resources that will be needed for the training activity
- the method of training activity
- the cost of the training activity
- the location of the training sessions

- who will provide the training sessions
- who has approved the training activity.

Consider the flow chart below.

The chart can be used as a step-by-step guide to your training and development activity. A simplistic way of looking at this is to establish your:

- training needs (staff appraisal)
- training plan (PDP)
- training/development objectives (SMART)
- decisions on 'who/where/how/when' elements of the training
- steps to gain approval for the training to go ahead
- evaluation of the training activity.

Your PDP should be used as a working document and be regularly monitored and reviewed.

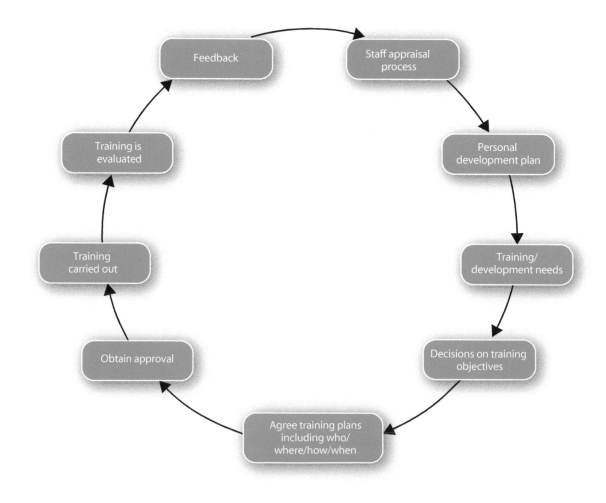

Figure A2.12 A step-by-step guide to your training and development activity.

Portfolio Task 5 45 minutes

Links to LO4: Assessment criterion 4.1

Using the personal development plan you completed in the previous portfolio task, prepare a training plan to show how you will organise your training activities in order to meet your objectives.

Discuss this document with your assessor.

PLTS

This activity will give you the opportunity to generate ideas and explore possibilities available to you (CT1).

Functional Skills

This activity will help you develop your Level 2 Functional Skills in English: Reading and Writing. You will need to present information and ideas in a logical manner using a suitable writing style.

You should try to identify how your development activity will assist, from the point of view of:

- yourself – how will it help you become more competent in what you do and help you achieve your goals, objectives and ambitions?
- your team – how will it help you to manage and lead your team more effectively?
- your organisation – how will it help your organisation to achieve its business objectives?

Activity 30 minutes

Examine how your identified development and training activities will assist you, the team members you manage, and your organisation to achieve work-related objectives. Write down your responses and share them with your assessor.

Remember

It is useful to obtain a copy of your organisational chart to examine the structure of your organisation. This will establish where you are positioned now and where you want to be in the future. This gives you a clear focus of where you want your career path to take you.

Explain how to monitor and review own personal development plan

It is important to monitor and review your development activities to establish how successful they have been and how useful your personal development plan has been.

You should focus on whether your plan has helped you to:

- close your skill gaps
- change your attitude towards the way you do things
- change your habits and the way you approach things
- build your confidence levels
- enhance your morale and motivation
- be more enthusiastic about learning and development
- work towards your personal objectives and career goals.

You might also consider to what degree your behaviour may have changed when dealing with customers, team members, suppliers and other stakeholders. Think about your own feelings, behaviours and needs and how these influence the way you behave towards others. Your development plan and subsequent activities may have encouraged you to think more about this.

Maslow's Hierarchy of Needs

You might find it useful to examine your own needs and how these influence your workplace behaviour. Consider Maslow's Hierarchy of Needs, shown in Figure A2.13 to help you with your assessment of this.

Figure A2.13 Maslow's Hierarchy of Needs.

- Biological and physiological needs – workers need to earn enough money to be able to survive and enjoy food, heating, somewhere to live and so on.
- Safety needs – workers look for job security, for example.
- Belongingness and love needs – workers need to be accepted by others in their team or workplace and they also need a culture of support.
- Self-esteem needs – workers feel the need to be respected by others in terms of what they do. They also need to feel that they have achieved something.
- Self-actualisation – Maslow suggested this is the highest order need. Workers need to know that they have fulfilled an ambition, or realised their expected potential.

> **Remember**
>
> When you identify your own needs, remember that the people you manage will have similar needs.

Monitoring your PDP

When monitoring your personal development plan you should:

- record results and outcomes of your training and development activities
- examine whether you have achieved your objectives on time
- examine why you might not have achieved an objective on time
- reflect upon what you have learnt
- assess how well you are progressing towards each of your objectives and targets identified in your plan.

At your staff appraisals you will examine the progress you have made and agree further development planning. It is important that you monitor your current PDP regularly so that you and your manager will be fully aware of your progress, and will be able to take steps to change.

The Blake Mouton grid

Management theorists Robert R. Blake and Jane Mouton devised a managerial grid model in 1964, which looks at behavioural leadership and can be used to assess your current managerial skill set and to monitor whether your personal development plan has enabled you to achieve additional skills as a manager.

The grid explores your:

- concern for people
- concern for tasks.

The Blake Mouton grid can help to plot a person's style of management and how they might develop themselves. The grid separates behavioural leadership styles into five distinct groups, varying from worst practice to best practice.

At the worst end of the scale, a manager will have no concern for getting the job done or creating a motivating environment in which to do the job. This is clearly not the style to aim for.

In contrast, Blake and Mouton then describe a manager who puts equal importance on production needs and people. Employees are involved in decision-making, which creates a team environment based on trust and respect and leads to high satisfaction and motivation, resulting in high production. This is considered to be the ideal style of management.

Activity 🕑 20 minutes

Research into the Blake Mouton managerial grid model and then think about the following:

- Where does your current style of management fit within the grid? Which of the five styles are you?
- What can you do to move further towards the ideal style of management?

Write notes on how you can plan your improvements. Try to include time frames for these improvements if possible.

As you monitor and review your personal development plan, you should consider how your activities may change or influence your management style. You may also wish to agree further development activities with your line manager to enable you to continue to work towards the ideal team management approach in Blake and Mouton's grid based on your findings from the previous activity.

Getting feedback

To examine whether you have successfully closed skill gaps and achieved the objectives in your personal development plan, you can obtain feedback from others. This helps you to review how your performance may have changed as a result of your development activities. It is a good idea to use a questionnaire and an example is shown below.

Feedback Evaluation Questionnaire on my Performance

(Your own name and position)

Recently I attended an Assertiveness Course at Healbridge College. In order to evaluate the effectiveness of this course, I would be very grateful if you could spend five minutes answering the following questions:

1. I am more assertive when allocating work

Yes   No

2. If yes, please explain how:

3. If no, how can I be more assertive?

4. Do you have any other comments on my assertiveness? Please add them here.

Thank you for taking time to complete this form.

Please return it to ....

by . ...

Figure A2.14 An example questionnaire for gathering feedback.

There are other steps you can take to review how successful your training and development activities have been. For example, consider the use of a self-assessment form, such as the one below, which you can use after you have attended training sessions.

By assessing yourself in this way, you can monitor and review to what extent your training and development is going to plan and what improvement has been made in the way you behave as a manager.

Remember

Your SWOT analysis, action plans, feedback forms and other documents you may use will all help you and your manager to assess the success of your development activities.

Personal Development Review

A final (and perhaps most important) document that should be used is a Personal Development Review (PDR) form. It is likely that you and your line manager will use a form, similar to the one shown in Figure A2.15, to review your past performance and development activity. You and your manager will complete this form together during your staff appraisal interview. This is an opportunity to review and evaluate the success of your PDP and the development activities you have undertaken as a result of your planning.

Management Skills – Self Assessment

Using the following scale to evaluate your team leading skills.

Scale: 1. Excellent 2. Very good 3. Good 4. Fair 5. Poor 6. Very Poor

Please circle the appropriate score.

Skills/Ability	Score
Communication skills	1 2 3 4 5 6
Decision making skills	1 2 3 4 5 6
Patient with others	1 2 3 4 5 6
Supportive	1 2 3 4 5 6
Able to work with colleagues	1 2 3 4 5 6
Honest and trustworthy	1 2 3 4 5 6
Treating colleagues and staff fairly	1 2 3 4 5 6
Respecting others views	1 2 3 4 5 6
Assertiveness	1 2 3 4 5 6

Knowledge Area	
Technical Knowledge	1 2 3 4 5 6
Staff members skills	1 2 3 4 5 6
Policies and procedures	1 2 3 4 5 6
Commercial Awareness	1 2 3 4 5 6

Figure A2.15 An example self assessment form.

Personal Development Review					
Dates of Training	What I did	Reasons why	What I have learnt	How I will use my new skills/ knowledge	What further development is needed in this area?

Figure A2.16 An example Performance Development Review form.

You should note that the last column, as seen in Figure A2.16, in your PDR form will feed into your next PDP.

Portfolio Task 6 — 45 minutes

Links to LO4: Assessment criterion 4.2

Discuss with your assessor how you intend to monitor and review your development plan. Explain how often it will be reviewed and what criteria you will use to establish if your objectives have been achieved.

Your assessor will record this discussion in order to generate evidence for your portfolio.

Unit A2 Manage own professional development within an organisation

Team talk

Tom's story

My name is Tom and I have been working for Canter Technologies for five years as a production line foreman. I am quite de-motivated at the moment as I am finding my job too easy and not challenging enough. I have approached my manager and she has agreed to have an appraisal meeting with me next month. Yesterday, I received an email from my manager telling me to prepare for this meeting and to bring along all the necessary documentation. She also informed me that she was on holiday now until the morning of the meeting.

In the five years I have been at Canter Technologies, I have never had an appraisal meeting and I have no idea what I need to take with me to the meeting.

Top tips

Tom may wish to speak to his colleagues, peers and other managers to obtain feedback about his current performance. This can be done by asking them to complete a feedback questionnaire. Also, Tom could complete a self appraisal form to help him identify his current skills and knowledge and any gaps he may have.

Ask the expert

Q	I want my appraisal meeting to be useful and productive and therefore need to prepare properly. What do I need to do?
A	Contact your human resources department to see if there are formal appraisal documents you should be using. For example, you will need a self-assessment form and perhaps an action plan template. If you have no response from the HR team, then you can prepare your own documentation. You will need to think about what your personal and career goals are. You may find conducting a SWOT analysis a useful activity whereby you assess your strengths, weaknesses, opportunities and threats. To help you with identifying your opportunities, it may be useful for you to obtain a copy of a job description and person specification of your future desired position, to establish the skills you may need in order to progress and develop. You may also find it useful to prepare a personal action plan. This will help you to set out where you are now, where you want to be and how you will get there. From this action plan you can then set out your own SMART objectives.

What your assessor is looking for

In order to demonstrate your competency within this unit, you will need to provide sufficient evidence to your assessor. You will need to provide a short written narrative or personal statement, explaining how you meet the assessment criteria. In addition, your assessor may need to ask you questions to test your knowledge of the topics identified in this unit.

Please bear in mind that there are significant cross-referencing opportunities throughout this qualification and you may have already generated some relevant work to meet certain criteria in this unit. Your assessor will provide you with the exact requirements to meet the standards of this unit. However, as a guide it is likely that for this unit you will need to be assessed through the following methods:

- One observation of relevant workplace activities to cover the whole unit.
- One witness testimony may also be produced.
- A written narrative, reflective account or professional discussion.
- Any relevant work products to be produced as evidence.

The work products for this unit could include:

- self appraisal form
- SWOT analysis
- personal development plan
- SMART objectives
- personal action plan
- examples of feedback from managers, peers, colleagues e.g. emails, completed questionnaires
- person specification and job description
- training plan
- personal development review.

Your assessor will guide you through the assessment process as detailed in the candidate logbook. The detailed assessment criteria are shown in the logbook and by working through these questions, combined with providing the relevant evidence, you will meet the learning outcomes required to complete this unit.

Task and page reference	Assessment criteria
1 (page 6)	1.1
2 (page 7)	1.2
3 (page 11)	2.1
4 (page 16)	3.1, 3.2
5 (page 19)	4.1
6 (page 23)	4.2

Unit B5 Set objectives and provide support for team members

This unit will assist you in developing your skills and knowledge to become a more effective team leader. The unit explains the principles and benefits of improving your team's performance and explores the value of effective communication in your team.

By empowering, supporting and valuing your team, you will be able to motivate and encourage your team members to meet their own work objectives, in turn meeting the overall objectives of the organisation.

The unit will explore different leadership styles and various team behaviours. There is also practical guidance to assist you in managing your team effectively.

What you will learn

- Be able to communicate a team's purpose and objectives to the team members
- Be able to develop a plan with team members showing how team objectives will be met
- Be able to support team members identifying opportunities and providing support
- Be able to monitor and evaluate progress and recognise individual and team achievement

Links to the Technical Certificate

If you are completing your NVQ as part of an Apprenticeship Framework, you will find the following topics are also covered in your Technical Certificate:

- Principles of team leading
- Developing working relationships with colleagues
- Coaching skills
- Getting results from your team
- Decision making
- Knowledge management in team leading

Be able to communicate a team's purpose and objectives to the team members

In this section we will look at the purpose of team working, how to communicate with your team members and how to set SMART objectives for your team.

Describe the purpose of a team

There are various definitions of what a team is. For instance:

A team is a number of people with complementary skills who are committed to working towards a common purpose, meeting performance goals and are accountable for their actions.

A key thing here is that a team will have a purpose. In a business environment, that purpose will link to what the organisation wants to achieve. Organisations set out their aims in their business plans, goals and objectives. They may also produce a mission statement, which will describe in a few words what they want to achieve. From this, objectives will be set and **strategies** employed to achieve their aims. Within the organisation, teams of people will all work towards achieving individual objectives that feed into the overall mission of the organisation.

> **Key Term**
>
> **Strategies** – Tools and processes used to achieve objectives.

Team member behaviours

Members of a team have two distinct roles. First they have to achieve the goals of the team and second they have to maintain an effective working relationship with each other. These two elements are interlinked because if the goals of the team are not met, then it will inevitably put pressure on the day-to-day working relationships within the team.

Through his extensive research in the late 1970s Dr Meredith Belbin devised a world-recognised model for team preferences, which can help us to understand why team members can behave in

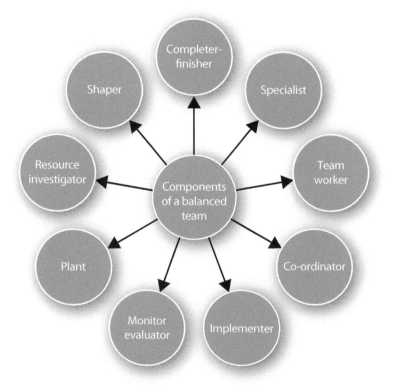

Figure B5.1 Belbin's team roles.

certain ways. He identified specific roles as shown in Figure B5.1 and outlined below.

In most teams, individual team members can take on several characteristics. Belbin argued that 'although one person can't be perfect, a team can be'.

The essential characteristics of each team member are:

- the completer-finisher ensures that nothing is overlooked and provides thorough attention to detail
- the specialist will be able to support the team on specialist issues and may sometimes work within a separate team
- the co-ordinator controls the activities of the team and is able to get the team working together as a complete unit
- the team worker promotes team spirit and encourages other team members through their supportive approach
- the implementer translates ideas into plans and breaks things down into tasks and actions
- the monitor/evaluator is a critical thinker, who is objective in their approach and can analyse ideas and suggestions
- the plant concentrates on the big issues and can be a source of innovation and ideas for the team; can be single minded
- the resource investigator harnesses resources for the team and networks with other teams and organisations
- the shaper makes things happen by injecting energy and strong direction.

As you can imagine, not all teams will have all of these types of people and some team members will have more than one attribute. However, these characteristics are all useful elements for a team to become fully effective.

There have been more recent studies by other experts who suggest similar personality types within teams as:

- action person
- caring person

- detail person
- co-ordinator
- creative thinker.

Again, some team members will have some or all of these attributes and don't forget, you are a member of the team as well.

For a team to be effective the team leader should recognise how each person's individual skills and abilities can help the team achieve its day-to-day objectives.

Portfolio Task 1 ⏱ 60 minutes

Links to LO1: Assessment criterion 1.1

Describe the purpose of a team. Consider your own team and check to see if you have any specific gaps, team-member types or characteristics and then try to think of a solution to resolve this. For example, if you don't think that you have many people in your team who think creatively, what can you do to improve this? Maybe you could have a brief creative session in your team meeting from time to time and ask the team to come up with any potential new and innovative ways of working.

PLTS

By arranging a team meeting and discussing creative issues, you will be developing effective team working and encouraging your team members to be independent enquirers by allowing them to work in a creative way (TW; IE; SM).

Set SMART team objectives with its members

The organisation will set SMART objectives and these are likely to be shown in the mission statement and the overall objectives for the organisation.

Different departments or divisions within the organisation will also set SMART objectives that feed into the overall objectives of the organisation. Different teams or team leaders will set SMART objectives or targets that feed into the departmental objectives.

Individual members of staff will also set targets in conjunction with their team leader to feed into their team's targets or objectives. Figure B5.2 shows how this would work in an organisation.

You and your team may not always realise it, but what you do on a day-to-day basis will link directly into the organisation's overall mission and objectives. If what you are doing does not link into the mission, why are you doing it?

Portfolio Task 2 60 minutes

Links to LO1: Assessment criteria 1.2, 1.3

Describe how you set SMART objectives for your team and explain how you communicate the team's purpose and objectives to the team members.

Your assessment could take the form of a written narrative or a professional discussion with your assessor. It could also include the production of workplace evidence.

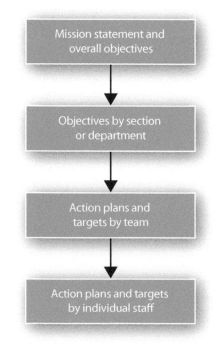

Figure B5.2 Linking organisational goals to individual targets.

Communicate the team's purpose and objectives to its members

The acronym KISS – 'keep it short and simple' – is an essential requirement in a business environment, both in terms of verbal and written communication. The basic principle of this approach is to:

● use fewer words
● use shorter words
● use pictures, graphs or charts where possible.

This approach can be linked to more general principles to ensure that you communicate effectively. Remember that you should:

● use the right language to fit the occasion
● use the right medium – verbal communication, emails or letters
● get the attention of the people that you are communicating with
● get your message across as you want it to be received – reduce the potential for misinterpretation or confusion
● maintain eye contact and observe the body language
● allow people to respond
● listen to what is being said to you
● be prepared to discuss issues
● don't allow team members to dominate team meetings and convince other team members that their opinion is right.

You may need to admit defeat where you are out-voted by your team. Collective decisions that the whole team agrees with are more powerful and more likely to work than decisions imposed by the team leader.

Team leadership and communication

You may have heard the statement that 'a team leader is only as good as their team'. There is some truth in this but in some ways the opposite is also true. A team is only as good as its leader – you. The key to success for the team leader is to shape and manage their team to ensure that the relevant

Behaviour	How to achieve this outcome	Possible evidence sources
You create a common sense of purpose	Involve the team in agreeing the goals and objectives	Team objectives or appraisal targets
You clearly agree what is expected and hold people to account	Agree objectives with each team member and manage their performance	Appraisal targets or performance management information
You seek to understand people's needs and motivations	Be sensitive to the needs and expectations of the team	Notes from discussions or personal statements
You make time available to support others	Put time aside to support the team both as a group and individually	Notes from one-to-one meetings or training events
You show respect for the views and actions of others	Involve the team in the decision-making processes	Team meeting minutes or 'away day' events
You develop an atmosphere of professionalism and mutual support	Be professional at all times and encourage team members to perform well and enjoy their job	Witness testimony or achievement of objectives
You show integrity, fairness and consistency in decision making	Foster team spirit and appropriate ethics and values in the team	Team meeting minutes, witness testimony or relevant procedures

Table B5.1 How to be an effective team leader.

outcomes are achieved and also to personally demonstrate behaviours that their team needs to aspire to attain. In simple terms, the team leader must:

- make sure that their team achieves its objectives
- demonstrate professional and supportive behaviours at all times
- lead by example
- communicate clearly.

Key Term

Outcomes – the things that have been achieved.

To be an effective team leader, you will need to gain the trust and support of your team. Table B5.1 shows some practical ways on how you can do this. It also includes suggestions for evidence, which you can include in your portfolio.

The benefits of effective communication

Collaboration means working together, and the key to effective collaboration is effective communication. By working together, team members can share their values and the vision of the organisation, develop a team spirit and absorb the information that they need to work well with each other. Trust, mutual respect and honesty between all team members is vital.

The principles of effective communication are to:

- make sure that it is a two-way process
- provide information that is clear, concise and in the right level of detail for the recipient
- ensure that everyone is clear about what is being communicated
- listen carefully to what is being said
- keep people informed on a regular basis, both in relation to general issues and their individual performance.

As a result of applying these principles, you and your team should reap the benefits and be able to work more productively. By building a positive working relationship with your team, you should see:

- less resistance to change
- improved commitment, co-operation and enjoyment of their roles
- increased output, productivity and efficiency
- improved supportive working within the team and across other team boundaries.

Listening skills

Listening is an often overlooked and underrated communication skill. How good a listener are you? Have a go at the following activity.

Activity 30 minutes

It is easy to hear someone speaking to you, but are you actually listening and understanding what they are saying to you? Complete the following short questionnaire by ticking the appropriate boxes.

When you are communicating with someone, do you:

Your behaviour	Always	Sometimes	Never
Finish off their sentences			
Think that you know the point that the other person is trying to make before they have finished			
Think about what you are going to say next while the other person is still talking			
Jump to conclusions before the person has finished talking			
Interrupt people while they are talking			
Get frustrated and wish that they would get to the point more quickly			

If you find that you have ticked the always and occasionally boxes, then try to identify these issues and set out how you can improve in these areas. If you have a personal development plan, it would be a good idea to include these issues and agree a timescale to complete them in. Set yourself a SMART objective to resolve each issue.

Portfolio Task 3 30 minutes

Links to LO1: Assessment criterion 1.3

Collect examples of all of the ways that you communicate with your team. For example, formal methods, such as appraisals or target setting and more day-to-day methods, such as emails and team-meeting minutes. These will provide useful evidence for your portfolio.

PLTS

By undertaking this task and collecting examples of how you communicate with your team, you will be demonstrating how you communicate effectively with your team and how you manage performance by setting clear goals and objectives (TW; CT; SM).

Be able to develop a plan with team members showing how team objectives will be met

In this section you will learn how to discuss how team objectives will be met and how to ensure team members participate in the planning process and think creatively. This will help you develop plans to meet team objectives and set SMART personal work objectives with team members.

Discuss with team members how team objectives will be met

Once you know the targets for your team as a whole, the next stage is to plan activities in conjunction with your team members. This involves team members agreeing targets and objectives with you and may be done as part of the annual appraisal meeting. If your company does not have an appraisal system in place, you may agree objectives on a less formal basis.

Once the individual targets are agreed, then specific activities can be planned and the resources put in place. Resources include time, manpower and equipment or facilities to do the job.

As the tasks are undertaken, it will be up to you to monitor and review the performance of individuals and the team as a whole. This can be explained by Figure B5.3 and the following worked example.

Imagine that you work for a telecom company and the company's mission is to be the 'number one telecommunications provider in the UK', with their main objective for the forthcoming year being to increase sales by five per cent. Other objectives include updating the existing customer database by the end of the year.

You manage part of the customer service team and some of your responsibilities involve updating the customer database for your geographical region. You have been assigned some objectives from your manager, one of which relates to updating the customer database. These objectives are:

- Overall organisational objective 'To update the customer database by 31 December 2012'.

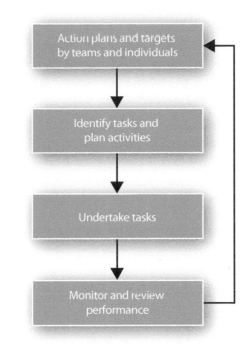

Figure B5.3 Managing team and individual targets and performance.

- As the team leader for the Eastern region of sales, your objective, set by your manager, is to complete the work required to update the database for your region by 30 November 2012.

You now need to involve your team in the process and set sub-objectives for your team members to achieve which should link into your objective.

So, how do you do it?

1. Work with your team and set sub-objectives for some or all of your team members. You may need to formulate a mini project plan to set out what you need to achieve by some agreed dates (milestones).

2. Meet with the team to explain what has to be done. This could be the whole team together, smaller groups or on a one-to-one basis as appropriate.

3. Once you have agreed a plan with your team then you need to manage and monitor their performance to ensure that they are making good progress and can meet your agreed deadline.

Be aware that you are not working in isolation. In this example other teams from different regions will also be working on their customer databases to ensure that the whole customer database is updated by the agreed date.

This is just one example and it is likely that you will have several objectives to achieve both as an individual and as a team as a whole, so careful planning is needed to ensure that you keep track of what you and your team are achieving.

Portfolio Task 4 60 minutes

Links to LO2: Assessment criteria 2.1, 2.2

Describe how you set objectives with your team members and explain how you ensure that team members participate in the planning process.

PLTS

By demonstrating that your team members actively participate in the planning process by setting targets and agreeing objectives, you will show how you allow your team to discuss how their objectives will be met. Relevant evidence, for example, appraisal documents or minutes of team meetings where you discuss these issues, will provide useful evidence for your portfolio (TW; IE; SM).

Ensure team members participate in the planning process and think creatively

In the 1960s and 1970s, Bruce Tuckman developed the team development cycle, which is still widely regarded as the definitive approach in helping us understand the different stages that teams can go through during their development. Most teams are likely to be part way through a team cycle at any given time. Tuckman suggests specific actions and strategies to adopt at the various stages. As a team leader or manager, you first need to recognise which stage your team is at and then adopt the relevant strategies for that phase. Always remember that a team is not necessarily at the performing phase just because it has been together for many years. Also bear in mind that teams who may be performing today, could, because of factors such as a lack of resources or staffing changes, move back to the forming stage at any time. Understanding the stage your team is at and managing them accordingly will help you to encourage their creativity and achieve full participation potential.

The following table shows the various stages, some of the team characteristics that you may experience and some ideas for how you can manage these stages effectively.

Stage	Team member behavioural characteristics	Your role as team leader
Forming	Polite, guarded, watchful, low level of involvement and participation, team members don't know each other	Establish clear objectives; build a supportive and open environment. Clarify the roles and expectations and get team members interacting with each other.
Storming	Difficulties can emerge, some team members opt out, resistance to change, sub-groups develop, different opinions voiced openly	Affirm your role, provide positive feedback, reiterate roles, responsibilities and objectives and manage conflict constructively.
Norming	Acceptance of roles and responsibilities, open exchange of information and opinions, active listening, working together and more co-operation	Encourage communication, tackle any issues, accept feedback, encourage ideas, creativity and innovation.
Performing	Team members are mutually supportive, high performance and increased productivity, give and receive feedback, openness, strong team identity, proud, feel secure and valued; team operating at maximum effectiveness	Encourage flexibility, delegate to and coach team members, leave the team 'to it' – empower and delegate.

Table B5.2 Team characteristics you may experience as a manager.

Activity | 30 minutes

Consider your own team and check what stage you are at. Can you develop some of the strategies and actions to maximise your team's performance?

The benefits of creativity and innovation

The benefits of encouraging and recognising creativity and innovation within a team is that they create an environment where people look at their role and the organisation differently and explore all aspects, not just accepting the status quo as the most appropriate solution.

You can encourage creativity and innovation by organising group sessions. If you get everyone involved in the process, it should ensure that the whole team is on board and no one feels intimidated or uncomfortable. If you hold these types of team events say once or twice a year, your colleagues can come up with new ideas, suggestions and creative ways of working that could potentially improve efficiency and productivity. All ideas should be considered and explored further where appropriate.

As your team develops into the performing stage then innovation and creativity should be more prevalent. Below is a brief checklist on how to encourage creativity and innovation.

- Your team members will only respond to requests for new ideas and initiatives as long as they are appreciated and never mocked.
- New ideas can involve risk taking and you need to be ready to take them on where appropriate.
- Allow team members time to think about creative ideas, for example, facilitate team events.
- Set up groups to explore ideas in greater detail.
- If an idea is approved and implemented always make sure that you thank your team member and put in place any new resources, training or support required to undertake the new or revised process.

Innovative ways of working should also be encouraged during normal day-to-day operations. Ask your colleagues if they can think of any ways to improve their job.

Creativity in a team could potentially improve efficiency and productivity.

Portfolio Task 5

🕐 30 minutes

Links to LO2: Assessment criteria 2.2, 2.4

Irrespective of the stage of development your team is currently at, how effective do you think that your team is? Complete the following questionnaire by scoring your team from 1 to 5 against each criterion and see if it identifies any issues for you to resolve.

How effective is my team?	Not effective				Very effective
	1	2	3	4	5
The team understands its objectives and targets					
Each team member understands their role and responsibilities					
A pleasant working atmosphere is in place and feedback is given and received by all					
Team members communicate well with each other					
Team members resolve disagreements					
All team members participate in discussions and the decision-making process					

Follow-up: If you have scored 2 or below in answer to any of the questions, it would be a good idea to address these issues.

PLTS

By completing this questionnaire, you will be identifying how effective your team is. As you work through each question, you will challenge each element in order to establish where any possible weaknesses may be. By undertaking this task, you will have the opportunity to proactively manage your team's effectiveness (TW; IE; SM).

Develop plans to meet team objectives

As we have explored, teams need a common purpose to ensure that they can link into the overall objectives of the organisation. Individual team members need to be committed to their own job, but at the same time be aware and understand how what they do ensures their team meets their objective, which in turn ensures the whole organisation meets its objectives.

Most organisations have an agreed working culture: this means 'this is how we do things round here'. It is also likely that there will be some **performance standards** in place, which you and your team will need to meet. These may include some specific targets and behaviours that you need to achieve on an on-going basis and also may include some general standards. For example, some general performance standards that all staff would need to meet may be:

- dealing with customers and colleagues quickly, courteously and efficiently
- treating everyone equally and fairly.

Some specific standards that you may set for your team may be on an individual basis, dependent on their current level of knowledge and ability, and these are likely to be linked to their targets and objectives. Your organisation may also have some specific performance targets, for example, to respond to all customer queries within five working days.

It is worth remembering that not all standards will be written down or communicated overtly and there may often be an assumption that all staff will just behave to this standard anyway.

One of the key elements for improving performance is to make sure that you and your team members are **self-motivated** and enjoy your jobs. This will improve your **job satisfaction** and should get you thinking about how you might be able to improve your job role and associated processes to become more efficient.

You and your team members should be accountable for your job and take responsibility for your actions. Adopting this frame of mind enables all team members to plan their work and to start to achieve their objectives.

Key Terms

Job satisfaction – enjoying your job on a day-to-day basis.

Performance standards – minimum performance standards which need to be met by you and your team.

Self-motivated – in work terms, coming into work each day in a positive frame of mind and you are able to complete the tasks by taking ownership of your job.

How to set objectives and provide support

Take a look at these issues and challenge yourself and your team. If you think that you can improve in some of these areas, then plan to resolve the issues.

- Ensure achievement of personal and team objectives – All team members should know what is required of them and you should know how to manage this, through regular reviews, one-to-one meetings or team meetings. You also need to know what to do when things go wrong and staff are not meeting the agreed standards of performance or achieving their targets and objectives.
- How effective is your team? – Do team members trust each other? Are you all open and honest with each other? Do team members support each other? Have any recent changes affected performance?

- Do you have the right resources in place? – You may be encountering problems if you do not have the correct resources in place – time, manpower, equipment, systems, etc. You may need to resolve some issues or investigate if any new technology can be used to improve the efficiency of your team.
- Knowledge and skills – Are your team competent in their roles? Do they have adequate skills and knowledge? Do they need further additional support? Are there any skills that the whole team lacks? Is your team ready for any future challenges?

Review the issues and ask yourself the following.

- Did we achieve our targets and objectives and if so how well did we do?
- What would we do differently next time?
- If we failed to achieve our targets and objectives, what went wrong?
- Did we spend enough time planning and securing the resources to achieve our objectives?
- Did we plan the activities well and did I manage performance effectively?

Always try to plan effectively. If you plan well, there is less chance of things going wrong.

Set SMART personal work objectives with team members

As part of your job, you will plan your own work and the team's work. For regular and routine jobs, you might prepare a 'to do' list of things that you need to do that day or that week. By prioritising your tasks you will be able to plan your work more effectively. However, as a team leader you will also need to plan resources in more detail for the whole team by identifying the work to be undertaken and then planning how you are going to achieve this with the resources that you have in place.

Use the following checklist to help you plan your tasks effectively.

- Write down all of your team objectives and targets and when you need to achieve them by.

Unit B5 set objectives and provide support for team members

- Highlight any specific deadline dates and try to achieve them by, for example, one week ahead of the deadline.
- For larger jobs, break down the tasks into more manageable elements or formulate a small project team.
- Classify your tasks by deciding how important they are and when they need to be completed by. You can use a system to help prioritise them.
- Identify at the outset any targets that may be difficult to achieve and try to negotiate extra time or resources if required.
- Manage your objectives, resources and the performance of your team through regular consultation and communication with team members, including team meetings and one-to-one meetings.
- Don't worry if a new urgent objective comes up, just slot it into your list and plan the resources required to complete it.
- Think about what you *must* do, *should* do and *could* do.
- Always review your plan at the end of each week.

The planning function of management is an important phase as if you make mistakes by not having adequate resources in place you will not achieve your objectives.

To ensure that you plan your resources effectively, you need to:

- focus on the organisation's mission and objectives
- be clear on your own and your team's objectives and targets and agree these objectives with your team
- identify the resources that you have in place – manpower, equipment, budgets etc.
- schedule your activities and prioritise the objectives
- agree processes and procedures to undertake the activities
- manage performance and budgets.

As the tasks are undertaken, it will be up to you to monitor and review the performance of individuals and the team as a whole. It is likely that meetings with various individuals and groups of people will take place at every stage of the performance management process.

PLTS

By pulling together any relevant workplace evidence, you will be showing how you interact with your team, allow your team to think creatively and independently (TW; IE).

Functional Skills

You may be able to use this personal statement as evidence towards Level 2 Functional Skills in English: Reading and Writing. You need to demonstrate that you have understood the process involved in how you set and agree SMART objectives.

Portfolio Task 6 ⏱ 60 minutes

Links to LO2: Assessment criteria 2.3, 2.4
Describe how you encourage your team to think creatively and work with you to develop their own plans to meet the team's objectives.

Gather any relevant evidence demonstrating how you set and agree SMART objectives with your team members. This will provide useful evidence for your portfolio.

Be able to support team members identifying opportunities and providing support

In this section you will identify opportunities and difficulties faced by team members. You will learn how to provide advice to team members to overcome difficulties and make the most of identified opportunities.

Identify opportunities and difficulties faced by team members

Teams are very powerful and as they grow stronger and more effective, they can begin to transform the whole organisation. As a manager, you will need to utilise the strengths and expertise of individual team members, which will in turn make your whole team more efficient and effective. You will need to be able to let go of some aspects to allow your team to develop and grow; this could involve supporting and coaching individuals to further develop their own skills and knowledge. You must harness positive energy in your team and encourage team members to take the lead on certain things. By doing this, you will be:

- developing the skills, knowledge and confidence of your team
- empowering and delegating by allowing team members to control some aspects of their own work
- encouraging team members to undertake other jobs (multi-tasking) by sharing their skills and experiences with other team members
- encouraging the team to take responsibility for their own role.

Delegating

As you plan your team's work schedule for the week, month or year, you will need to identify specific members of your team who will undertake specific tasks. By delegating authority and allowing members of the team to undertake specific tasks,

you are giving the team members responsibility over some parts of their job. This can often be a motivating factor for staff as they will enjoy the control over elements of their job and they will like the fact that they can make certain decisions.

Unfortunately, not all managers are good delegators and some managers are unable or unwilling to delegate tasks. Also, some team members do not enjoy having additional responsibilities when a task is delegated to them. These team members may need additional support and reassurance as they learn to take on new tasks and responsibilities.

When you delegate, you need to be aware that it may take your team member longer to undertake the task than it would take you and also that they may not perform the task to as high a standard or mistakes may occur. However, you need to be supportive and build in additional time for your team member to guide them through the process, particularly if they are doing something new for the first time. Think back to when you were learning something new. An easy option is to think 'I can do that job much quicker, I'll just get it done'. This is not the best option. It is likely that as a team leader you will have a high workload and not enough hours in the day to get the work completed. If you do not delegate, the problem will be compounded and you will just get busier and busier and your team will be less and less effective as you try to control all of the tasks.

Always remember that as a team leader, you can delegate specific ad hoc tasks as well as regular tasks. Ask yourself 'Am I the most suitable person to be undertaking this task?'. Also bear in mind that it is not appropriate to delegate some tasks. For example, if you had some interviews planned and it was important for you to make the appointment yourself, you would not normally delegate this type of task.

> **Remember**
>
> Delegating work shows confidence in your team and frees you up to do other tasks.

Portfolio Task 7

30 minutes

Links to LO3: Assessment criteria 3.1, 3.2

How good a delegator are you? Complete the following questionnaire. This will provide useful evidence for your portfolio and might highlight some development needs that you can also include in your development plan.

My behaviour	Agree	Disagree
Some of my team members are not motivated and find their roles mundane		
Some of my team members say that they are not always that busy		
I work really long hours, but I find it difficult to delegate work to my team members		
I don't have enough time available to coach and support my team members		
I'm unhappy if my team members make mistakes		
It is quicker to do the task myself and I can get it right first time without any mistakes		

In summary, delegation gives a person the freedom and authority to undertake certain tasks or elements of their own job without the need to constantly refer issues back to their manager for a decision. They are able to make certain decisions and as a result, they are empowered and able to work more on their own initiative. They are also likely to be motivated, more effective and more productive.

By implementing the elements in Figure B5.4 you are more likely to become an effective delegator.

Discuss identified opportunities and difficulties with team members

As a team leader, you will need to be able to provide moral support, for example, if someone has personal difficulties that they need assistance

with. You will also be required to provide practical support, for example, if a colleague is struggling to meet a specific deadline.

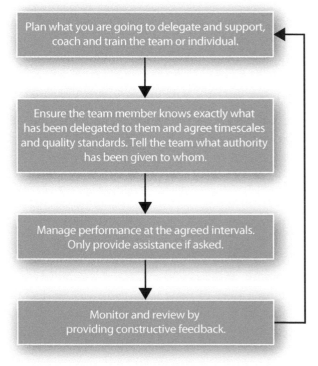

Remember

Always utilise the skills and knowledge of your team. Some team members are likely to have very detailed specialist skills. Encourage and utilise these skills to best effect.

Figure B5.4 Effective delegation.

The level of support required will vary significantly from team to team and also individually. Some team members will require little or no support, whereas other team members may require regular assistance, advice and support. Care needs to be taken here as you need to be clear in your own mind what represents a reasonable level of support. For example, if a person needs regular support in relation to a routine task, then it could be because they are not competent in their role and it may be appropriate in these circumstances to review their capabilities through a formal procedure. However, if a team member needs support in relation to a new task or change in circumstance, then this is perfectly acceptable. Also remember that your colleagues can provide support to each other as specific staff with specialist knowledge may be better placed than you to provide relevant support.

Remember

Communicate effectively at all times. You never want your team members to say 'We're always the last people to know' or 'We never get to know about anything'.

The types of support and advice that your team may need will depend on a number of factors including:

- the type of organisation that you work for and the policies and culture in place
- the rewards and benefits available to staff
- the ability of your team to meet its objectives
- the mix of personalities in your team and the degree of competiveness within the team
- the personal circumstances of your team members.

Be prepared to give time and support to any of your team members as and when they require it. Meet with them on their terms, perhaps at their workstation rather than in your office, and always be sympathetic to their needs.

Don't just think about individual support: you can support the whole team, through team building sessions, specific problem-solving meetings, team briefings, clarifying the overall objectives and planning the work to be undertaken.

Provide advice and support to team members to overcome difficulties and challenges

It is inevitable that you will have to deal with disagreements or conflicts, either within your own team or conflicts between your team and other teams. Generally speaking, these disagreements can be classified into either task-based challenges or people-based challenges.

- Task-based challenges are normally easier to solve than people based problems as they are less complex. Task-based problems relate to doing the job and examples include meeting tight deadlines, lack of skills, equipment or resource breakdown or staff absences.
- Examples of people-based challenges can include personality clashes, problems over the allocation of roles, lack of support between team members, team members blaming each other or some staff deliberately being disruptive.

Difficulties can also arise in times of uncertainty such as during periods of economic downturn or the reorganisation of a team. During these times, staff may be worried about the security of their jobs and it will be up to you to keep them informed at all times and provide relevant support and advice as required.

While you need to steer your team successfully through these challenges, you also need to recognise that you cannot control everything. As we have discussed earlier, teams are influenced by individual personalities, beliefs, personal feelings and attitudes. You can do your bit, but things which may be outside your control may sometimes go wrong.

Sometimes you may need to impose a decision or introduce a new system or process that proves unpopular. The best way to undertake this is to have an open and frank discussion with all members of the team and explain the reasons for the proposed changes. Listen to the concerns of your team members and take on board any relevant issues. If people know why something is happening and it is explained to them in person, they are much more likely to accept the changes even if they do not agree with them entirely.

Make sure that team members are supported when doing a task they have not taken on before.

Provide advice and support to team members to make the most of identified opportunities

It is critical to ensure that as a team leader you are respected by your colleagues and:

- have a positive attitude
- are an effective communicator
- are competent in your role as a team leader
- able to motivate, influence and encourage the team
- able to harness and develop the skills and knowledge within the team
- know and understand individual team members strengths and weaknesses
- able to link the team goals to the overall objectives of the organisation.

Remember to value your team. In principle, you are only as good as the team that works for you. Your team is your resource to respect, work with and hopefully achieve your objectives. Make the most of any opportunities that may arise. These could include expanding your team, developing new and innovative ways of working, creating more efficient and effective systems and keeping your colleague's skills and knowledge up to date. By doing this, you will be helping to improve the organisation overall, which should assist in providing stability longer term.

Portfolio Task 8 — 90 minutes

Links to LO3: Assessment criteria 3.1, 3.2, 3.3, 3.4

1. Describe what opportunities and what difficulties are faced by you and your team.
2. Describe how you communicate and deal with any difficult situations.
3. Describe how you develop opportunities for your team members and explain the structure of how this works.
4. Think of some recent examples of when you have given support to individual team members or the team as a whole. This could be through a team briefing or maybe during a one-to-one meeting.

PLTS

By describing and explaining the ways in which you interact with your team on a day-to-day basis, you will be demonstrating how you develop opportunities within the team and also how you communicate with your team effectively (TW; IE; EP; SM).

Activity — 30 minutes

Think about your team and check if you possess any of the traits listed. If you think that you have any specific areas for development, make a note of them and build them into your personal development plan.

Functional Skills

You may be able to use this personal statement as evidence towards Level 2 Functional Skills in English: Reading and Writing. You need to demonstrate that you have understood the process involved in how you support your team.

Checklist

How to steer your team through difficulties and challenges.

- Recognise that difficulties and challenges will naturally occur within any team.
- Identify the simple task based issues first, e.g. lack of resources or time, and then propose a solution to resolve these issues.
- Try to encourage the team to be proactive and look for solutions to problems rather than focusing on the problem.
- Destructive conflict, which involves people insulting or criticising each other or refusing to communicate, cannot be tolerated.
- Insist on open negotiations between the various parties and try to achieve a win-win solution for all parties.
- Be able to think of a completely different solution or idea in order to diffuse the situation if required.
- Check that all parties agree with the outcome and any agreed action at the end of the discussion.

Be able to monitor and evaluate progress and recognise individual and team achievement

In this section you will look at how to monitor and evaluate individual and team activities and progress and provide recognition when individual and team objectives have been met.

Monitor and evaluate individual and team activities and progress

Managing performance is critical. You will need to monitor and evaluate individual and team performance on a regular basis. You may undertake this through some or all of the following.

- Gathering and interpreting performance information from the relevant internal systems in your organisation.
- By discussing performance with your team members on a one-to-one basis for example, through individual discussions, more formalised regular performance meetings or perhaps an annual appraisal meeting.
- By discussing performance with your team members in a group environment for example, through a daily 'stand up' ten-minute meeting or a more formalised regular team meeting.

By motivating, supporting and empowering team members, you will be allowing them to take an active role in shaping your team. It is worth remembering that a team is like a living thing: you

will be able control most elements but not all, and while you will be able to manage the team to some extent, there are other dynamics in place that you may not have control over. Ultimately the team operates on a day-to-day basis based on a number of factors including:

- your own management style
- the development stage that the team is at (forming, norming, storming, performing)
- the dynamics of the team members, including the skills, knowledge and motivations of individual team members
- your interaction with other teams and the interaction that takes place with your customers
- the resources in place and the objectives that you need to achieve with these resources
- your ability to manage performance and link it to organisational objectives
- individuals' understanding their job roles.

Empowerment is the process of allowing your team members to take control over their work and also become involved in the decision-making process.

By empowering employees, you can assist in preparing the organisation towards long-term success by developing key individuals and teams who may generate a competitive advantage for the organisation. This can be achieved by the organisation having more effective employees as a result of them being more skilled and trained than their competitors.

You will need to have a good understanding of the systems and processes in place in your organisation, as a key part of your role will be to monitor and evaluate performance. Once you have interpreted the information, you will need to know what to do next in order to take the most appropriate action.

Provide recognition when individual and team objectives have been met

By trusting and supporting your colleagues, they can become more and more efficient and should begin to strive towards achieving excellence.

By working closely with your team you will develop their skills, knowledge and career aspirations. You can do this by:

- providing training which will develop their knowledge, skills, and competencies
- providing positive and constructive feedback on their performance
- involving team members in the decision-making process and agreeing objectives collectively
- coaching team members on a one-to-one basis and supporting their individual development
- creating a friendly environment where team members feel that their input is valued and welcomed
- creating an open-door policy whereby you make yourself available to all staff at all times
- communicating effectively with your team, by making sure that all team members know what is happening all of the time.

Once you have all of these practical elements in place, it is very likely that your team will be empowered and motivated on a day-to-day basis.

Motivating your team does not have to cost much. You may be able to offer flexible working or incentive schemes. Discuss ideas with your manager and your team. It is sometimes difficult to give monetary rewards, but think of alternative ways to reward your staff.

Your team members don't just need reward, they also need recognition. You should put time aside to speak with each team member individually to acknowledge any good work they have done and see how you might improve the scope of their role or provide them with additional development opportunities.

Portfolio Task 9 60 minutes

Links to LO4: Assessment criteria 4.1, 4.2
Write a personal statement describing how you monitor and evaluate the performance of your team. Explain what processes you undertake (and their frequency) in order to ensure that performance is managed effectively.

Describe any recent achievements that your team has made and also support this with any relevant evidence.

PLTS

By demonstrating how you manage the performance of your team, you will also be detailing how the team members work together and how they participate in the performance-management process on a day-to-day basis. You may also be able to present any relevant evidence, for example any targets you have set a team member or any reviews of performance that you have undertaken (TW; EP; SM).

Remember

Give praise to your team and thank them when they do a good job.

Functional Skills

You may be able to use this personal statement as evidence towards Level 2 Functional Skills in English: Reading and Writing. You need to demonstrate that you have understood the process of how to monitor and evaluate progress and recognise individual and team achievement.

Unit B5 Set objectives and provide support for team members

Team talk

Jodie's story

My name is Jodie and I'm employed as a team leader in a bank in Leicester and I manage a team of eight part-time staff. I've only recently joined the company and it is the first time that I have managed a team. Part of my role is to set and agree objectives with my team and to manage their performance. I agree specific targets with each team member as part of their annual appraisal meeting, but this is something that I have not done before, so I was a little unsure what I needed to do.

I decided to arrange a meeting with my manager to ask her exactly what performance targets we were working towards achieving and how I could manage the process effectively. I knew about some of our performance targets and standards, but I needed everything to be clarified. Before the meeting, I decided that I needed to clarify:

- the exact corporate performance standards that were in place
- the specific targets that were in place for my team to achieve
- when I needed to complete the appraisals by
- how the company dealt with any training requests.

At the meeting, my manager was pleased that I had taken the time to prepare for the meeting and she explained everything to me in detail. I learnt a lot of new things about the company and as a result I was able to structure the appraisal meetings well and set and agree a number of objectives and targets with my team members. I also agreed a process to have a 30 minute one-to-one meeting with each member of my team on a monthly basis to help me manage their performance.

Top tips

Jodie did well to write down a list of all the issues. This demonstrated that she had thought about everything, and by preparing a list she was starting a structured process towards setting and agreeing the objectives and managing the team's performance.

Jodie could have researched the performance targets and objectives in a bit more detail before she met with her manager. By doing this, she would have had more of an overview of the performance standards and objectives that are already in place.

Can you think of anything else that Jodie could have done better?

Ask the expert

Q	I have to formulate a series of SMART objectives for my team. What do I need to do?
A	Begin by clarifying the team's objectives with your manager and then begin to prepare a list of objectives by considering the following items. ■ How will your objectives link to the organisation's overall mission and objectives? ■ How will you prioritise the objectives? ■ Plan your resources – can you complete the objectives alone or do you need any specialist support? ■ Agree dates for completing the objectives. ■ Consult with your team and finalise the objectives. ■ Agree the objectives with the team. ■ Manage the process to ensure that you complete the objectives within the agreed time frame.

What your assessor is looking for

In order to prepare for and succeed in completing this unit, your assessor will require you to be able to demonstrate competence in:

- understanding and being able to describe the purpose and benefits of teamwork

- understanding and being able to describe the purpose of communication in teams and how to communicate effectively

- understanding the purpose and being able to plan with team members how objectives will be met

- valuing a team and being able to demonstrate how to respect and support them

- being able to monitor and evaluate team and individual achievement and provide relevant opportunities to support team members.

You will demonstrate your skills, knowledge and competence through the four learning outcomes in this unit. Evidence generated in this unit will also cross-reference to the other units in this qualification.

Please bear in mind that there are significant cross-referencing opportunities throughout this qualification and you may have already generated some relevant work to meet certain criteria in this unit. Your assessor will provide you with the exact requirements to meet the standards of this unit. However, as a guide, it is likely that for this unit you will need to be assessed through:

- one observation of relevant workplace activities to cover the whole unit

- one witness testimony may also be produced

- a written narrative, reflective account or professional discussion

- any relevant work products to be produced as evidence.

The work products for this unit could include:

- your individual and team's objectives or targets

- relevant research that you have undertaken

- emails or other communication methods that you have used in your team

- copies of any team meeting agendas and minutes

- your organisational structure

- any feedback that you have received on your performance

- your appraisal document

- examples of any creative or innovative working methods.

Your assessor will guide you through the assessment process as detailed in the candidate logbook. The detailed assessment criteria are shown in the logbook and by working through these questions, combined with providing the relevant evidence, you will meet the learning outcomes required to complete this unit.

Task and page reference	Assessment criteria
1 (page 29)	1.1
2 (page 30)	1.2, 1.3
3 (page 32)	1.3
4 (page 34)	2.1, 2.2
5 (page 36)	2.2, 2.4
6 (page 38)	2.3, 2.4
7 (page 40)	3.1, 3.2
8 (page 42)	3.1, 3.2, 3.3, 3.4
9 (page 44)	4.1, 4.2

Unit D5 Plan, allocate and monitor work of a team

Working as a team can provide enormous benefits in terms of productivity, achievement of business goals and creating good working relationships. Teams can achieve work goals that would be impossible for individuals working alone. However, the key to successful teamwork lies in how well its activities and tasks are planned and allocated to the different team members. Good monitoring and management of teamwork processes are also essential in the achievement of the team's work goals.

In this unit, you will investigate some of the best ways of planning teamwork objectives and managing your team effectively to keep on target. You will also look into the issues you need to think about when allocating tasks to the various members of your team. Individual skills, current workload and personalities are all vital elements that you will need to take into account when scheduling and allocating tasks to team members.

What you will learn:

- Be able to plan work for a team
- Be able to allocate work across a team
- Be able to manage team members to achieve team objectives
- Be able to monitor and evaluate the performance of team members
- Be able to improve the performance of a team

Links to the Technical Certificate

If you are completing your NVQ as part of an Apprenticeship Framework, you will find the following topics are also covered in your Technical Certificate:

- Motivating the work team to perform
- Planning and monitoring work
- Team performance

Be able to plan work for a team

Effective planning is a vital first step in scheduling the work of a team so that it can then get on with its tasks efficiently. Working well together and being organised are also central to the achievement of your team's goals. When you plan the work of your team, you will need to think about how to ensure the team members work together in the most effective manner possible and how they can be best organised to get their tasks completed.

Agreeing team objectives with your own manager

Before working out a plan or a schedule for your team's work objectives, you first need to set and agree the objectives with your own line manager. This is the very first step in the objective setting process. It is important because the objectives and targets of your team need to be a good fit with the overarching aims and strategy of the business. This ensures that the individual tasks and activities of each and every team member contribute towards the overall achievement of the business's goals.

Aligning team objectives to the wider business goals

Your line manager will be fully briefed on the wider plans and goals of the business and is therefore well placed to oversee the team

objective-setting process. Securing the agreement of your line manager in this respect ensures that together, you are establishing team objectives that are aligned to the wider business goals.

Negotiating with your manager

A key element of any successful meeting with your manager to set out your team's objectives will involve you having to negotiate effectively with them. This will mean that you have to be **assertive**, stand your ground and defend your team where, for example, your manager has perhaps overestimated the possible work rate of the team or underestimated the equipment costs or numbers of staff required for a particular task. This is all part of good business communication, which is a critical skill for you to develop to become an effective manager.

> **Key Term**
>
> **Assertive** – speaking up for yourself and stating your opinions firmly but not aggressively.

Never be afraid to speak up if your opinion on some aspect of your team's work differs from that of your manager. Your manager is, after all, one step removed from the day-to-day workings of the team, whereas you have more direct, hands-on knowledge.

Negotiating problems or issues in situations such as these can be a very good opportunity

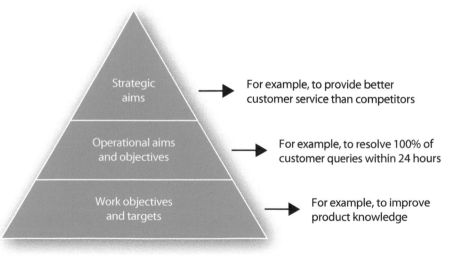

Figure D5.1 Work objectives must fit within the wider goals of the organisation.

for you to demonstrate your professionalism and management skills. You should present your issues to your line manager along with carefully considered alternatives. This way, you are giving your line manager both the problem and a range of possible solutions.

If you fail to flag up any unrealistic expectations on the part of your manager during your objectives setting meetings, you will only be creating problems for yourself and your team members further down the line. This is why it is essential to have any such issues aired at the outset and more realistic solutions found.

> **Activity** ⏱ 15 minutes
>
> Write a brief summary describing the key areas that you would need to discuss with your manager in an objective-setting meeting. Which, if any, of these areas might you be likely to disagree on and why?

> **PLTS**
>
> Reflecting on and evaluating your experiences of meetings will help you to develop your skills as a reflective learner (RL).

Developing a plan for a team to meet agreed objectives

Once you have agreed your team's objectives with your own line manager, you know exactly what is expected of you and your team. The next question is 'How are you going to make it happen?'

The key to your success lies in careful and well thought out planning and in establishing clear work targets that can be easily understood by your team members. In this section, you will look at the planning process, the benefits of careful planning and the various planning tools you can use.

The planning process

During the planning process you will need to think about issues such as:

- the number of team members available to you
- the specific skills and expertise needed and those available
- equipment requirements

- the available budget
- any training or recruitment requirements
- the schedule and any key **milestones**
- any possible **bottlenecks** or hold-ups which may arise along the way – and how you could deal with these.

Taking time out at the beginning to plan your team's work objectives also means that:

- you are less likely to overlook important aspects of the work
- you can think about 'what if' scenarios and build in **contingency plans** to allow for these
- you can apply a **proactive** approach to your planning, rather than merely reacting to – and firefighting – events as you go along.

Essentially, time to plan allows you clear thinking space, so that you can prepare well and manage your team to the best of your ability.

> **Key Terms**
>
> **Bottlenecks** – areas where progress slows or stops due to one part of a process becoming overloaded.
>
> **Contingency plans** – back-up plans in case your main plan has to change.
>
> **Milestones** – key stages within a project.
>
> **Proactive** – thinking ahead and initiating events rather than waiting for things to happen.

> **Remember**
>
> A good planning process helps you to:
> - co-ordinate activities for maximum effectiveness
> - allocate tasks and resources in the best way
> - identify 'what if' scenarios and work out how best you would deal with them.

Breaking down plans into clear work targets

Suppose that your organisation had the overall plan of increasing your team's sales by 15 per cent over the next twelve months. What would you do to translate this business aim into individual work targets for each of your team members? Assume that you have exactly the same number of staff as the previous year and that recruiting additional team members is not an option for you.

One approach could be to examine individual sales achievements for the previous year and work out exactly how many additional sales each team member needs to achieve per annum in order for the team to meet this 15 per cent improvement. Once you have worked out this annual figure, you can then break it down into monthly, weekly and even daily sales targets for each individual.

For example, if the previous year's sales amounted to 120,000 units, then the new target for the following year is 120,000 + 15%, which equals 138,000 units. If you have ten team members, then each person must achieve 13,800 unit sales over the year in order for your team to achieve the new target. Further dividing this figure down, you can see that each team member must achieve 1,150 sales per month, or 57.5 sales per day.

Breaking down the figures in this way allows your team to clearly see what they are expected to achieve on a daily basis. They can also easily measure their own achievements against this figure.

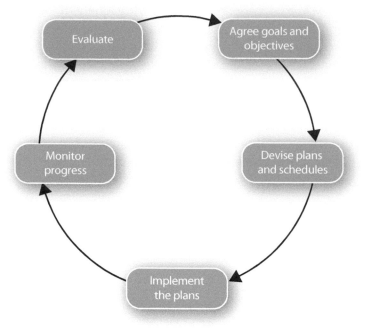

Figure D5.2 Why do you think it is important to use a framework for the planning process?

(its capacity), bearing in mind any existing work commitments, as well as examining individuals' specific skills and abilities in different areas (capabilities). There is little point in setting work plans that are unachievable, so a careful and honest assessment of the team's strengths and weaknesses is critical at this stage. It may also throw up useful indicators of:

* recruitment needs for the team, either now or in the future
* training needs for certain team members, including possibly multi-skilling to create a more **versatile** team
* resourcing problems, such as a lack of adequate equipment.

Any issues that come to light may need flagging up to your line manager to identify the best options for addressing them.

Activity — 15 minutes

Identify one of the current business aims for your organisation that will impact on the work of your team. How would you go about translating this business aim into practical work targets for the team? Sketch out some plans on paper and discuss them with your assessor.

Stages of the planning process

A standard business planning process might look like the one shown in Figure D5.2. It consists of a series of steps or stages, which ensure that all of the essential elements of planning are undertaken.

Capacity and capabilities of the team

It is essential that any work plans that you make for your team take full account of the team's **capacity** and **capabilities**. This means thinking about how much work the team can realistically get through

---

Key Terms

Capabilities – skills and abilities.

Capacity – availability to take on further tasks.

Versatile – capable of carrying out a variety of different tasks.

Activity ⏱ 30 minutes

Look af Figure D5.2 showing the stages of the planning process. For each of the five stages, list the things that you currently do – and any additional actions that you could implement in the future – to manage each stage of the planning process.

PLTS

Reviewing your current actions and exploring new solutions will help you to develop your skills as a creative thinker (CT).

Useful planning techniques

You can start your planning very simply by sketching out your team's work plan on a piece of paper. However, it is recommended that you also keep a computer-based copy of your plan in some form: this will be useful, will appear more professional when presenting to higher management and is very easy to update and amend when required.

There is a variety of different planning tools you can use, such as:

- critical path analysis
- flow charts
- Gantt charts.

Trying out different tools will help you to decide which is most convenient and useful for you for the type of planning work that you need to carry out.

Activity ⏱ 30 minutes

Carry out an analysis of your team's current capacity and capabilities for their work goals and targets. Make brief notes to highlight any issues, such as recruitment or training needs, that you have found. Keep a copy of your analysis for your portfolio as it will be a good source of evidence of your planning skills.

PLTS

Analysing and evaluating your team's capacity and capabilities will help you to develop your skills as an independent enquirer (IE).

Critical path analysis

Critical path analysis (CPA) is a very useful tool for planning larger or more complex projects. Its key benefit, as the name implies, is that it identifies the **critical path** through your project – in other words, the key activities and deadlines by when each must be completed for the project to come in on time.

Key Term

Critical path – a critical path shows the sequence of tasks through a project that must all be conducted on time for the project to complete on time.

Figure D5.3 shows a series of numbered circles, or nodes, representing each task. Each node gives the earliest and latest start and finish times for that task. Where the earliest and latest times are the same, this is where there is no slack at all in the project and gives you your 'critical path'. Tasks that have different earliest and latest start and finish times are the places where there is slack time (sometimes also called float) and some capacity for delays in beginning specific tasks, without impacting the final completion date of the project.

One drawback of CPA is that it looks quite complicated and technical, so it is potentially more difficult to understand than a Gantt chart. A critical path analysis is not normally appropriate for smaller projects.

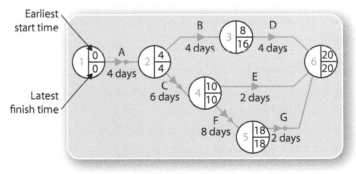

Figure D5.3 Critical path analysis.

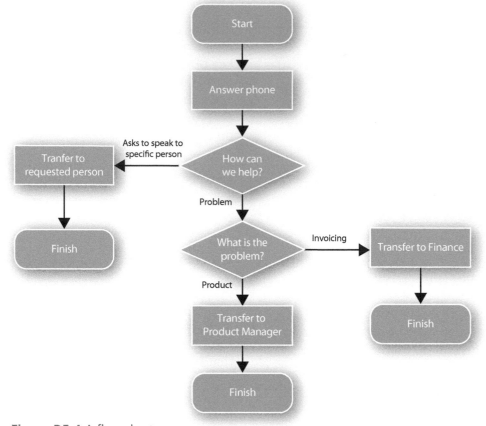

Figure D5.4 A flow chart.

Flow charts

A flow chart is a simple diagram showing all the steps required in a process in the order they need to be completed. Flow charts consist of two different types of steps – actions and decisions. Actions are shown in oblong boxes and decisions in diamond boxes. The start and finish points are shown in rounded boxes. The example in Figure D5.4 shows the process by which receptionists should route incoming calls to a business.

Gantt charts

A Gantt chart is a very widely used method of charting a project. It allows you to list each main task, along with the time needed for it to be completed. It also shows which tasks must be completed before others can begin. Dependency is when one task cannot begin until another has finished. For example, if you are making a cup of tea, you cannot pour the water into the cup until you have boiled the kettle, so pouring on the water is dependent on having first boiled the kettle!

A Gantt chart gives you a very good visual overview of the whole project, along with a clear picture of the key milestones along the way. Time is usually plotted along the x-axis and the tasks are plotted along the y-axis. Gantt charts are commonly used in all areas of business to present project plans to senior management and clients. You can easily put together a simple Gantt chart using Microsoft® Project or other similar software.

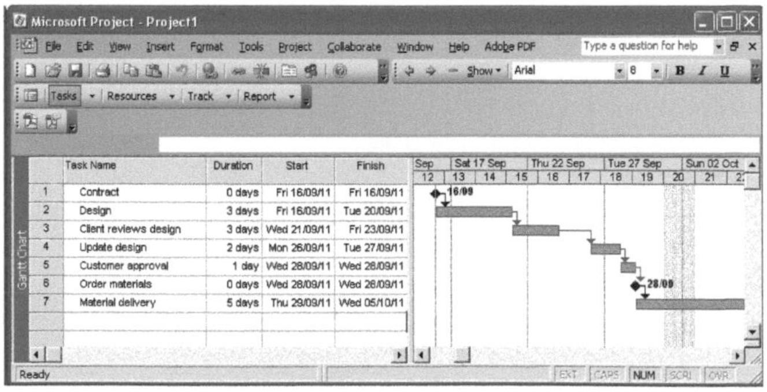

Figure D5.5 A Gantt chart.

Activity
30 minutes

Carry out research to find more information on at least three planning tools and techniques. You can research the techniques mentioned in this section, or you can find out about others if you wish. Write a brief, one-paragraph summary on each of the techniques which you research. Some useful websites you could visit for information include www.businessballs.com and www.mindtools.com. Ask colleagues at work if they use any specific planning techniques that may also be useful for you.

Functional Skills

Taking part in a professional discussion with your assessor as part of your assessment will allow you to practise your Functional English Speaking and Listening skills.

PLTS

Analysing and evaluating the different planning tools which you could adopt for your job will help you to develop your skills as an independent enquirer (IE).

Portfolio Task 1
1 hour

Links to LO1: Assessment criteria 1.1, 1.2

1. Describe the reasons why it is important to agree team objectives with your own manager. Give an example of an occasion when you have done this and include any relevant work documents to support your answer. If you have not yet agreed team objectives with your manager, say what you think would be the key issues to cover and why.

2. Describe the steps involved in developing a plan for a team to meet agreed objectives, taking into account capacity and capabilities of the team. Show how the development of your plan fits into the stages of the planning process model outlined in this section. You will also need to show that you understand what is meant by the terms 'capacity' and 'capability' and outline how you have accounted for these elements in your plan.

Your assessment could take the form of a written narrative or a professional discussion with your assessor. It could also include the production of workplace evidence, work-based observations or the use of witness testimonies, as appropriate.

Be able to allocate work across a team

The way in which you communicate your plans with your team will have a huge influence on how motivated your team are about them. Openness, enthusiasm and a positive approach on your part will be more likely to result in a successful start to your team's project. Allocating work according to individual team members' skills and aptitudes is also a critical consideration in determining the success of the team's work.

Discussing plans with your team

It is important that you take the time to brief your team on your plans for their work. The better the communication process, the more likely your team are to:

- understand what is required of them
- be committed to the team's goals
- feel involved and motivated.

Remember, your team cannot hope to perform well if they have not been told clearly the overall goal which they are working towards. Give them the big picture and this will help them to understand specific work objectives.

Effective team briefing helps your team understand their work goals.

Briefing meetings

Set up a briefing meeting with your team to tell them about the plans. Make sure you are well prepared for your meeting by collecting together all of the information that you will need beforehand. Produce a **meeting agenda** and circulate it to your team in advance to give everyone time to read it. Give yourself time to think about how you will present to your team and practise your delivery in a warm, open and informative way.

Communication

Remember that you need to establish two-way communications with your team so they feel able to speak up, ask questions and give their own suggestions. **Participation** increases motivation!

Key Terms

Meeting agenda – a list of the main points to be discussed in a meeting.

Participation – actively taking part.

Checklist

The golden rules for successful team meetings are:
- be very clear
- encourage participation
- set out team rules and processes
- check everyone understands.

Commitment

Aim to get 100 per cent agreement on – and commitment to – the team's plans as early as possible. Allowing your team to input into this process helps to give them ownership of it, which is a great method of increasing motivation.

Clarity

Most of all, you need to remember to make the briefing meeting as clear as possible, so that everybody understands what is going on and can see how their individual contribution to the team is valuable. This is also a perfect opportunity for you to assert your skills as team leader and set out the ground rules and working guidelines for the team's processes.

Activity ⏱ 15 minutes

How well do you handle team briefings? Look at the following list and make notes on how well you carry out each of the following tasks. Then, list some of the things you could do in the future to improve your team communication skills.

- I always set a clear purpose for my team meetings.
- I aim to get full agreement on team goals.
- I actively encourage contributions from each of my team members.
- I listen to my team.
- I establish the ground rules on how team processes will work.

Agreeing work allocation and SMART objectives with team members

Allocating the work tasks to your team members is an area requiring skill and judgement. On one hand, you need to assign tasks in such a way that the work can be completed efficiently, on the other, you also need to think about being seen to be fair. Questions that you need to consider include the following.

- Do your team members have the required skills to complete the work you are allocating to them – or will additional training be needed?

	Monday	Tuesday	Wednesday	Thursday	Friday	Saturday	Sunday
Sophie	Kitchen 8–1	Kitchen 8–1	Kitchen 8–1			Kitchen 8–1	Kitchen 8–1
Charlie	Kitchen 10–7		Kitchen 10–7	Kitchen 10–7	Kitchen 10–7	Kitchen 10–7	
Marcus	Kitchen 1–9	Kitchen 1–9		Kitchen 1–9	Kitchen 1–9		Kitchen 11–7
Rhys		Bar 9–3	Bar 9–3	Bar 9–3		Bar 5–11	Bar 5–11
Olivia	Bar 5–11	Kitchen 10–7	Bar 5–11		Bar 5–11	Kitchen 1–9	
Stephen		Bar 5–11	Bar 5–11	Bar 5–11	Bar 9–3	Bar 9–3	
Ashleigh				Bar 5–11	Bar 5–11	Bar 12–7	Bar 9–3
Deena	Bar 9–3			Bar 12–7	Bar 12–7		
Sanjay	Bar 12–7	Bar 12–7	Bar 12–7			Bar 5–11	Bar 12–7
Gabriela	Bar 5–11	Bar 5–11	Kitchen 1–9	Kitchen 8–1	Kitchen 8–1		

Figure D5.6 A staff rota showing a team's work allocation for the coming week.

- Are the team happy with the tasks allocated to them? If not, you need to address this issue quickly to keep morale from dropping and to prevent conflict arising.
- Has the workload been allocated evenly to each of the team members? Have you taken into account the time, effort and skill-set involved in each task?
- Is there a dependence on certain team members to complete key tasks? Can you deal with this by coaching or training other team members?

Once you have agreed the work allocation among your team, you should have a list of who will do what and by when. You may have this information in the form of a rota or schedule. Make sure to recap the task assignments to the team once they are finalised and use this as an opportunity to take questions and clarify any points needing explanation. Once the final amendments are complete, remember to circulate the schedule to the team.

Delegation

By allocating tasks to your team members, you are delegating work to them. **Delegation** is a vitally important management skill and it is essential that you do it well. When you delegate work to a team member, you are assigning work – and authority – to them, although you retain ultimate responsibility for the overall completion of the task. Delegation is a necessary activity for the simple reason that you cannot do everything yourself. That's why you have to employ management skills such as delegating tasks to others.

Key Term

Delegation – assigning tasks or responsibilities to someone else to complete.

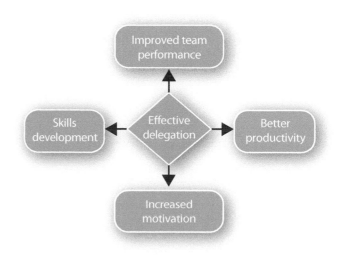

Figure D5.7 Delegation.

Benefits of effective delegation

Effective delegation has many benefits: it is central to improved team performance, better productivity and increased motivation as staff enjoy being given more responsibility. Staff are also given the chance to experience new and challenging tasks and to develop additional skills. This is of great benefit to the team and even to the business as a whole, as it will ensure smooth **succession planning** with suitably skilled and experienced staff moving easily into more senior positions when they become available in the future.

Establishing your level of delegation

It is possible to delegate in different ways. Let's suppose, for example, that you ask one of your team to research an issue for you so that a decision can then be made. You could:

- make the decision yourself based on the findings
- allow your team member to make the decision
- make the decision together, after discussing the findings with one another.

Whichever approach you decide to take with delegation, make sure that you are absolutely clear about this to your team beforehand. This avoids any misunderstandings and makes sure that

Checklist

The golden rules for effective delegation are:

- delegate as much as you can to your team
- trust them to get on with the tasks
- be clear with them on your delegation rules
- match tasks to team skills and preferences
- do not keep the best tasks for yourself.

everyone knows what is expected of them. Also, be very careful to avoid the common error of **micro-managing** your team once you have delegated a task to them. You simply have to trust them to get it done in the manner they find most suitable.

Key Terms

Micro-managing – closely monitoring and controlling the work activities of others.

Succession planning – planning for future staffing requirements.

Agreeing SMART objectives with team members

You are probably already familiar with SMART objectives, as they crop up in many of the units. SMART stands for:

- Specific – exactly what needs to be completed and to what standard (within 24 hours, within three rings, with no more than 5 per cent error rate)
- Measurable – including a number, such as 100 sales, 15 phone calls, 20 customer complaints resolved
- Achievable – objectives need to be achievable by the vast majority of staff, not just the top 5 per cent, so don't set goals that only your best salesman can ever hope to achieve
- Realistic – objectives must be firmly founded in reality
- Time-bound – have a time by when the objective must be completed (this is usually over a relatively short time frame and should always be within 12 months).

Activity 🕐 10 minutes

Look at the following list and think about how good your delegation skills are. Identify any areas where you are strong and any areas where you may have development needs. Write a short comment against each of the criteria so that you can show it to your assessor.

- I let my team know clearly the level of delegation which I use.
- I show my team that I trust them to get on with the work.
- I consider individual skills and preferences when I am deciding which tasks to delegate to whom.
- I do not keep the best tasks for myself.
- I allow extra time for team members doing tasks for the first time.

Agreeing SMART objectives with your team members breaks down the overall aims and mission of the team into individual, manageable work tasks, complete with all of the information they need to ensure they can achieve them.

> **Remember**
>
> High-performing teams always have clear and understandable objectives in place. Without these, people will not be able to work together effectively as a team.

Take a look at the following example of an objective for an events co-ordinator role in a marketing company:

Secure at least 500 attendees at the annual national telemarketing conference, which takes place on 30 November. This will be achieved by sending invitations to all registered members of the professional association by 30 June. The list of registered members is available from the administration department.

Look to see how this objective satisfies the SMART criteria:

Specific	– to secure attendees for the annual national marketing conference
Measurable	– 500 attendees is a measurable target
Achievable	– the list of registered members is available
Realistic	– inviting guests in June to attend a conference in November is realistic
Time-bound	– invitations need to be sent by 30 June.

> **Activity** 🕐 30 minutes
>
> Make a list of at least three objectives that you have, or could set for your team members. For each one, address the five elements of the SMART acronym to show how your team's objectives satisfy these criteria. If any of your objectives are not SMART, or could be improved, this is a good opportunity for you to develop them.

Agreeing standard of work required by your team

Standards of work refer to the precise performance details that are required in a given task. For example, a customer service agent position may have the following standards:

- answer the phone within three rings
- speak in a polite and friendly manner to all customers
- return calls to customers within 24 hours
- resolve all customer complaints or, where this is not possible, refer them to a line manager before the end of the business day.

Notice in the example above that some standards refer to precise numbers (answer the phone within three rings, return calls to customers within 24 hours), whereas others are more general. Standards with numbers attached to them are sometimes also referred to as targets, although they essentially mean the same thing.

Standards are very important for you to be aware of as a team leader because:

- they provide the guidelines by which people know when they have succeeded in completing a task correctly
- they ensure consistency in work output over time, no matter who is performing a given task
- they help staff to know exactly what is required of them
- they will provide the basis for your subsequent checking and monitoring of work.

> **Activity** 🕐 10 minutes
>
> List three examples of work tasks that your team needs to complete. For each one, state the standards that are applied to that task. Explain how team members are made aware of these standards. If there are no existing standards in place, devise new standards of your own and say how these will be communicated to staff.

Negotiating with team members

A key part of agreeing the standards of work required by your team will involve negotiating with them – either individually or as a group. Negotiations will most likely concern the allocation of tasks to be completed.

For example, what if one of your team members had a particular preference for one task over another? How would you go about securing their agreement and commitment to their work? One approach could be that you decide to switch task allocation around to other members to accommodate preferences. A note of caution here – remember to be seen to be equally fair and accommodating to all of your team if you do this.

You cannot negotiate with one of your team and refuse to be accommodating to another.

Switching tasks may also be necessary due to the individual skill sets of the various team members. One person may be very good at closing sales, for example, but not so efficient at administration. Allocating tasks according to skill sets is an effective way of improving team efficiency, especially in the short term.

Functional Skills

If you produce a written report as part of your assessment, this will allow you to practise your Functional Skills in English: Writing.

Portfolio Task 2
⏱ 2 hours

Links to LO2: Assessment criteria 2.1, 2.2, 2.3

1. Explain the reasons why you think it is important to discuss team plans with your team. Write a short checklist, which could be used to train new team leaders, showing the essential 'dos and don'ts' relating to such team discussions.

2. Explain how you would go about agreeing work allocation with your team members. What issues might you come across during this process? Say how you would deal with these.

3. State the reasons why you should always agree SMART objectives with team members. Include examples of work-based SMART objectives which you have, or could have, set for your team to demonstrate how you might go about this process.

4. Give reasons to explain why it is essential to agree standards of work required by your team. If possible, show evidence of standards which you could use with your team.

Your assessment could take the form of a written narrative or a professional discussion with your assessor. It could also include the production of workplace evidence, work-based observations or the use of witness testimonies as appropriate.

Be able to manage team members to achieve team objectives

Management involves many different skills and activities, such as leading, delegating, co-ordinating, checking, monitoring and evaluating. In this section, you will investigate how you can apply your management skills to ensure that your team achieve their objectives and operate as a high-performing unit.

Supporting team members to achieve objectives

Providing support to your team members will be an ongoing responsibility for you as team leader. Supporting team members helps keep everybody on track and can bring a halt to any issues that are slowing down productivity.

Providing support involves:

- coaching
- providing timely one-to-one feedback
- conducting regular group update meetings.

Coaching

Coaching is the provision of support and guidance in order to help people to improve their performance. It is an informal process where a person with more experience helps new and inexperienced team members to become fully competent in their job. Coaching is an **on-the-job** process, which is based on good relationships and a caring approach.

Key Terms

On-the-job – taking place while doing the job, i.e. not away from the workplace, for instance in college.

Timely – something that occurs exactly when it is needed.

As team leader, if you notice that one of your team is struggling with a certain aspect of their job, you should consider coaching as an effective approach for performance improvement and one that provides very quick results. The main drawback, however, is that it is an expensive and potentially time-consuming technique, especially as only one person is being coached at a time.

If you do not have the time to coach others yourself, you could consider nominating other, suitably experienced, members of your team as coaches to help newer members of staff. This can also be an excellent way of building good relationships among team members.

Activity — 15 minutes

Do you employ coaching, either yourself, or via more experienced members of the team? If so, give examples of the types of coaching that occur in your team. If you do not currently use coaching, talk about whether and how it could be used in your team.

Providing timely one-to-one feedback

A key ingredient of providing effective support to your team involves giving **timely** one-to-one feedback. There are two reasons for this. First, your team members value their one-to-one time with you, as this is a good sounding board for discussing things they may not like to mention in front of the whole team. Second, keeping your team informed about their current progress on a regular basis is vital, so that they have up-to-date knowledge about how they are doing. These feedback sessions need not take long, nor should they be at all formal.

Remember

Even if there are no issues to discuss and the feedback meeting is just to say that everything is fine, it is still important to keep feedback regular. It is also a good opportunity to recognise successes.

Conducting regular group update meetings

The key to supporting your whole team is providing them with regular information on the team's overall progress with a focus on collective, rather than individual, contributions. A short, weekly meeting is often suitable for this purpose, although the frequency will depend on your particular company or industry.

Regular group update meetings are an excellent forum for recognising team achievements, reinforcing the team purpose and encouraging contributions from each team member. They are also a good source of identifying any issues and addressing them before they cause damage to the team's morale and its productivity.

For example, in a retail store, you would be able to get feedback from the shop floor sales team on how well a product is selling, which products your customers prefer or which products are being regularly returned to the store.

Activity ⏱ 15 minutes

What types of useful information would you be able to obtain from your team by having regular meetings with them? Make a list of some of the key issues relevant to your team or department.

Portfolio Task 3 ⏱ 30 minutes

Links to LO3: Assessment criterion 3.1

Explain why it is important to provide support to all team members in order to achieve team objectives. Give examples of the ways in which you either do, or could, provide ongoing support to your team. Include any relevant work documents to support your answer.

Your assessment could take the form of a written narrative or a professional discussion with your assessor. It could also include the production of workplace evidence, work-based observations or the use of witness testimonies, as appropriate.

Functional Skills

If you use computer-generated documents to provide evidence towards your assessment, this will allow you to practise your Functional Skills in ICT: Developing, presenting and communicating information.

Regular team updates keep everyone informed on progress against targets.

Be able to monitor and evaluate the performance of team members

Performance monitoring is an essential part of effective team management and you will need to have suitable procedures in place to provide you with reliable performance indicators for your team. In this section, you'll take a closer look at how to go about the process of effectively monitoring and evaluating the performance of your team.

Assessing work against agreed standards and objectives

Earlier in the unit, you looked at both objective and standard setting for your team. Together, these objectives and standards will provide the basis upon which you will carry out assessment of your team's work. Conducting your assessment based on objectives and standards ensures **objectivity**, fairness and consistency, so that each member of your team is treated equally when being assessed.

It also ensures that the criteria on which you are basing the assessment are directly related to the key outcomes required for the team. In other words, these are the important **performance indicators** on which your team will be judged by senior management. Some examples of performance indicators might include:

- number of outbound calls made
- value of sales made
- number of complaints resolved.

Key Terms

Objectivity – based on facts, neutral and unbiased.

Performance indicators – measures that show the achievement of objectives.

There will be two aspects to your assessment – individual and whole team assessment. We'll begin by looking at individual assessment.

Individual team member assessment

Assessment can be done using a form such as the one on the next page, which is based on the objectives and standards for that role. The example below is for a customer service agent.

Forms such as the one below are useful ways of assessing individual team member's performance against objectives and standards. Results for all of the team can then be compiled to create a team assessment profile. This will give you a very clear, detailed picture of the strengths and weaknesses of your team.

Team member assessment form

Team:	Customer service team
Team member name:	Leanne Evans
Role:	Customer service agent
Team leader:	Brian Fieldings

Assessment rating key:

Unacceptable	Satisfactory	Good	Very good	Outstanding
1	2	3	4	5

Role objectives and standards	Rating
Speak politely and cheerfully to customers	5
Answer the phone within three rings	5
Answer ten calls per hour	3
Keep the call-waiting queue to no more than six	3
Resolve complaints received by phone from customers or, if not possible, refer them to a line manager the same day	5

Key strengths:	Always professional and polite in all dealings with customers. Very efficient at resolving customer complaints.
Areas for development:	Needs to attempt to get through more customer calls per hour. Needs to focus on reducing the call-waiting queue.
Comments:	Overall, a very good performance assessment with strong evidence of outstanding performance in some areas. Leanne has an excellent track record for successfully resolving all types of customer complaints. A focus on increasing the speed of dealing with each case would make for an overall outstanding assessment next time.

Figure D5.8 An example team member assessment form.

Team-based assessment

Carrying out the assessment of the team's work will require a combination of:

- ongoing observation of performance
- data collection and analysis.

Activity ⊘ 30 minutes

What do you think are the key areas on which your team should be assessed? Research any existing assessment documents for guidance or, if there is nothing currently available, put together a team assessment checklist of your own.

Ongoing observation of performance

Ongoing observation of your team's performance will give you immediate information on any gaps where standards are, for whatever reason, not being met. It is your responsibility to provide the necessary support to bring about improvements in such situations. These **performance gaps** can occur for many reasons and the support that you put in place needs to be sensitive to this.

For example, it may simply be that someone has not understood clearly what they were supposed to do. This is a straightforward issue to put right. It may be, however, that someone is having personal issues which are having an impact on their performance. In this type of situation, you would be wise to seek advice from your own line manager before trying to deal with it, especially if you are new to this type of situation. It may be appropriate in such cases to refer the matter to the human resources department within your organisation so that they can refer the employee for counselling or provide other supportive measures.

Activity ⊘ 15 minutes

Think about what you would do if you encountered a performance gap in your team. Describe what you think is the correct way to deal with this situation.

Data collection and analysis

Part of your ongoing monitoring and evaluation will require you to gather data on your team's work output. Depending on the nature of your team and the industry in which it operates, this may include collecting figures for things such as:

- sales made
- complaints resolved
- units produced
- services provided to customers
- commissions earned from sales made.

These figures give you a measurement of the actual work output of your team. You can look at the figures over time to see whether output is increasing or decreasing overall, identify any peaks or troughs in output and any seasonal, monthly, weekly or even daily variations. You can also further break down the figures to identify output per employee.

This kind of analysis helps you to plan ahead for appropriate staffing levels, to avoid the problem of too few or too many staff on certain shifts. It also allows you to plan ahead for the ordering of the correct amount of materials and stock, as well as looking at ways of making the best use of time during quieter periods.

You will also need to collect figures for issues such as:

- usage of materials including wastage
- number of customer complaints
- number of product defects
- error rates
- production **downtime**.

Key Terms

Downtime – time lost at work due to machinery or system failure or personnel problems.

Performance gap – a gap between the current and the required performance standards.

By including issues such as these in your data analysis, you can identify areas where costs can be reduced or downtimes can be improved, to increase the overall productivity of your team.

Using graphs to analyse your figures

The best way to analyse your team's output figures is to put them into graphical format. You can easily do this using a program such as Excel® or other similar software. The longer the time period over which you can collect data, the more meaningful any analysis will be. For example, figures for output for one single month of the year will only provide you with a brief snapshot of performance. However, if you have the figures for the whole of the last twelve months, you will be able to gain very useful information which will help you plan for the following year.

Take a look at the following graph, which shows factory output over a 12 month period.

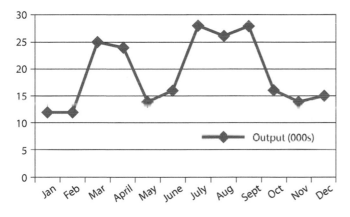

Figure D5.9 Factory output over a year.

If you look closely at the figures over the year, there are two main findings you can draw. The first thing to note is that there are two major peaks in output over the year. The first occurs in March to April and the second occurs in July to September. During these two peak periods, output is almost double that of the other months.

The second key finding is that, overall, you can see a general upward trend in output over the year. You could reasonably expect this general trend to continue in the following year.

You can produce similar graphs to show your team's performance figures for complaints, defect

rates and any other aspect of team performance that you need to monitor. This is a good method of identifying improvements against targets over a set period of time.

Identifying and monitoring conflict

Disagreements are inevitable among team members at times, especially when they are under pressure, or feel passionately about something. However, when such disagreements become a permanent feature of working life, or disrupt the ethos of the team, then this is where disagreement has descended into conflict and needs resolving.

Possible sources of conflict

Conflict can arise from many areas, but the following are often key triggers:

- personality clashes among team members
- power battles and overly competitive team members
- team members focused more on their individual goals than those of the team
- hidden agendas
- communication problems within the team
- unclear goals
- low morale among team members.

From your own experience as a team leader, you could probably add more issues to this list.

Monitoring conflict

It is essential for you to keep a close eye on the functioning of your team, including levels of harmony. You need to spot the difference between healthy debate and serious disagreements and conflict in the team. If left unresolved, conflict will ruin the effectiveness of the team and undo all of your hard work and team-building efforts.

Things to watch out for include the following:

- Tasks – are there particular tasks or processes that are the source of constant argument among the team? If so, you may need to evaluate your team's current processes and implement new working arrangements which eliminate this issue.

- People – are there any particular people who are the source of conflict or aggression? If this is the case, and personality clashes are the root cause of the problem, maybe a change of team membership could be the solution.

- Behaviour – is there evidence of bullying, harassment or any other inappropriate behaviour within the team? If so, you must address this immediately and decisively. You would be advised to speak to your human resources department in situations such as these.

Checklist

Remember, when dealing with conflict to:

- identify the problem by fact finding
- speak to everybody concerned
- listen to the issues
- decide on the most appropriate solution
- monitor the situation afterwards.

Activity ⏱ 15 minutes

What would you do if you encountered examples of conflict within your team? How do you think you would handle the situation? Find out what the specific guidelines are in your organisation for dealing with such issues. It is important for you to be aware of these to ensure you act in accordance with organisational guidelines if any such circumstances occur.

Dealing with conflict

The specific way in which you handle a conflict situation will depend on its circumstances and its root cause. However, the following are some principles that are useful in most conflict handling situations.

1. Be assertive.

2. Get all of the facts from the affected parties before you decide on the solution.

3. Try to get agreement from opposing parties on the solution but if this is not possible, use your leadership position to take the decision and implement it quickly.

4. Act decisively.

5. Carefully monitor the situation afterwards to be sure that it has, in fact, been resolved.

Ensuring the conflict has been resolved

It is part of the conflict-handling process to make certain that all issues have been resolved and that no **grievances** linger afterwards. Unresolved conflict can escalate into further aggression and even physical violence in the workplace, resulting in serious disciplinary action and even prosecution. This is reason enough to follow up on all such situations and to ensure that they have been dealt with satisfactorily.

Organisational policies for managing workplace conflict

Conflict can have an impact on other areas such as health and safety, discrimination, equality and diversity, as well as grievance and discipline, which are all specifically covered by employment legislation. Where an employee raises a grievance as a result of conflict, then the conflict has moved from an informal to a formal position and the organisation must then invoke its workplace policies and procedures for dealing with it.

ACAS recommends that, for this reason, organisations should put in place specific conflict-handling policies that are separate from the grievance and disciplinary procedure. They also recommend including **mediation** as a stage in the conflict-handling process. Mediation is carried out by an independent and impartial person, which could be a member of the organisation, such as a representative from the human

---

Key Terms

ACAS – Advisory, Conciliation and Arbitration Service – a statutory, independent body that offers advice to employers and employees on many workplace matters including grievances and disputes.

Grievance – a cause for complaint, which can be the result of a wrongdoing or a hardship suffered.

Mediation – help from an independent third party in reaching agreement between opposing individuals or groups.

resources department, or it could be carried out by an outside body. The aim of mediation is not to impose a solution, but instead to help the individuals or groups involved in the conflict to reach agreement on an acceptable solution.

Consulting with employees

Many organisations have established structures in place for consulting with employees on issues that are often the cause of conflict. These can include working groups, which are temporary groups set up on an ad hoc basis to look at a specific issue, and staff councils, which are permanent groups established to periodically review issues on an ongoing basis.

Dispute resolution procedures

Where conflict cannot be resolved through consulting with employees, organisations can turn to their dispute resolution procedures. These might include:

- written agreements between the organisation and its recognised trade union on the methods which will be used in resolving disputes
- approaching another third party, such as ACAS, to assist in the dispute resolution process.

Identifying causes for team members not meeting team objectives

There are a number of possible reasons why team members may fail to meet their objectives. For example, team members may be completely overloaded with work at a given point and feel unable to live up to the expectations made of them. They may have misunderstood their objectives, or they may have health or other personal issues which are having an impact on their performance. As team leader, it is your responsibility to identify the reasons for poor performance and to take steps to put them right, if this is possible.

Your first task, having identified an underperforming team member, is to speak to them about it. Point out the issue and see if they can help identify the reasons. They may well have a perfectly valid reason for the underperformance.

For example, it could point to a lack of adequate training or a lack of direction. Perhaps the objectives which were set were too complicated or too demanding. Issues such as these are fairly easy to put right, with a little investigation on your part. Other issues, such as personal problems, may require the intervention of the human resources department, as they have expertise in this area and are probably better placed to provide the necessary help and support to the team member.

Portfolio Task 4 — 60 minutes

Links to LO4: Assessment criteria 4.1, 4.2, 4.3

1. Explain the reasons why it is important to assess team members' work against agreed standards and objectives. Give examples of the ways in which you either do, or could, go about this process as part of your job. Include any relevant work documents which provide evidence of your team assessment activities to support your answer.

2. Describe the steps you could take to identify and monitor conflict within your team. Explain why monitoring conflict within a team is so important. Discuss any work-based rules or guidelines for dealing with conflict situations that exist in your organisation.

3. Identify some of the main causes for team members not meeting team objectives and say how you would deal with each of these issues. If you have experienced your own team members failing to meet objectives, discuss these examples in your answer.

Your assessment could take the form of a written narrative or a professional discussion with your assessor. It could also include the production of workplace evidence, work-based observations or the use of witness testimonies, as appropriate.

Functional Skills

If you produce a written report as part of your assessment, this will allow you to practise your Functional Skills in English: Writing.

Be able to improve the performance of a team

In this section, you'll investigate various ways in which you can make your team more productive and effective and the benefits of this. You will look at methods of providing constructive feedback to aid performance as well as investigating how to implement performance improvement measures.

Identifying ways of improving team performance

Improving your team's performance has many benefits, both to the team and the business, including:

- improved efficiency
- increased morale among staff
- reduced waste
- more streamlined processes
- staff are less likely to leave the team.

But however successful your team may currently be, there is always room for improvement. Having a clear focus on certain factors will reap enormous benefits to your team's performance. You could:

- find ways of increasing collaboration
- focus on collective team spirit rather than individual achievement
- set clear and challenging goals and objectives
- encourage participation in decision making
- aim to get 100 per cent agreement to goals and processes
- nurture a positive team culture.

All of these factors aim to increase team motivation as the basis for better performance.

Motivating your team

Motivation is what makes us want to do something. So, how do you make your team want to do something? There are various theories on the subject. We will take a brief look at some of these so that you have an appreciation of the thinking behind certain systems of job design, rewards and bonuses adopted by organisations.

Taylorism

Frederick Winslow Taylor put forward the theory of **scientific management**. This argued that workers were naturally lazy, unwilling to work hard and were mainly motivated by money. From this, he developed a system of paying workers based on their output. This was called a **piece rate** system where, the harder a worker worked and the more they produced, the greater the pay they received. This type of thinking is behind many sales pay structures, where salespeople are paid either a basic wage plus a **commission** on each sale made or even paid commission-only.

Key Terms

Commission – a monetary reward, often a set percentage of the value involved, paid to an agent in a commercial transaction.

Piece rate – a payment system where workers are paid per unit produced or per sale made.

Scientific management – a theory of management that used science to improve work efficiency.

Mayo's Hawthorne studies

Elton Mayo studied workers in a factory in Chicago. He changed various aspects of their working conditions to see what effect this had on their productivity. He found that workers were motivated by:

- working in groups rather than working alone
- greater involvement from management
- better communication with management.

Mayo's work was hugely influential and began the development of personnel or human resources departments in organisations, which had the aim of looking after the interests of employees.

Activity
15 minutes

To what extent do you think that Mayo's theory of motivation has been adopted by your own organisation? How much are group working, involvement and communication used as motivators by management? Decide whether you think motivation could be improved by increasing the use of these methods and give examples to support your opinion.

Maslow's hierarchy of needs

Abraham Maslow put forward a theory of motivation with a focus on workers' different levels of need. He argued that there was a hierarchy of five different levels of needs with basic survival at the bottom and **self-actualisation** at the top. He argued that the needs at the bottom of the hierarchy had to be fulfilled before moving up to the next level. So, a worker who was not earning enough money to feed his family and therefore not yet having his basic need for survival satisfied, would hardly be expected to be concerned with matters such as status, recognition and self-esteem. Maslow's theory argues that, as workers progress up each level of the hierarchy their focus moves away from the most basic and onto the achievement of increasingly prestigious aims.

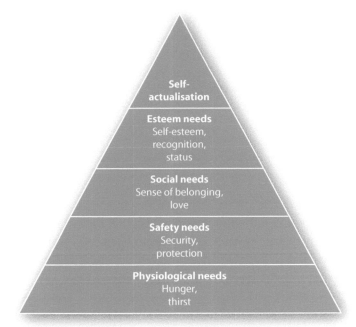

Figure D5.10 Maslow's hierarchy of needs.

Key Term

Self-actualisation – achieving your highest career potential.

Activity 15 minutes

Apply Maslow's theory to your own organisation. For each of the five levels of need that Maslow identified, think of a way in which your organisation tries to satisfy this need. Use a table like the one below to record your thoughts. Some suggestions are included under the table to help you. The first example has been completed for you.

Need	How my organisation tries to satisfy this need
Physiological needs – hunger, thirst	A basic wage
Safety needs – security, protection	
Social needs – sense of belonging, love	
Esteem needs – self-esteem, recognition, status	
Self-actualisation	

Suggestions: job security, a team culture, benefits such as company cars and bonuses, opportunities for career advancement and self-development.

Herzberg's dual factor theory of motivation

Frederick Herzberg put forward a theory of motivation consisting of two elements:

- motivators – aspects of the job itself, such as opportunities for interesting work, responsibility and promotion, which made people want to work harder

- hygiene factors – not directly concerned with the job itself but with issues surrounding the job, such as pay and safety conditions at work.

Herzberg argued that if hygiene factors were not provided, dissatisfaction would arise. However, just providing these basic elements did not bring about motivation, it just removed dissatisfaction.

Herzberg thought that organisations should therefore focus on designing jobs in ways to bring about motivation at work including job enlargement (providing a variety of tasks for interest), job enrichment (providing increasingly challenging tasks for a sense of achievement) and empowerment (increased responsibility for decision making).

Providing constructive feedback to improve performance

Constructive feedback is designed to focus on positives and on producing improvements. It is intended to be helpful and not to be personally critical in nature. Constructive feedback can nevertheless be used to discuss both good and bad aspects of performance.

The key to effective constructive feedback lies in its delivery. Negative aspects of feedback are conveyed in a careful and non-offensive way, so that the focus is clearly on how to bring about any necessary improvements and on what help can be given to achieve this. With constructive feedback the performance may be criticised, but never the person. The following are examples of how negative aspects of performance can be dealt with in a constructive way.

'I've noticed that you seem to be having a little trouble getting to grips with the new payroll system. Perhaps some further training would be helpful for you. I can speak to human resources to sort this out for you. How would you feel about that?'

'Your paperwork is sometimes a little late in being completed. Perhaps it would be a good idea to set aside the last hour of each day and use this to complete your forms. Do you think this would be helpful to you?'

Activity ⏱ 15 minutes

List three performance issues you think you may potentially have to deal with when providing feedback to your team members. For each one, practise the wording you could use in order to raise the issue with them in a constructive way, focused on helping them to improve.

The constructive feedback process

The usual process for constructive feedback is as follows:

- begin with a positive area by congratulating an achievement
- mention a less positive area of performance and offer help and support to bring about the required improvements
- end on a positive note, maybe by summarising an overall good performance or by mentioning some positive feedback received from a colleague, manager or customer.

This process is sometimes referred to as a feedback sandwich, or a caring sandwich.

Figure D5.11 Feedback sandwich.

Why do you think it is important to begin and end on a positive note when providing constructive feedback?

Implementing team performance improvement measures

Team performance improvement measures can be concerned with many different aspects of the team's work including:

- production output
- error reductions
- cost savings and reduction in waste
- team absence and punctuality
- quality improvements to both goods and services.

For example, suppose that you are going to implement a performance improvement measure to increase the quality of your customer service so that 99 per cent of all calls are correctly dealt with within 24 hours.

The following shows one approach to implementing this measure.

1. Hold a team meeting to announce the measure.
2. Get commitment from everyone involved – this could include providing **incentives** such as bonuses for achieving the new targets.
3. Set clear targets for each individual, along with time limits for reaching them.
4. Arrange any training needed by team members.
5. Examine the performance figures as soon as they are available to you and monitor performance improvements against target.
6. Keep the team regularly updated on their progress against targets and make sure you reward achievements.

Key Term

Incentives – any items (monetary or otherwise) that motivate a particular action.

Activity ⏱ 15 minutes

Think about one way in which you could implement a team performance improvement action. Describe what the area of performance is and say how you would go about implementing the measure including how you will measure the result to identify the extent to which it has improved.

PLTS

Setting performance improvement measures will help you to develop your skills as a reflective learner (RL).

Portfolio Task 5 ⏱ 60 minutes

Links to LO5: Assessment criteria 5.1, 5.2, 5.3

1. Identify some of the different ways in which you could go about improving team performance. Explain which specific aspects of team performance would be improved using these methods and the benefits this would bring.
2. Give examples of ways in which you could provide constructive feedback to team members to improve their performance.
3. Describe how you would go about implementing identified ways of improving team performance.

Your assessment could take the form of a written narrative or a professional discussion with your assessor. It could also include the production of workplace evidence, work-based observations or the use of witness testimonies, as appropriate.

Functional Skills

If you take part in a professional discussion with your assessor, this will allow you to practise your Functional Skills in English: Speaking and Listening.

Unit D5

Plan, allocate and monitor work of a team

Team talk

Rob's story

My name is Rob Joynson, I'm 26 years old and have been a team leader at Ashley Manufacturing Ltd for nearly two months. I've inherited an existing team of manufacturing operatives and am beginning to worry about their performance. The team has not hit one of its targets since I arrived and morale seems incredibly low. The operatives always seem to be arguing among themselves and nobody takes pride in their work. Last week, we were meant to have 1,000 pallets of products completed and shipped to a major client in Europe. However, the quality of the finished products was so bad that many pallets had to be recalled and replaced, all of which delayed the order being shipped. This also increased the costs of the project significantly.

I really need to get to the bottom of the problems with my new team before their underperformance starts to reflect badly on me. I am on six months' probation in this position and I need to turn this team around before the end of my probationary period. The trouble is, I don't know where to start.

Top tips

Taking over an existing team, with all of its politics, personalities and legacy issues, can be a daunting experience. In order to begin managing these various factors to mould your team into a high-performing one, you need to assert your role as the new team leader. Talk to the team members, set the ground rules for processes and decision-making, and open up two-way communications. The sooner you get your team working effectively together, the sooner you will have a productive team. Remember, enthusiasm breeds enthusiasm (and vice versa!) so the more you exude positivity, the more it will spread among the team. Set clear roles, objectives and deadlines. Hold regular meetings to measure improvements and have a focus always on celebrating successes with recognition, rewards and praise.

Ask the expert	
Q	I have recently begun a new team leader role but have quickly discovered that my team are not performing well. I do not know how to go about bringing them back on track.
A	You need to implement some team-building and performance-improvement strategies to refocus the team and inject a fresh positive approach. However, you cannot do this until you have the facts on the root cause of the problems. Start by getting the team together for a meeting to ask for their opinions on the problems currently being experienced. You may be surprised by what you find out! Set new performance goals and objectives for your team and make sure team members input into the process and feel a sense of ownership of it. Set regular team meetings for the next three months so that you can keep a close eye on target achievement as well as morale. Take every opportunity to reward achievement and focus on positives.

What your assessor is looking for

In order to prepare for and to succeed in completing this unit, your assessor will require you to be able to demonstrate competence in:

- planning work for a team
- allocating work across a team
- managing team members to achieve team objectives
- monitoring and evaluating the performance of team members
- improving the performance of a team.

You will demonstrate your skills, knowledge and competence through the learning outcomes in this unit. Evidence generated in this unit will also cross-reference to the other units in this qualification.

Please bear in mind that there are significant cross-referencing opportunities throughout this qualification and you may have already generated some relevant work to meet certain criteria in this unit. Your assessor will provide you with the exact requirements to meet the standards of this unit. However, as a guide, it is likely that for this unit you will need to be assessed through:

- one observation of relevant workplace activities to cover the whole unit
- one witness testimony

- a written narrative, reflective account or professional discussion
- any relevant work products to be produced as evidence.

The work products for this unit could include:

- your team's objectives or targets
- your team's work plans, rotas or schedules
- assessments which you have made of your team members' work against agreed standards
- examples of feedback you have given to team members on their performance.

Your assessor will guide you through the assessment process as detailed in the candidate logbook. The detailed assessment criteria are shown in the logbook and by working through these questions, combined with providing the relevant evidence, you will meet the learning outcomes required to complete this unit.

Task and page reference	Assessment criteria
1 (page 55)	1.1, 1.2
2 (page 60)	2.1, 2.2, 2.3
3 (page 62)	3.1
4 (page 67)	4.1, 4.2, 4.3
5 (page 71)	5.1, 5.2, 5.3

Unit B10b Manage risk in own area of responsibility

In this unit you will learn why health and safety is important to you as a manager. You will explore the relevant legislation and how the Health and Safety at Work Act 1974 places a legal duty on both employer and employee. You will look at health and safety policies in organisations and how they ensure compliance with all relevant legislation, as well as the individual health and safety responsibilities of directors and supervisors.

The unit will look at carrying out risk assessments and take you through the 'five steps to risk assessment' framework adopted by the Health and Safety Executive. It will also provide useful advice on how to eliminate specific risks and hazards. Non health-and-safety risks, including risks of financial loss and risks to reputation, will be briefly discussed.

Finally, we will look at identifying stakeholders and the importance of recognising how stakeholders are affected by a business's operations.

What you will learn:

- Be able to undertake a risk evaluation for current and planned activities within own area of responsibility
- Be able to minimise the impact and likelihood of potential risks occurring in own area of responsibility
- Be able to communicate identified risks

Links to the Technical Certificate

If you are completing your NVQ as part of an Apprenticeship Framework, you will find the following topics are also covered in your Technical Certificate:

- Why health and safety legislation impacts on organisations
- How a risk assessment can be undertaken

Be able to undertake a risk evaluation for current and planned activities within own area of responsibility

The best way to evaluate risk is by undertaking a risk assessment. You will find that there are many tools you can use to feed into a risk assessment and formulate a risk evaluation, including questionnaires, feedback from colleagues and probability matrices. Risk assessments are an important tool to use in business to ensure the safety of you and all other employees. Before beginning the risk assessment process it is, however, useful to understand the surrounding legislation and your role in ensuring the safety of all employees.

Health and safety legislation and procedure

The Health and Safety at Work Act

The Health and Safety at Work Act 1974 places a legal duty on both employer and employee to be aware of and manage risks. Employer and employee have different roles to play in adhering to this act.

The role of the employer

Employers must safeguard, as far as reasonably practical, the health, safety and welfare of their employees. The employer must ensure that safe systems of work are in place to manage workplace activities and machinery, equipment and substances used. The organisation must ensure that:

- all relevant employees are adequately trained
- regular and routine risk assessments are carried out
- **personal protective equipment** (PPE) is provided as necessary
- dangerous substances are moved, stored and used safely

- adequate welfare facilities, including toilets and washing facilities, are provided
- health and safety issues are communicated to employees
- employees are able to raise any concerns with their manager or a health and safety representative
- relevant systems and processes are in place to manage fires and first aid
- accidents are recorded.

The role of the employee

Employees have a duty to take reasonable care to avoid harm to themselves and others and should work with their employer and others to meet their health and safety obligations. Employees must not interfere with or misuse anything provided for them in the workplace. Employees must ensure that they:

- attend all relevant training
- work safely and within the framework/process/ safe system of work set out by the organisation for that particular activity
- take care of the health and safety of themselves and their colleagues
- co-operate with the organisation in relation to health and safety issues
- use equipment and tools as instructed
- report any hazards, ill health, accidents and near accidents
- wear/use any protective equipment (PPE) provided
- comply with all relevant legislation and take a proactive approach in relation to managing health and safety.

It is important for employees to follow health, safety and security procedures to ensure the:

- safety of themselves, colleagues, customers and visitors to the work premises
- physical security of themselves and others
- protection of personal data relating to themselves, colleagues, customers and the organisation.

As a manager, you will be responsible for managing risk in your own area of responsibility and must make yourself familiar with the current health and safety legislation. You must also have a good practical knowledge and understanding of the organisation's health and safety policy and procedures.

Workplace (Health, Safety and Welfare) Regulations 1992

The Workplace (Health, Safety and Welfare) Regulations 1992 cover a wide range of health, safety and welfare issues and apply to most workplaces, with the exception of workplaces involving construction work. These regulations detail many of the day-to-day aspects of ensuring that your workforce's health and safety is maintained. Some of the important elements covered by these regulations are:

- adequate ventilation
- maintenance of minimum temperatures for indoor work
- adequate lighting to enable people to work and move about safely
- keeping workplace, furniture, furnishings and fittings clean and tidy
- sufficient volume of workrooms and adequate free space to allow people to move about with ease
- suitability of workstations to the work required and the workers' needs
- adequate seating support for the lower back and provision of footrests if required
- maintenance of the workplace, equipment, devices and systems

- sufficient traffic routes to allow people and vehicles to circulate safely with ease
- openable windows, skylights and ventilators which, when open, should not pose any undue risk to anyone
- suitable, sufficient and accessible sanitary conveniences and washing facilities; kept clean, adequately ventilated and lit with running heated and cold water, soap and hygienic drying facilities
- adequate supply of high-quality drinking water
- suitable, sufficient and secure space to store workers' own clothing and special clothing
- suitable, sufficient and readily accessible rest facilities with seats provided for workers to use during breaks in a place where PPE need not be worn.

Remember

Since 1 July 2007, it has been against the law to smoke in virtually all enclosed public places and workplaces in England, including most work vehicles. Similar legislation exists in Scotland and Wales.

European Union Directives

Health and safety is affected by some European legislation. Probably the most important EU legislation to be aware of is the Working Time Regulations, which implement the European Working Time Directive into British law. The legislation is concerned with protecting excessive working which has been linked to causes of stress, depression and illness. This detailed directive creates the right for EU workers to:

- a minimum number of holidays per year
- paid breaks at work
- rest of at least 11 hours in any given 24 hour period.

The legislation also restricts excessive night work and work on a Sunday and gives an employee a default right to work no more than 48 hours per week.

The Health and Safety Executive (HSE)

The HSE is the regulatory body for all issues relating to health and safety. It provides advice, information and support by telephone, email or post and produces a wealth of reasonably priced and free publications available by mail order or online from www.hsebooks.co.uk. Free leaflets can also be downloaded from www.hse.gov.uk.

The HSE also enforces safety-related legislation and is responsible for accident investigation and accident reporting.

Health and safety policy

Compliance with all health and safety legislation is not a luxury; it is an essential requirement for all businesses. For organisations employing five or more people, a formal written health and safety policy must be put in place.

Such a policy outlines how health and safety issues are organised. Individual responsibilities for directors and supervisors should also be included. The policy will also detail the specific arrangements and processes that will ensure that

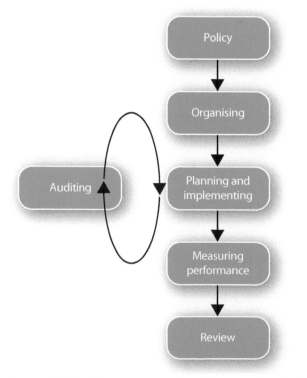

Figure B10b.1 The stages involved in managing health and safety effectively.

health and safety is managed effectively. Figure B10b.1 shows the flow of how health and safety performance is measured and the need to regularly review these issues. A review would normally happen annually. It is fairly common in larger organisations to have a formal audit of health and safety; this is normally annual and may be undertaken by an internal or external health and safety specialist.

Identify potential risks in current and planned activities within own area of responsibility

What is a risk assessment?

On a practical level, risks assessments are probably the most important tool that you will use to manage risk. A risk assessment is a process of identifying any potential **hazards** that may cause harm and then assessing those **risks** and putting in place control measures that will reduce the risks to an acceptable level. Once you have reduced the risks to an acceptable level and have an agreed working process or method in place, this is often referred to as a 'safe system of work'.

> **Key Terms**
>
> **Hazard** – anything that may cause harm, such as chemicals, electricity, working from ladders or a trailing cable.
>
> **Risk** – the chance, high or low, that somebody could be harmed by these and other hazards, together with an indication of how serious the harm could be.

A risk assessment is important for protecting your team and business, as well as complying with the law. It helps you focus on the risks that really matter in your workplace – the ones with potential to cause real harm – so that you can weigh up whether you have taken enough precautions or should do more to prevent harm. Workers and others have a right to be protected from harm caused by a failure to take reasonable control measures. Accidents and ill health can ruin lives and affect your business too, for instance if output is lost, machinery is damaged or insurance costs increase.

In many instances, straightforward measures can readily control risks, for example ensuring spillages are cleaned up promptly so people do not slip, or keeping cupboard doors and drawers closed so people do not walk into them. The law does not expect you to eliminate all risk, but you are required to protect people as far as is reasonably practicable.

Carrying out a risk assessment

You can assess risks by carrying out a visual check, but it is essential to assess your main hazards and risks through a formal written process, usually using a standard risk assessment form. It is likely that your organisation will have a risk assessment form in place that you can use, but if not, an example of a blank form can be found on page 95, Figure B10b.8.

Try not to overcomplicate the process. In many organisations, the risks are well known and the necessary control measures are easy to apply. You probably already know whether, for example, you have employees who move heavy loads and so could harm their backs, or where people are most likely to slip or trip. Even so, check that you have taken reasonable precautions to avoid injury.

You don't have to be a health and safety expert to manage risk effectively. If you work in a larger organisation, you may have a health and safety adviser to help you. If you are not confident, get help from someone who is competent. In all cases, you should make sure that you involve your staff and their representatives in the process. Your team will have useful information about how the work is done that will make your assessment of the risk more thorough and effective. But remember, as their manager you are responsible for seeing that the risk assessment is carried out properly.

Use the following five steps to carry out your risk assessment.

Step 1: Identify the hazards

The first thing to do is to work out how people could be harmed. When you work in the same location each day it is easy to overlook some hazards, but if you follow the steps outlined here you should notice any hazards that are present.

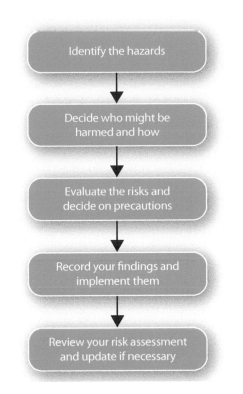

Figure B10b.2 A risk assessment process.

- Walk around your workplace and look at what could reasonably be expected to cause harm.
- Ask your team if they have noticed anything – they may have seen something that is not immediately obvious to you or which is only present at certain times.
- Visit the Health and Safety Executive website (www.hse.gov.uk) for practical guidance on where hazards occur and how to control them. If you are a member of a trade association you should contact them, as many produce very helpful guidance.
- Check the manufacturer's instructions or data sheets for all chemicals and equipment in the workplace. They can be helpful in highlighting related hazards.
- Look back at your accident and ill-health records – these often help to identify the less obvious hazards.
- Think about long-term hazards to health e.g. high levels of noise or exposure to harmful substances.

Step 2: Decide who might be harmed and how

For each hazard you need to be clear about who might be harmed; it will help you to identify the best way of managing the risk. That doesn't mean listing everyone by name, but rather identifying groups of people (e.g. people working in the storeroom).

In each case, identify how they might be harmed, or what type of injury or ill health might occur. For example, shelf stackers may suffer back injuries from repeated lifting of boxes.

Remember that some workers, such as new or young workers or new or expectant mothers, have particular requirements and people with disabilities may face different risks from others.

You should also think about people who may not be in the workplace regularly, such as cleaners, contractors and maintenance workers. Visitors or members of the public could also be hurt by your activities. If you share your workplace with another company you will need to think about how your work affects them and vice versa – talk to them.

Step 3: Evaluate the risks and decide on precautions

You now have to decide what to do about the hazards you have identified. The law requires that you do everything reasonably practical to protect people from harm. The easiest way of doing this is to compare what you are doing with good practice. There are many sources of information about good practice, such as the HSE website www.hse.gov.uk.

First, look at what you're already doing; think about what controls you have in place and how the work is organised. Next, compare this with the good practice and see if there is more you should be doing to bring yourself up to standard. In asking yourself this, consider the following questions.

- Can I get rid of the hazard altogether?
- If not, how can I control the risks so that harm is unlikely?

When controlling risks, apply the following principles:

1. Try a less risky option. For example, switch to using a less-hazardous chemical.
2. Prevent access to the hazard (e.g. by guarding).
3. Organise work to reduce exposure to the hazard (e.g. place time limits on specific relevant operations).
4. Issue personal protective equipment (e.g. clothing, footwear, goggles etc.) and provide welfare facilities (e.g. first aid and washing facilities for removal of contamination).

Improving health and safety need not cost a lot. For instance, placing a mirror on a dangerous blind corner to help prevent vehicle accidents is a low-cost precaution considering the risks. Failure to take simple precautions can cost you a lot more if an accident does happen.

Involve all of your team members in your decision making, so that you can be sure that what you propose will be accepted by the team and won't introduce any new hazards.

Step 4: Record your findings and implement them

Putting the results of your risk assessment into practice will make a difference when looking after people and your business. Writing down the results of your risk assessment, and sharing them with your team, encourages you to do this. Risk assessments do not need to be perfect, but they must be suitable and sufficient.

You will need to be able to show that:

- a proper check was made
- you considered and asked who might be affected
- you dealt with all the significant hazards, taking into account the number of people who could be involved
- the precautions in place are reasonable and the remaining risks are low
- that you involved your staff and/or their representatives in the process.

If you find that there are any improvements you could make, both big and small, don't try to do everything at once. Make a plan of action to deal with the most important things first. Then as you complete each action, tick it off on your plan. Health and safety inspectors acknowledge the efforts of businesses that are clearly trying to make improvements.

Checklist

A good plan of action often includes a mixture of different things such as:

- a few cheap or easy improvements that can be done quickly, perhaps as a temporary solution until more reliable controls are in place – these are often referred to as 'quick wins'
- long-term solutions to those risks most likely to cause accidents or ill health, particularly those risks with the worst potential consequences
- arrangements for training employees on the main risks that remain and how to control them
- regular checks to make sure that the control measures stay in place
- identifying clear responsibilities – who will lead on what action, and by when.

Step 5: Review your risk assessment and update if necessary

Few workplaces stay the same. Sooner or later, you will bring in new equipment, substances or procedures that could lead to new hazards. It makes sense, therefore, to review what you are doing on an on-going basis. When you are busy managing a team it's all too easy to forget about reviewing your risk assessments until something has gone wrong and it's too late. Why not set a review date for your risk assessment now? Note it in your diary as an annual event.

Having said that, if there is a significant change between annual assessments, don't wait. Check your risk assessment and, where necessary, amend it. If possible, it is best to think about the risk assessment when you're planning your change – that way you leave yourself more flexibility.

Remember

If there are any new or significantly revised operations or processes, it will be necessary to undertake a new risk assessment.

When reviewing your risk assessment consider if there have been any changes. Are there improvements that you still need to make? Have your colleagues spotted a problem? Have you learnt anything from accidents or near misses? Make sure your risk assessment stays up to date.

Getting help

If you get stuck when undertaking a risk assessment, ask you manager or health and safety adviser if you have one for assistance. There is also a wealth of information on the HSE website: www.hse.gov.uk. You may also find the following publications very useful:

- Health and Safety Executive (HSE) *Essentials of health and safety at work* (Fourth edition), HSE Books, 2006, ISBN 978-0717661794
- Health and Safety Executive (HSE) *Five steps to risk assessment*, HSE Books, 2011. ISBN 978-0717664405

Frequently asked questions

What if the work I do varies a lot, or workers have to move from one site to another?

Identify the hazards you can reasonably expect to occur and assess the risks from them. This general assessment should stand you in good stead for the majority of your work. Where you do take on work or a new site that is different, cover any new or different hazards with a specific assessment. You do not have to start from scratch each time.

Do my employees have responsibilities?

Yes. Employees have legal responsibilities to co-operate with their employer's efforts to ensure health and safety (e.g. they must wear protective equipment when it is provided), and they must look out for each other.

What if one of my employee's circumstances change?

You'll need to look again at the risk assessment. For instance, you are required to carry out a specific risk assessment for new or expectant mothers as some tasks (heavy lifting or work with chemicals for example) may not be appropriate. If an employee develops a disability then you are required to make reasonable adjustments. People returning to work following major surgery may also have particular requirements. If you put your mind to it, you can almost always find a way forward that works for you and your team.

What if I have already assessed some of the risks?

If, for example, you use hazardous chemicals and you have already assessed the risks to health and the precautions you need to take under the Control of Substances Hazardous to Health Regulations (**COSHH**), you can consider them 'checked' and move on.

Key Term

COSHH – control of substances hazardous to health regulations that apply to certain products and chemicals. COSHH data sheets will be provided by the supplier or manufacturer for substances covered by these regulations. This will detail the contents of the product and its potential to cause harm and how it should be stored.

Portfolio Task 1 2 hours

Links to LO1: Assessment criteria 1.1, 1.2

Consider your own team and operational activities. Identify all of the activities that you undertake and determine if a risk assessment needs to be undertaken. For any activities where a risk assessment is required, complete an action plan to detail what actions you will undertake. Agree a timeframe and complete the action plan as soon as you can. This will provide essential evidence for your portfolio.

Assess the nature of identified risks and potential consequences

A hazard can be defined as something with the potential to cause harm. The identification of hazards is the first step in controlling risks as every hazard has the potential to cause a health problem and/or result in an accident.

Different types of hazard

There are many different types of hazard in the workplace and you need to be able to identify those relevant to you and your team's operation. Hazards can be grouped into four main categories:

1. Physical e.g. equipment, machinery, noise, electrical shock and heat.
2. Chemical and biological e.g. acids, alkalis, asbestos, dust, viruses or disease.
3. Ergonomic e.g. physical discomfort or injury.
4. Psychological e.g. stress or anxiety.

It is important to understand that some hazards are generic to any workplace while specific hazards might only apply in a particular environment. For example trip hazards could occur in any organisation, whereas exposure to chemicals or high levels of noise would be specific only to certain workplaces.

You can identify hazards by:

- observing the physical conditions and activities carried out at your workplace
- communicating with your colleagues
- inspecting relevant documentation detailing hazards, e.g. risk assessments or COSHH data sheets.

Some examples of the main types of hazards that can exist in workplaces are shown below. Please note that this is not an exhaustive list and other hazards may exist.

Fire

Fire is a risk for all businesses and has the potential to cause serious injury or death. A major fire can have significant consequences and could result in the organisation going out of business.

Electricity

If electricity passes through the body, it can cause convulsions, heart failure and internal or external burns. Any combination of these can result in serious injury or death.

Work equipment

This includes any machinery, equipment or tools used in the workplace with the potential to cause harm. Examples include hand tools, power tools, other electrical equipment, shredders, grinders, cutters, lifting equipment and ladders.

Vehicles

Vehicle hazards are complex and include the movement of vehicles either on-site or off-site. They include the potential harm caused to you or by you, any injury or damage caused while driving a vehicle and by the loading, unloading and re-fuelling of vehicles. Reversing vehicles are a serious hazard.

Housekeeping

This relates to keeping your workplace clean and tidy and free from obstructions, particularly of fire doors or routes. Personal hygiene is also important to reduce the potential for the spread of disease or infection.

Slips, trips and falls

These are very common hazards and include trips or falls on the level or falls from height. Accidents resulting from falls from height are the most common cause of death and serious injury in the workplace.

Manual handling

Manual handling hazards are common in the workplace and they can occur as a result of lifting, carrying, lowering, pulling or pushing items. Manual handling injuries include cuts, strains and sprains. Crush injuries can also occur, but these are less common.

Display screen equipment

Display screen equipment (DSE) hazards relate to the operation of computer workstations. Continued and prolonged use of DSE can result in upper limb disorders, posture problems and eye strain.

These can be managed effectively by having a self-assessment risk assessment process in place and by rotating of duties and enforcing regular breaks.

Noise

Noise hazards do not exist in many organisations. However, you will need to assess if there are any noise hazards in your section. High levels of noise can destroy parts of the ear.

Chemicals

Chemicals can cause harm by entering the body through a number of routes including direct contact with the eyes or skin, swallowing or ingestion and by breathing in fumes.

These hazards all have the potential to cause harm of varying severity. However, a formal process of regular and routine written risk assessments will ensure that you identify all potential hazards. The next stage is to identify the specific severity of the hazard and the likelihood of its occurrence. The final stage is to put the necessary control measures in place.

Non health-and-safety risks

In terms of day-to-day operations, your main focus will be to ensure that you are managing health and safety effectively. However, it is worth briefly introducing the concept of managing non health-and-safety related risks. For example, reputation is important to all organisations because if reputation is damaged it can have disastrous consequences, for instance, falling sales and diminishing market confidence.

Also, many sectors have to work to a particular code of practice and if that code is breached, an organisation could be fined a significant amount of money. This can have a particularly serious effect on smaller organisations. For example, a global bank would probably be able to absorb a £1m fine, but a small company may go into liquidation if they were fined £50,000.

Non health-and-safety risks can be classified as:

- financial risks e.g. a significant trading loss
- adverse publicity (reputation)
- fraud by an employee

- legal implications (prosecution)
- claims against the organisation by a third party or employee.

It is important to consider all of your activities and to make sure that your working practices comply with all relevant legislation, agreed practices and codes of conduct.

Many organisations adopt a risk management strategy to manage all risks, including non health-and-safety risks. Through this type of strategy, an organisation would:

- satisfy all mandatory, regulatory and statutory duties and responsibilities
- ensure compliance with health and safety legislation
- promote safe working practices aimed at the reduction or elimination of risk
- establish a systematic and consistent approach to risk assessment
- maximise the efficient use of available resources and minimise the costs associated with risks
- conduct all operations in a lawful manner
- safeguard all its assets.

Many organisations manage this process by formulating risk maps. These identify the risks, assign responsibility for them to an individual person (risk owner) and then provide an action

plan detailing how the risks are managed at a level acceptable to the organisation.

An example of how a risk management framework would work is shown in Figure B10b.3.

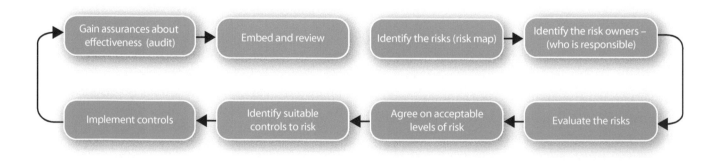

Figure B10b.3 Managing risk effectively.

Evaluate the probability of identified risks occurring

A common phrase associated with managing risks is 'reasonably practicable'. This means putting in place controls and safe systems of work to allow for a common sense and practical approach towards managing that hazard. The amount of time, effort and cost associated with implementing an agreed safe system of work needs to be proportionate to that particular risk. For example, measures to counter a low-risk hazard can be completed over a period of time for a low cost, but a hazard assessed as high risk should be dealt with immediately and all reasonable costs agreed. The following examples demonstrate how the level of detail and resources required will vary dependent on the risk.

Example of a low-risk hazard:

Some of your team members occasionally lift boxes.

You therefore need to:

- undertake a risk assessment
- identify any training needs and PPE to be worn e.g. gloves
- deliver any relevant training
- review annually (or whenever significant changes are made)
- train all new employees.

Example of a high-risk hazard:

Your warehouse holds very heavy items at low and high heights. Fork lift trucks are used to move them.

You therefore need to:

- undertake regular risk assessments for all activities
- put in place detailed and clear safe systems of work and procedures
- put in place guard rails, floor markings and fixings
- ensure all staff are trained, competent and training is kept up to date

- manage the health and safety risks in a proactive way through regular consultation with the team and daily 'walk round' visual checks
- provide all mechanical and manual lifting devices
- issue relevant PPE and enforce its use
- adequately maintain lifting devices
- ensure that the floor is always clean and not slippery
- ensure that the whole area is clean, tidy and free from hazards
- ensure that access in the warehouse is restricted to relevant employees.

Don't worry if this second example appears overwhelming and you are struggling to see the difference between the two scenarios, as someone within your organisation will have overall responsibility for health and safety management. They will be able to advise you on any queries. The learning point here is to ensure that adequate steps are taken to minimise the risk of the hazard.

Likelihood and severity

When you undertake a risk assessment, two key factors, likelihood and severity, need to be considered.

Likelihood

This refers to the probability of the hazard causing some type of loss or injury. You will need to assess:

- where the hazard is
- who will be affected
- how knowledgeable those people are
- how often the hazard occurs (frequency)
- what the exposure times to the hazard are.

Most organisations categorise the likelihood as:

3 – high (where it is certain or nearly certain that harm will occur)

2 – medium (where harm will occur frequently)

1 – low (where harm will rarely occur).

Unit B10b Manage risk in own area of responsibility

Severity

This refers to the possible outcome of the hazard and the resulting potential loss or injury. Most organisations categorise the severity as:

3 – major (for example significant injury or death)

2 – medium (where injuries would result in an employee being off work for three days or more)

1 – slight (for all other minor injuries resulting in no lost time or absence for only up to three days).

Probability matrix

Once the likelihood and severity have been assessed you can categorise the risks. A common method used to assess likelihood and severity is a probability matrix and your organisation may already have this in place. This will assist you in identifying those high level risks that must be dealt with first. To calculate the risk factor, you multiply the likelihood rating by the severity rating to give a number between 1 and 9. Clearly those risks with a high number will have to be dealt with first and are also likely to need more resources to control the risk.

Risk ratings

When you have carried out your initial risk assessment each hazard can be rated in terms of likelihood and severity. It is likely that for most,

if not all of your activities, you will have some systems, processes and controls already in place. However, the starting point when completing your risk assessment is to imagine that there are no controls currently in place and assess the likelihood and severity on that basis. This will give you an initial risk rating.

The second stage is to consider the existing systems and controls that are already in place. Make sure that you ask the following questions.

● Can the hazard be eliminated altogether?
● Can the hazard be reduced to a level below the acceptable threshold?
● Can the exposure to the hazard be controlled by means of physical barriers e.g. PPE or organisational barriers, reducing the time of exposure?

Once you have assessed the existing controls, you can complete a second (revised) risk rating (1 to 9) based on the current activity using the current control measures. From this you will be able to determine any additional actions or control measures that may need to be implemented. You may decide at this stage to suspend any activities that are causing you concern until the additional control measures have been implemented, or you may decide to continue with the activity, but agree an action plan to implement the new controls within an agreed period.

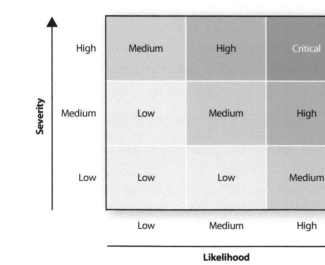

Figure B10b.4 Example of a probability matrix.

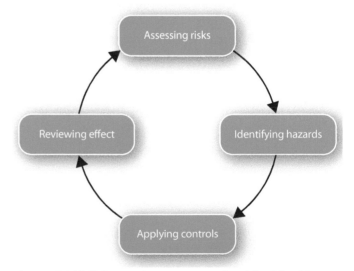

Figure B10b.5 Remember to assess the risks, identify the hazards, put control measures in place and review annually.

Case Study

A worked example of rating

Aled manages a team of window installers. His team installs UPVC windows in domestic houses and commercial premises and works from height on a daily basis.

Aled has completed his initial risk rating, assuming that there are no control measures in place. The severity is 3 as a fall from height could result in serious injury or death. The likelihood is also 3 as harm is almost certain to occur if no control measures are in place. This gives a maximum risk rating of 9 (3 times 3). Aled's choices are to:

1. temporarily suspend the activities as there are inadequate controls in place

2. continue with the current activities with no changes

3. continue with the current activities subject to some further new or updated control measures to be implemented within an agreed timeframe.

In these circumstances, if no control measures were in place, he would need to suspend all operations as the risks are at an unacceptable level. Aled now considers the control measures that are already in place. These are:

- fully trained and competent staff
- equipment meets agreed standards and is regularly maintained
- staff all use PPE
- staff use specialist safety devices e.g. safety harnesses
- scaffolding is used when required
- all ladders secured or footed by a colleague.

After reviewing all of the work and control measures already in place, Aled revises the risk rating to 3. Therefore there is no need to suspend activities, which can continue as normal subject to annual review of the risk assessment.

Portfolio Task 3 ⏱ 2 hours

Links to LO1: Assessment criteria 1.1, 1.2, 1.3

Work through the following points, considering the policies, systems, processes and procedures that are in place within your own organisation and include all relevant workplace evidence, for example, any risk assessments that you have undertaken.

1. Explain how you identify the potential risks in the current and planned activities within your own area of responsibility.

2. Explain how you assess the nature of the identified risks and their potential consequences.

3. Explain and detail how you evaluate the probability of the identified risks occurring.

PLTS

By explaining how you work with your team to manage health and safety in a proactive way, you will demonstrate how you work well as a team and encourage each other to think creatively to find solutions to specific hazards. Additionally, the risk assessment evidence will show how you manage the process effectively (TL, CT, IE, SM).

Be able to minimise the impact and likelihood of potential risks occurring in own area of responsibility

By implementing agreed safe systems of work, you will be minimising the impact of any loss or injury to your workforce. A safe system of work will be the agreed way of undertaking a particular process or task. Figure B10b.6, on the following page, illustrates a practical way that this would work.

A safe system of work is an agreed method to undertake a task that all relevant parties know and understand. It is likely that not all of the hazards will have been eliminated and there will be some residual risk. However, this residual risk will be at an acceptable level for all parties.

When assessing if an existing safe system of work is adequate, consider the following elements:

- People – are they trained, competent and knowledgeable and do they protect each other?
- Equipment – is the right equipment in place and is it adequate and well maintained?

- Materials and substances used – are there safer alternatives/substitutes that could be used and is PPE in place?
- Environment – is it safe, adequately lit and maintained and able to provide protection?

Observe the current process/activity
- Check how the current process works
- Identify all risks and hazards
- Consider the current controls already in place

Undertake a risk assessment
- Work through the process
- Identify any improvements and implement any changes

Implement an agreed safe system of work
- Agree the new process with all relevent parties
- Identify any new equipment or resources required
- Ensure your staff are trained and are competent

Figure B10b.6 Implementing a safe system of work.

Identify ways and means of minimising the impact and likelihood of potential risks

The way that the risks are minimised will vary depending on the specific risk. Most risks are minimised by a combination of ways. For example, the risk of a moving part on a machine can be minimised by putting a guard rail in place to protect the operative. However, the operative will also need training on the how the machine works and they may also need goggles and gloves.

Some of the generic ways to control risks are considered on the following pages.

Training and communication

Ensure that your staff are competent. Make sure that they know how to undertake all of their day-to-day activities in a safe manner.

When new employees start, spend time with them through a formal induction to explain the systems, processes and any safety signs and identify and action any training needs.

Safety signs that all staff should be familiar with.

Communicate regularly with your team on health and safety issues. For example, have health and safety as a standing item on your monthly team meetings. Ensure that all members of your team know they can approach you if they have any concerns regarding health and safety issues and that you will action these issues immediately. It is also important to display all relevant signs, as seen on the photo above.

Supervision

All staff should be adequately supervised. Implement a process to ensure that no employees are exposed to any unnecessary risks, for example lone working. Pay particular attention to young and inexperienced workers and provide one-to-one supervision if necessary.

Personal protective equipment

Issue personal protective equipment (PPE) as appropriate and enforce its use. There may be some resistance within your team, but you need to emphasise the importance of PPE in providing vital protection to your workforce.

A safe working environment

Apply a common sense approach. Don't issue safety glasses to everyone if it is not appropriate. Assess the risks and identify those people who could be harmed then provide the relevant support, training or PPE for those specific employees. Keep all areas clean, tidy and uncluttered. Mark floors or bays as appropriate, use guard rails where required and prohibit access into specific areas for certain staff if they are not adequately trained or do not have the relevant PPE. Provide a safe working environment with adequate welfare facilities including toilets and a kitchen area. Ensure that no employees are exposed to excessively low or high temperatures or noise. Always store chemicals in a secure environment.

Testing

Regular testing of equipment and practising of safety procedures, will identify any shortcomings that you need to resolve. It also keeps employees' memories jogged in what to do in the event of an emergency or evacuation. Test all electrical equipment on a regular basis. This is called portable appliance testing or PAT testing. Make sure that you have got trained first aiders in place within your organisation.

Specific risk assessments

As well as completing your regular and routine risk assessments on an annual basis, you should also complete specific risk assessments for:

- any new or significantly changed activity or process
- all young people within your team
- any expectant or new mothers
- anyone newly disabled or recovering from significant illness.

Clear processes and effective health and safety management

Make sure that all members of your team understand the agreed processes, systems, procedures and safe systems of work that are in place in your organisation. You and your team should take a proactive approach towards managing health and safety – don't wait for something to go wrong and then resolve it. Be aware at all times of any potential problems, risks or hazards and resolve them as quickly as possible. Encourage your team to speak to you at any time if they have any concerns. Make sure everyone in your team is competent and understands the importance of health and safety. Make them aware of any relevant issues and ensure that they understand the different types of safety sign.

Review

Learn from previous mistakes including any accident or incident reporting. Learn from any near misses which may have been brought to your attention – this is when something could have happened, but was avoided. In this instance, take any relevant action to resolve the issue.

The Health & Safety (Safety signs signals) Regulations 1996

These regulations provide the legal means to require employers to provide safety signs in a variety of situations where there is a significant risk to health and safety which has not been avoided or controlled satisfactorily by other methods.

Know your safety signs

 Prohibition signs (Do not do)
Signs prohibiting certain behaviour
e.g. No Smoking

 Warning signs (Caution, Danger)
Signs which indicate a specific course of action is to be followed
e.g. Danger high voltage

 Mandatory signs (You must do)
Signs which indicate a specific course of action is to be followed
e.g. Safety helmets must be worn

 Safe Condition Signs (Safest way)
Signs giving information about safe conditions, doors, exits and escape routes
e.g. Fire exits

Fire signs (Fire fighting equipment)
Signs indicating the location of fire fighting equipment
e.g. Fire point

Types of safety sign.

Also consider any health checks or medical screening that you may want to undertake. For example it is useful to identify if a new employee has any existing health conditions.

How to minimise risks and hazards

In addition to the general ways in which risks and hazards can be minimised, there are some more detailed control measures that can be put in place. These are shown in Table B10b.1.

Hazard	How to minimise risk
Fire	• Never leave heat sources unattended • Keep heat sources and fuel apart • Store flammable liquids and gases safely • Have regular fire drills • Have extinguishers in place • Never block fire doors or evacuation routes
Electricity	• Never overload circuits • Never work on or near live surfaces • Regularly visually check wires and cables • PAT test relevant equipment • Ensure all staff are appropriately trained and competent
Work equipment	• Ensure all staff are appropriately trained and competent • Ensure guard rails are used where necessary • Ensure the correct use of PPE • Ensure that all ladders and other lifting devices are regularly maintained • Ensure that the workplace is well lit, ventilated and at the correct temperature
Vehicles	• Minimise the need to reverse vehicles • Clearly mark pedestrian routes • Consider loading and unloading of vehicles and re-fuelling operations • Ensure all staff are appropriately trained and competent including compliance with legislation and regulations e.g. fork-lift-truck driver training
Housekeeping	• Keep all areas clean and tidy • Have regular practice drills
Slips, trips and falls	• Keep all areas clean and tidy • Clear up spills straight away • Keep all areas free from obstacles
Manual handling	• Ensure all staff are appropriately trained and competent • Risk assess each operation and each person to assess the capability of that person • Use mechanical aids where appropriate • Use more than one person to lift heavy or awkward items
DSE	• Ensure that all DSE users complete a self-assessment and implement any required actions • Rotate staff and give regular breaks • Ensure that the workplace is ergonomically correct for each person
Noise	• Where possible eliminate operations with a high level of noise or reduce the noise • Carefully assess and check exposure to noise • Use PPE – earplugs and ear defenders
Chemicals	• Only use and store approved chemicals which hold a data/COSSH sheet • Avoid direct contact with chemicals • Do not use chemicals in confined spaces • Store chemicals in a locked secure place at the correct temperature • Display clearly any safety instructions regarding what to do in the case of a spillage or direct contact

Table B10b.1 Control measures – ways of minimising risk.

Allocate responsibility for risk management to relevant individuals within own area of responsibility

Managing risks is everyone's responsibility. Your organisation's policy must clearly define responsibilities and arrangements. For example, the chief executive or board members may have overall responsibility, but some day-to-day tasks will be delegated to team leaders and managers. It is important that you understand your own responsibilities and you must ensure that your team members know their own responsibilities.

All employees have a **duty of care** to themselves and others and any potential risks or hazards need to be identified at the earliest stage. It is not acceptable to ignore something that could potentially cause harm to you or one of your colleagues. It is important to promote risk awareness throughout the organisation. This can be achieved by using a mixture of formal training, past experience, good practice guides, results of audits and risk assessments and effective policy implementation.

The diagram detailed in Figure B10b.7 (from the document, HSG65) has been produced by the Health and Safety Executive and outlines how an organisation should manage and control its risks.

Responsibility for risk management should be assigned to individuals through their job description. This will give a clear outline of any specific responsibilities that you and your team may have. In addition, it may be necessary to delegate and/or share some of those responsibilities with your team members. You may do this through an annual appraisal

meeting, whereby you assign specific objectives to individuals. You might then manage this through regular one-to-one meetings with your team to track progress and ensure that performance in relation to risk management is at an acceptable level.

Risk management issues could be included on the agenda at team meetings to provide the opportunity to identify and discuss risks, using the team's own perceptions and experiences. Where appropriate, solutions can be agreed, assigned to an individual and then acted on.

> **Key Term**
>
> **Duty of care** – a general legal duty on all individuals and organisations to avoid carelessly causing injury to other persons.

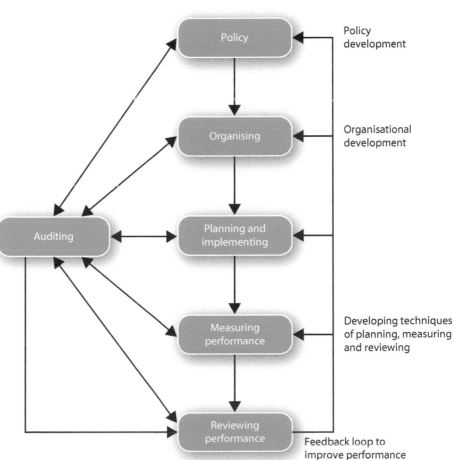

Figure B10b.7 Successful health and safety management.

At an operational level, the manager, team leader or supervisor must take responsibility for their team's health and safety and well-being by:

- enforcing the use of the correct equipment, materials and PPE
- ensuring that all employees work in ways that do not compromise each other's safety
- assessing competence and capability on an individual basis and planning any relevant training
- maintaining high standards at all times
- working with and mentoring team members to improve their health and safety awareness
- being proactive in managing health and safety.

Portfolio Task 4 — 2 hours

Links to LO2: Assessment criteria 2.1, 2.2

1. Explain the various ways and means of minimising the impact and likelihood of risks.

2. Explain how you allocate responsibility for risk management to the relevant individuals within your own area of responsibility.

When you are working through these questions, consider the policies, systems, processes and procedures that are in place within your own organisation and include any relevant workplace evidence, for example any risk assessments that you have undertaken, discussions or team meetings that you have had with your team members and copies of any relevant objectives that have been agreed. These will provide essential evidence for your portfolio.

PLTS

By explaining how you work with your team to minimise the impact and likelihood or risk, you will be demonstrating how you work well as a team together and encourage each other to think creatively to put forward solutions to specific hazards. Additionally, the risk assessment evidence will show how you manage the process effectively and allow your team to input (TW, CT, IE, SM).

Be able to communicate identified risks

Communication is a key factor in managing health and safety successfully. It must be two-way and regular. All employees must be able to communicate with their manager or supervisor at any time both on an informal day-to-day basis and also more formally, perhaps at a regular team meeting or to the **health and safety committee**. All relevant risks identified should be acted on.

Key Term

Health and safety committee – a regular meeting to discuss health and safety issues. Attended by all relevant staff including the director responsible for health and safety, the health and safety adviser, relevant team leaders, managers and supervisors and union representatives.

A health and safety committee structures and formalises an organisation's approach to health and safety and is encouraged by the HSE. Regular and specific items are discussed and it can create a positive health and safety awareness throughout the organisation whereby employees take a proactive approach thus reducing the potential for accidents or loss.

Provide information on identified risks to relevant stakeholders

A stakeholder is a person, group or organisation who affects or can be affected by an organisation's actions. All stakeholders need to be made aware of and understand your organisation's systems, procedures and processes.

Managers and certain stakeholders also have specific responsibilities.

- Employers – responsible for protecting people from harm caused by work activities. This includes the responsibility not to harm contractors working on your site. As a manager, you will have specific responsibilities in this area for your team and their activities. Employers must ensure that employees are trained and clearly instructed in their duties.

- Employees – must co-operate with their employer on health and safety matters and not do anything that puts them or others at risk.
- Suppliers of chemicals, machinery and equipment – must ensure that their products or imports are safe and they must provide information on this.

Contractors working on your site

If you have any contractors working on your premises, it is important to understand how to manage them effectively. Any work undertaken for you by a contractor is usually covered by a formal civil contract and it is good practice for the health and safety requirements to be written into the contract.

Remember

The Management of Health and Safety at Work Regulations 1999 are of particular importance in any client/contractor relationship. These set out requirements for a health and safety management system in all workplaces and the accompanying Approved Code of Practice gives advice on compliance.

In any client/contractor relationship, both parties have duties under health and safety law. Similarly, if the contractor employs sub-contractors all parties will have some health and safety responsibilities. The extent of the responsibilities of each party will depend on the specific circumstances.

As the client, you must clearly identify all aspects of the work you want the contractor to do. The level of risk will depend on the nature of the job. Whatever the risk, you will need to consider the health and safety implications of the job you want undertaken. This will involve selecting someone suitable to do the job, assessing the risks, deciding what information, instruction and training is required, how co-operation and co-ordination between all parties is achieved, how the workforce is to be consulted and the level of management and supervision required.

If you are involved in the selection of contractors, you will need to satisfy yourself that the contractors are competent to do the job safely and without risks to health and safety. The degree of competence required will depend on the work to be done.

Checklist

Make sure contractors know your expectations by:
- explaining your health and safety arrangements to them
- showing them your procedures, systems and processes
- showing them the agreed safe systems of work and your health and safety policy statement and make sure they understand and will act in accordance with it.

Clients, contractors and sub-contractors must consult with their employees on health and safety matters. Where there are recognised trade unions, consultation should be through safety representatives appointed by the unions. Trade unions have an important role to play and can provide expertise to help in the area of health and safety. Where there is no recognised trade union, different arrangements will have to be made e.g. through representatives elected by their employees.

You may already have risk assessments for the work activities in your team, but the contractor must assess the risks for the contracted work and then the two of you must consider any ways that each other's work could affect the health and safety of the other team or anyone else. Together, agree the risk assessment and make all new preventative and protective steps that are needed.

You are responsible for communicating any changes to your team and the contractors are responsible for their own employees. However, you should still exchange clear information regularly about any risks arising from the planned operations, including relevant safety rules and procedures, and dealing with emergencies. This exchange of information should include details of any risks that other parties could not reasonably be expected to know about.

The client should set up liaison arrangements with all parties. This could take the form of regular meetings or briefings. Liaison is particularly important where variations of the work are proposed or where more than one contractor or sub-contractor is engaged. You must also decide what you need to do to effectively manage and supervise the work of the contractors. Both the client and the contractor should review the work after completion to see if performance could be improved in future.

Employees

All of your team members must be aware of the risks that could affect them. You will need to ensure that you communicate this information to them on a regular and structured basis. You should cover all health and safety issues with new employees, assess their competence and plan any relevant training.

Checklist

Keep employees updated by:

- communicating information by displaying relevant signs and posters in prominent locations
- ensuring staff are made aware of information relating to risks and where they can find that information e.g. in the health and safety policy, staff handbook or on the intranet
- encouraging consultation through formal methods e.g. health and safety committee meetings
- demonstrating a commitment to safe working practices by having health and safety as a standing item at every team meeting.

Employees working off site

Ensure that all employees working off site are made aware of the risks that could affect them, e.g. working alone or late at night for which special arrangements may need to be implemented. Employees need to be aware that if they work at another organisation's premises or site, they need to make themselves aware of and comply with the relevant health and safety in place in those locations.

Suppliers

Suppliers of chemicals, machinery and equipment have to make sure that their products are safe and they must provide written information on this. If you do not receive the relevant documentation from your supplier relating to a particular product, then you must return the goods as you cannot risk compromising the safety of your team members by using a product or item of machinery that may have risks that you are not aware of.

Reporting accidents

Organisations are responsible for reporting serious accidents to the Health and Safety Executive (HSE). The process is called **RIDDOR** reporting and you need to be aware of it. Put simply, if someone you employ or someone working on your site has an accident, you must:

- notify the HSE contact centre immediately if the accident is fatal or involves a major injury, such as a fracture, amputation or loss of sight
- report any work-related accidents that result in more than three days off work, including if a visitor is killed or sent to hospital as a result of an accident on your site
- record all accidents in your accident book.

The free HSE leaflet *RIDDOR Explained* (HSE3) gives more details including contact numbers.

Key Term

RIDDOR – Reporting of Injuries, Diseases and Dangerous Occurrences Regulations 1995. This act places a responsibility on organisations and employers to report all relevant accidents to the HSE within specific timeframes.

Visitors and the general public

It is likely that from time to time you will have members of the public and visitors on your premises. This is particularly true in a retail environment where you will have members of the public in your building during your normal trading hours. Always make sure that visitors and members of the public are provided with adequate up-to-date information to enable them to visit your premises safely. Ensure that their safety is not compromised.

Portfolio Task 5 🕐 90 minutes

Links to LO3: Assessment criterion 3.1

Explain how you provide relevant information on identified risks to relevant stakeholders.

When you are working through this, consider the policies, systems, processes and procedures that are in place within your own organisation and include relevant workplace evidence of how you communicate with stakeholders. Discuss your findings with your assessor.

Functional Skills

If you write up any of your research on health and safety issues, you could use it as evidence towards Level 2 Functional Skills in English: Reading and Writing. You need to demonstrate that you have read and understood the process involved in the particular policy or procedure and that your spelling and punctuation is correct.

XYZ LIMITED – RISK ASSESSMENT FORM

Team/Department	Date of assessment:	Review date:

Definition of activity, process or operation	What are the identified hazards?	What risks do they pose and to whom?	Initial risk rating*	What existing control measures are in place?	Revised risk rating	Any further action required and Implementation dates
1.						
2.						

Name of the person undertaking the risk assessment _____

    Signature _____

Name of the person undertaking the manager _____

    Signature _____

* The initial risk rating is calculated assuming no controls are in place. Likelihood rating 1 to 3, multiplied by the severity rating 1 to 3. Maximum score is 9.

Figure B10b.8 A risk assessment form template for your use.

Team talk

Jessica's story

Jessica is the new manager of a call centre team. She has only had the job for a few months and she has decided to carry out risk assessments relating to their operations. She has to undertake:

- a general risk assessment of the main office environment
- individual risk assessments for each person.

Jessica used self-assessment for the individual assessments. She designed a form and asked each member of her team to assess their working environment by completing it. Jessica told the team members that she would resolve any issues identified.

One worker, Daniel, identified problems in his self-assessment. He had developed an aching shoulder and neck and with sore eyes and a headache. Daniel uses a computer and display screen equipment (or DSE) to update customer records and make service calls. He also records messages on the system and responds to emails.

The risk assessment identified the following problems.

- While talking on the phone, Daniel would often hold the handset between his shoulder and ear and type at the same time.
- On bright days, Daniel's screen was difficult to read because of reflections and glare through the window. He was constantly adjusting his posture and working position to avoid the glare.

From the risk assessment, simple and cost effective measures were introduced by Jessica.

- Daniel was provided with a hands free telephone headset to eliminate his neck and shoulder problems.
- An eye test was arranged to identify if Daniel had any vision problems.
- Daniel's workstation layout was rearranged to minimise the glare on his screen from the window.
- Jessica's arranged for regular DSE training sessions for all staff, so they were aware of the health problems associated with computer use and how to prevent them by adjusting their chairs, arranging their workstation appropriately, and taking regular breaks.

Daniel is now much happier, his health problems have diminished and his productivity has increased.

Top tips

Jessica could have solved the problems earlier by putting a system in place for undertaking risk assessments on a regular and routine basis. She could have also checked what risk assessments (if any) were already in place. She could have contacted the health and safety officer or spoken to other managers for advice or support, for instance to ask them about alternative equipment, such as headsets.

Ask the expert

Q I've recently been promoted to a team leader, what should I do to make sure that my team are all comfortable at their workstations?

A Speak to your team to ask them if they have any issues with their workstations. You could do this at a team meeting or you could speak to them individually. You could also get them to complete a workstation self-assessment form. Results can then be discussed at team meetings and any problems rectified.

Remember to use any relevant in house risk assessment forms that exist and liaise with your health and safety officer who will be able to offer advice and support.

What your assessor is looking for

In order to prepare for and succeed in completing this unit, your assessor will require you to be able to demonstrate competence in:

• identifying all risks in your area of responsibility

• proactively managing risks

• minimising the impact of risks occurring

• being able to communicate information relating to risks and hazards to relevant stakeholders.

You will demonstrate your skills, knowledge and competence through the three learning outcomes in this unit. Evidence generated in this unit will also cross reference to the other units in this qualification.

Please bear in mind that there are significant cross-referencing opportunities throughout this qualification and you may have already generated some relevant work to meet certain criteria in this unit. Your assessor will provide you with the exact requirements to meet the standards of this unit. However, as a guide it is likely that for this unit you will need to be assessed through the following methods:

• An observation of relevant workplace activities or a witness testimony.

• A written report or reflective account.

• A professional discussion.

• Any relevant work products produced as evidence.

The work products for this unit could include:

• copies of any risk assessments that you have undertaken

• a copy of any relevant agendas and minutes from any meeting which you have attended where risks and or health and safety issues were discussed

• any written communications in relation to risks. This could include emails that you have sent or received.

Your assessor will guide you through the assessment process as detailed in the candidate logbook. The portfolio tasks will provide relevant opportunities to meet certain elements of the learning outcomes.

Task and page reference	Assessment criteria
1 (page 82)	1.1, 1.2
2 (page 84)	1.1
3 (page 87)	1.1, 1.2, 1.3
4 (page 92)	2.1, 2.2
5 (page 95)	3.1

Unit B10b Manage risk in own area of responsibility

Unit D10 Manage conflict in a team

As a team leader you may encounter conflict with your team members or others from both inside and outside of your organisation. This unit will give you the opportunity to explore some of the main causes of conflict and the steps you can take to minimise them.

You need to understand the importance of supporting your team members and how effective communication can be key to helping you manage and resolve conflict situations. You will learn about strategies for dealing with conflict and some of the techniques that you can use to encourage team members to resolve their own conflicts.

Policies and procedures are likely to exist within your organisation to assist you when managing conflict and this unit examines the importance of these along with the necessity of maintaining complete, accurate and confidential records of conflicts.

What you will learn:

- Be able to support team members' understanding of their role and position within a team
- Be able to take measures to minimise conflict within a team
- Be able to understand how to encourage team members to resolve their own conflicts
- Be able to understand legal and organisational requirements concerning conflict

Links to the Technical Certificate

If you are completing your NVQ as part of an Apprenticeship Framework, you will find the following topics are also covered in your Technical Certificate:

- Roles of a team and stages of team development
- Why it is important to be professional and encourage team participation
- Adopting a positive approach and resolving work related difficulties
- Dealing with conflict within a team
- Understanding self managed teams

Be able to support team members' understanding of their role and position within a team

Your team members will feel more confident in their working environment if they are clear about what is expected of them. Their work roles and responsibilities must be communicated to them in an appropriate format, such as job descriptions, rotas and work schedules.

It is important that your team members can approach you with any concerns they have and that you show you will support and guide them through any difficulties.

Effective two-way communication is necessary if morale and motivation is to be maintained, so you need to examine how you communicate and which techniques you should use in particular circumstances.

Communicate standards of work required

Productive working relations with your team members largely depend upon your ability to communicate effectively with them. The **standards** you expect your team to work towards must be made clear – if you don't explain to your team members exactly what you expect from them, you can't expect them to achieve what you want them to.

The purpose of setting standards with your team is to:

- make sure everybody is working towards the same quality standard
- ensure the customer or end user receives the same quality level.

In order for this to happen the standards required must be effectively communicated.

During team meetings, supervision meetings or one-to-one discussions, you may find opportunity to communicate your expectations regarding standards of performance and behaviour. As a

follow up to face-to-face meetings, you could reinforce the importance of working to these standards by:

- sending group emails, informing the team where they might find policies, procedures and standards expected electronically (for example, on the organisation's intranet)
- pinning copies of policies and procedures on notice boards to be read
- signposting the team to hard copies of policies, procedures and standards – perhaps kept in lever-arch folders on shelves in an office where they can be easily inspected.

In addition, these documents may form part of the organisation's **staff handbook** and might also be contained in the induction file that each employee receives when they start their job in your organisation.

Key Terms

Staff handbook – information pack for employees containing the organisation's policies and procedures.

Standards – rules used as a basis for comparison or judgement.

It may be necessary to allocate time – perhaps during an induction day or a team meeting – for each team member to read through the index of policies and procedures that the organisation has, and then to read the contents of those you consider most applicable to the work of your team (for example, the health and safety policy, dress code, fire procedures). It is a good idea to produce a form for each employee to sign and date that they have read and understood the contents of the policies and procedures you consider important and appropriate.

Policies and procedures need to be revised from time to time to meet changing demands of industry customers and the economy. It is important that you keep your team members updated of any reviewed policies, procedures and standards. A useful time for you to do this is when you conduct staff appraisals with your team members.

Don't forget to communicate to your team the following:

- changes to policies and procedures
- the purpose of the policies and procedures
- where they can be found e.g. intranet, notice board.

Remember

It is not enough for employees to just know that policies and procedures exist – they should all be encouraged to read and understand them.

It is important that you communicate to your team members a list of the policies and procedures that exist in your organisation, what their purpose is and where they can be found.

In some industries, organisations adopt an approach to standards which identifies them as:

- standard costs – this is the desired cost of producing an item or providing a service
- standard time – this is the desired time an employee takes to complete a given task when producing an item or providing a service.

The standard time can be multiplied by how much per hour an employee working on a task is paid, which results in a total labour cost for that task.

The standard – or desired – costs and time can later be compared to the actual costs and time taken, to establish how well the organisation or team, is performing. These results should then be communicated to the employees and any difference between what was expected and what actually happened can be discussed in detail.

The process of quality assurance serves to ensure that quality standards will be met. These standards should be discussed and agreed with your team members with a focus on customer or end-user satisfaction. For this purpose you may use a team meeting as a vehicle to brainstorm ideas from the team. This is an opportunity for you to let the team know that views and ideas are welcomed and that all opinions are equally valued. In turn, team members may feel more motivated, which could automatically increase workflow and output for

which they should receive recognition, praise and perhaps reward. Then as morale increases further so will output, and a positive cycle of workflow can be sustained.

Clear channels of communication and using the right methods and techniques at the right time, can help to keep your team informed and updated of what is expected of them and what has been achieved.

Remember

When discussing expected standards and targets with your team, build in milestones, so that progress towards completed tasks can be measured and communicated at intervals through the process.

Encouraging good communication and standards of behaviour

By making your team members fully aware of the standards of work and behaviour that is expected of them, you can go some way to helping to reduce the possibility of conflict situations occurring.

The behaviour you expect from your team members must be made clear. How they behave in the workplace can have an impact on meeting targets and expected standards of quality.

In your role as team leader, you must communicate effectively and stress to your team members that it is important for them to communicate effectively with each other too! Doing this can encourage a **holistic** approach to meeting targets and standards, and can promote a positive team spirit and complementary behaviours.

Key Term

Holistic – looking at all parts of the team's efforts so that individuals work closely together to achieve the same overall goals of the team.

Failure to communicate in the right way and at the right time, may lead to negativity in the team and in particular:

- confusion
- mistrust
- distress.

These factors can adversely effect team dynamics and behaviours.

In your organisation, standards may apply to work performance and behaviour. You may be able to identify policies and procedures in your workplace that relate to behaviour. A policy informs employees what senior management consider acceptable, or not acceptable, behaviour or actions (for example an equal opportunities and diversity policy). Procedures however, can be described as sets of step-by-step instructions to follow when undertaking specific tasks. This ensures that everyone carries out these tasks in exactly the same way, resulting in a consistent approach towards achieving recognised and expected standards. There may also be a code of conduct and even a dress code in force to guide employees.

Remember

Effective communication means getting the right message to the right people at the right time, and obtaining feedback.

Activity · 45 minutes

Research the purpose of the policies and procedures listed below and identify your own definition of each.

- Equal opportunity and diversity
- Bullying and harassment
- Unacceptable behaviour
- Health and safety
- Grievance
- Disciplinary
- Code of conduct (if appropriate)

Culture and communication

Culture is often referred to as 'the way we do things here' and this is often influenced by the attitudes and behaviours of employees at all levels and the policies and procedures that are in place.

If you reflect upon the culture you work in, you may establish that it is, for example, a pleasant working culture in which everyone gets on well with each other. Alternatively, it is possible that

you may work in a negative workplace culture (for example, a blame culture).

The team that you lead may, in turn, develop its own culture and the attitudes and behaviours of each team member will play a part in the development of this. As part of its own distinct culture, teams may adopt their own way to operating (their norm) in an effort to achieve standards and targets. They may also develop their own use of language and jargon within the team and perhaps create nicknames for each other. An advantage of this is to create a strong team identity and a culture that is supportive of team members, but a disadvantage might be a tendency to become inward looking and exclusive and a reluctance to accept new members into the team.

Portfolio Task 1 · 20 minutes

Links to LO1: Assessment criterion 1.1
Explain to your assessor how you communicate the organisation's standards of work to your team and outline the behaviour that is expected of them. Provide examples of methods of communication where you are setting out the standards of work. Examples of these could include minutes of meetings, emails, appraisal documentation.

PLTS

Through discussions with your assessor, you will generate ideas and explore opportunities that will enable you to communicate standards you expect your team to work towards (CT1; EP2).

Activity · 30 minutes

1. Reflect on your team members and identify whether there are any behaviours you think could be changed. Alternatively you could reflect on your own behaviours – what would you like to change?
2. How often do you think you should make time in meetings or get your team together to discuss behaviours at work and how things can be changed for the better? Give reasons for your responses.

Discuss your responses with your assessor.

How team members can work together and support each other

Encouraging effective team working and bonding has many benefits. These include increased levels of morale and motivation and mutual respect between team members. Team members should be given the opportunity to share ideas and best practice during team meetings as this will encourage a holistic approach. The more that people feel part of the team and have a sense of belonging, the more likely they are to support each other on a day-to-day basis, but particularly during difficult times in the workplace.

For various reasons, team members will display behaviours that may be of a positive or negative nature. Negative behaviour might be associated with their work role or their working environment (for example, disagreements with other team members) while positive behaviour might be associated with job satisfaction and clearly defined job roles.

Team members' behaviour

Your observation of your team members' behaviours may enable you to categorise each of them as:

- passive – a person who feels their opinions are not as important as those of other people in the team
- assertive – a person who accepts that everyone in the team is entitled to an opinion that is no more or less important than any other team member
- aggressive – a person who thinks that their opinions are more important than anyone else's in the team.

Activity 🕐 20 minutes

Write a statement saying whether you think these different types of people need managing in a different way. Explain your reasons and discuss your thoughts with your assessor.

Within your team you may find personality clashes because of different attitudes, mind-sets or ways of thinking. If such clashes are not managed effectively they can sometimes escalate to potentially damaging conflict situations. It may help to be aware that in any workplace there is likely to be a mix of:

- 'can't do' people – these people want to perform well, but are currently not capable of doing so, until they receive further support, training or guidance
- 'won't do' people – these people simply don't want to be at work and their motivation is solely to receive their pay at the end of the month. Regardless of capability or support, they have no interest in performing well.

As a team leader you can support, guide and encourage your 'can't do' people but your 'won't do' people will be harder to manage. By being aware of 'won't do' people in your team you can take steps to intervene when, for example, other willing team members are having to compensate by trying to do their own work and take on some of the work that the 'won't do' person should be doing. As you might imagine, if you don't intervene to prevent escalation of bad feeling, then conflict between team members may arise. Further, your team members may not feel they are getting the support they should from you, potentially creating conflict between you and them.

Remember

When dealing with difficult situations, be aware of your own limits of authority. It is not a weakness to advise your line manager of difficult situations and seek support when you feel you need to.

Douglas McGregor's Theory X and Theory Y

In the 1960s Douglas McGregor, a management theorist, carried out some research into types of workers. He identified two different categories, which he called Theory X and Theory Y.

Theory X workers are considered to be lazy and are only motivated by earning money rather than job satisfaction or the challenge of working as part of a team. They often need to be supervised closely and generally respond to detailed directions and instructions. Theory Y workers are committed to the work of the team and enjoy the challenge of working towards targets and objectives. They seek responsibility and enjoy problem solving to improve the work of the team.

Activity ⏱ 60 minutes

Conduct some research into Douglas McGregor's Theory X and Theory Y workers and discuss your findings with your assessor.

To promote a holistic approach to work and to the meeting of targets, it is important that you encourage your team members to work well together and support each other in every way possible.

To achieve this, consider to what degree you:

- empower your team members to take the lead
- praise individuals for working well
- praise the team for working well
- encourage creative thinking and formulation of ideas in the team
- advise your team members, as soon as possible, of difficulties or changes that will affect them
- agree and negotiate different ways of doing things with your team.

if your team is armed with up-to-date information relating to targets and expectations, then members can take steps to organise themselves and focus on supporting each other. There will be times when team members are emotional or angry over something that has happened in the workplace or at home. In situations like this it may well be fellow team members who intervene and offer support in the first instances.

Because you will have already communicated the expectations and targets for the team, your team members will realise that by supporting each other during difficult or challenging times, they are more likely to achieve what is expected of them.

A culture of support is likely to develop in the team if members:

- are prepared to listen to each other's concerns
- step in to help a teammate who may get overloaded or behind with their work
- build rapport and trust in the team (e.g. encouraging openness)
- respect everyone else's views
- ask each other for honest feedback
- communicate effectively with each other
- share team problems and difficulties
- respect diversity in the team.

Remember

The way team members interact and communicate with each other is likely to affect how supportive the team culture is.

Management theorists Andrew Leigh and Michael Maynard conducted research into team development and suggested that a team will work through six development stages.

1. Starting – integrating new team members and building relationships.
2. Sorting – there may be conflict as members compete for a position in the team.
3. Stabilising – the team adjusts to accept the workplace culture and adheres to rules and regulations. At this stage, members usually agree the best way for the team to do things.
4. Striving – the team starts to perform well and aims to meet its targets.
5. Succeeding – the team achieves its objectives, meets targets, standards and expectations and examines way to enhance performance
6. Stopping – members of the team leave, are promoted or transferred, or perhaps a one-off project is complete. Team members may be saddened by these events.

Refer also to Unit B5 to also examine the work of Bruce Tuckman and Meredith Belbin in relation to teams and team building. Tuckman, for instance, came up with a similar idea of stages in team development, naming them Forming, Storming, Norming, Performing and Mourning.

Leadership styles

For team members to support, respect and value each other, it is necessary for you as the team leader to promote the fact that you are part of the team. Team members need to understand and respect that you are the leader, but this doesn't stop you taking turns with unpleasant tasks to muck in with the team occasionally and supporting them when things get difficult.

Kurt Lewin, a management theorist, identified the three following styles of leadership.

- Autocratic – people do things your way only. Useful in times of a crisis, but some people find this style demotivating.
- Democratic – you allow people to be involved in the decision-making process and value their opinions. You however will make the final decisions.
- Laissez-faire – you trust the capabilities of the team, so that you can stand back and leave them alone to get on with the work.

Being aware of your preferred leadership style can help you to reflect on to what degree you empower your team to make their own decisions and support each other. The term 'preferred leadership style', is used because you may from time to time change your style to suit circumstances as they happen, for example a machine breakdown needs urgent action – you may become autocratic.

Portfolio Task 2 — 20 minutes

Links to LO1: Assessment criterion 1.2

Having your team members working together and supporting each other is important for an effective team. Using your own workplace examples, explain to your assessor how your team members work and support each other. Your evidence to support your discussion could include examples of minutes of meetings where your team agree their roles and responsibilities.

Be able to take measures to minimise conflict within a team

Being able to identify a potential conflict situation can give you the opportunity to step in to take action that will prevent it from escalating further. Knowing what to look for isn't always easy, but having an understanding of some of the factors that can lead to conflict between your team members can help you to take measures to minimise the possibility of it happening.

How organisational structures, systems and procedures can give rise to conflict

On a day-to-day basis the activities that your team members undertake can be the cause of conflict. For example, your organisation's policies and procedures may be outdated and need reviewing, which may result in team members ignoring them and working in slightly different ways. People may begin to argue over the best way to approach a task which can lead to conflict.

Similarly, the way your organisation is structured can lead to conflict if, for example, communication is ineffective or if it is not clear who should report to whom or who has the authority to make decisions.

Organisational structures

Very often, the way an organisation is structured can influence how effectively people communicate with each other. Poor communication can lead to situations of conflict and some examples of this will be discussed later in this unit.

Organisational structures are not static. As a business operation expands its range of products or services, its structure will evolve. This may be due to an increase in demand from the market place, the result of a merger or takeover, or perhaps because new contracts have been won. Whatever the reason, as the business grows the structure may change accordingly. If not managed properly, such change can result in conflict.

Depending on the nature and type of business activity, the number of staff and the number of customers, organisations are likely to be structured in one of the following ways:

- hierarchical (or pyramid)
- geographical
- product
- matrix.

These different types can be best illustrated by an organisational chart, a pictorial or visual method of communication to inform staff of who does what in the organisation and who reports to whom. The chart shows how many managers there are working at different levels in different departments, and how many operatives there are in each department.

A hierarchical (pyramid) structure is the most common type of structure found in many organisations, as seen in Figure D10.1. It is developed over time as an organisation grows larger with layers of employees at different levels. Authority and decision-making power increases up the pyramid.

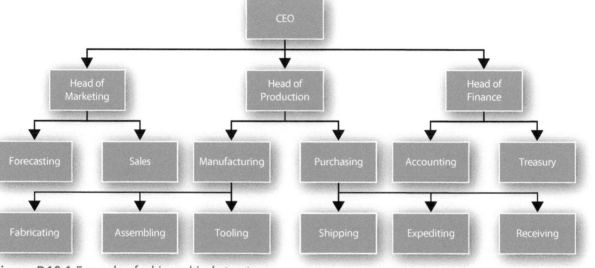

Figure D10.1 Example of a hierarchical structure.

A geographical structure is often used by large retailers who have many branches in many different regions of the UK (for example, Tesco or B&Q), as seen in Figure D10.2.

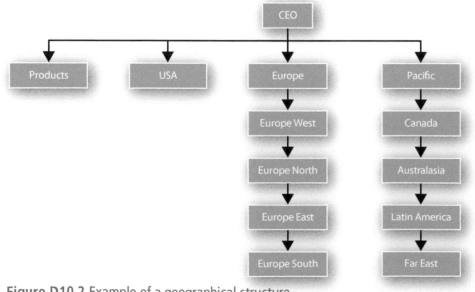

Figure D10.2 Example of a geographical structure.

A product structure is likely to be used by an organisation that makes a variety of related products. For example, a pharmaceutical organisation may produce different types of specialist medicines, vaccines and sterile supplies.

A matrix structure is often used for one-off projects such as motorway bridge building or perhaps a car manufacturer producing a limited edition. An example matrix structure is shown in Figure D10.3, below.

As a team leader, you need to know and understand the structure of your organisation and exactly how many team members should report to you. Everyone should know how many layers of management exist and what the other departments are in the organisation. Sometimes, the boxes used in a chart will show names of employees working in their positions, other times, the chart will show only the job title and perhaps how many positions are held (for example, '21 × sales representatives' might be written in one box).

Consider that a sales manager has a meeting with their team leaders to discuss sales targets. The manager will expect the team leaders to convey this information down the hierarchy to their team members. Remembering that in the first place the sales manager would have been instructed by their own manager to increase sales, this is known as the **chain of command**. The sales manager cannot be expected to manage the workload of each sales assistant in each team. Therefore, the sales manager will only be concerned with managing each team leader and in turn each team leader will be concerned with managing their own team members.

Key Term

Chain of command – the line of authority.

Chain of command

If a chain of command is too long and there are too many layers for messages or instructions to travel through, then difficulties with channels of communication can occur.

- Messages can be distorted as they go either up or down the chain of command. Each person in the chain might interpret the message differently and repeat it to the next person in a slightly different way.

- The more people in a chain of command then the longer the person who sent the original message may have to wait to receive a reply; this might ultimately affect staff morale or customer expectations.

- It may be easier for someone in the chain to hold on to bad news, complaints or a problem, hoping they can resolve it themselves before others in the chain find out about it and consider that person unable to do their job properly.

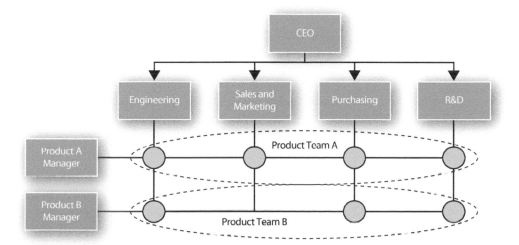

Figure D10.3 An example matrix structure.

> **Remember**
>
> It only takes one member of the team to ignore the procedures in place to undo the good work of the rest of the team as a whole.

Portfolio Task 3 30 minutes

Links to LO2: Assessment criterion 2.1

Give examples to your assessor of possible issues with organisational structures, systems and procedures that have or could cause conflict in your team. Provide examples of policies, procedures, structures and/or minutes of meetings which explain the main cause.

Copies of your minutes of meetings, organisational structural charts, policies and workplace procedures will provide evidence for your portfolio.

These examples illustrate how easily workers can become dissatisfied, frustrated and demotivated if communication is poor in the chain of command. In extreme cases, conflict can arise and some organisations may re-structure themselves in an effort to de-layer their organisational structure, reducing the length of the chain. This means that middle managers will often be removed (either redeployed or their positions made redundant). Teams may be empowered or organised into self-managed teams, meaning that the need to retain all supervisors and team leaders will be reduced.

> **Remember**
>
> A large percentage of work-related accidents – some very serious ones – happen when people ignore procedures in an effort to rush something or cut corners.

The importance of policies and procedures

Ignoring procedures can be dangerous and harmful and may also lead to conflict between team members. If one team member cuts corners, to get a task finished quickly then not only can this adversely affect the quality of the product or service, it could put other workers at risk.

It is therefore vitally important that you emphasise the importance of following procedures, for instance, in your team meetings. If procedures are not followed by a minority, the rest of the team may become frustrated and feel let down by their colleagues. These situations may begin by the perpetrators being jokingly chastised by the rest of their colleagues, but if the consequences of not following the procedures are serious – affecting the whole team – then conflict in the team may occur.

It may be useful to examine the procedures you and your team use. If they have not been reviewed recently it may be time to rewrite them, as changes in your industry and equipment you use may warrant this. Your team members should be involved in this **process**, after all they are the ones doing the tasks you are reviewing.

This can only be good for morale, as team members will appreciate that you value their opinions. It can also help to minimise the risk of conflict in your team as you should obtain 'buy-in' from members.

The ownership they have of their procedures should encourage everyone to abide by them and the importance of this should be reinforced during the one-to-one discussions and staff appraisals you conduct with each team member.

> **Key Term**
>
> **Process** – a series of actions to achieve a desired objective.

Identifying potential causes of conflict

Generally, conflict can occur as a result of:

- organisational problems – the workload may be too challenging or perhaps not challenging enough. This may lead to frustration or boredom and some team members may take their frustration out on others. Ineffective communication and unfair working practices can also be problematic between team members.

- structural problems – insufficient reward and recognition may cause some members of your team to question 'Why do I bother?'. They may withdraw from their usual effective way of working resulting in their team resenting them as they are prevented from meeting targets. Experiencing abuse of power from others and generally not enjoying their job may also trigger situations of conflict in the team.

- personal problems – your team members may be experiencing bullying, harassment or be on the receiving end of constant teasing from others in the team. Perhaps colleagues are inflexible towards them when they try to encourage a holistic approach to meeting targets. These circumstances can easily escalate to conflict situations.

Being aware of potential conflict situations between team members. You may need to intervene and quickly put corrective action in place to remedy the situation before morale and performance is affected.

Conflict can occur for many reasons. You may have experienced or witnessed some of the following examples:

- Not respecting others' values or beliefs.
- Disagreeing on how tasks should be carried out.
- Resources not being shared out fairly.
- Regular absences of a team member, with others having to cover their work on top of their own.
- Inadequate procedures to follow.
- Favouritism towards a team member(s).
- Unclear job roles/no job description.
- Confusion over work roles – who should be doing what?
- People in the team feeling their work is more important than others'.

Remember

When 'change' occurs, for example a restructure or a new shift pattern, employees can become demotivated and frustrated leading to conflict unless the reasons and details of the change are communicated effectively.

Add to the list, poor communication, not involving team members in the decision-making process and personality clashes, and its easy to understand how conflict can arise between team members. In addition, the culture of the team or workplace cannot be overlooked. For example, managers creating an unhealthy blame culture or an 'us and them' culture can be particularly damaging to team spirit and lead to conflict.

Team members exposed to conflict will look to you, as team leader, to take steps to rectify these situations. Failure to do so may result in you losing the faith your team have in you and you may lose their respect.

Be aware of the limits of your authority when dealing with conflict situations. You may need to inform your manager if the situation is becoming serious or if you need support. It's always a good idea to keep your managers fully aware of any situations.

Team morale versus conflict

Allowing conflict situations to continue can damage team morale. Even those team members not directly involved may find the atmosphere difficult to work in or may even find themselves being encouraged to side with one party or another. This can result in sub-groups forming in your team, seriously affecting morale, motivation and performance. If standards and targets are not being achieved as a result, questions will be asked of you, and your manager will want answers. Perhaps worse, customers' expectations may not be met and they may find other suppliers for their goods and services placing the job of everyone in the team at risk. This highlights the importance of managing conflict in a team.

It may be useful to take a step back and analyse how you deal (or think you might deal) with conflict in your team. Perhaps everyone does react differently, but being aware of your own management style and aiming to develop your own approach may be useful.

Examine Figure D10.4 on the next page. Management theorists Kenneth W. Thomas and Ralph H. Kilmann devised this model in 1974 to recognise stages of conflict that can occur.

Unit D10 Manage conflict in a team

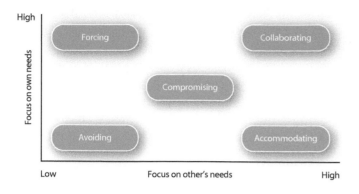

Figure D10.4 Stages of conflict.

Conflict management

In 1983, theorist M. A. Rahim carried out some research into conflict management. Rahim suggested that five conflict-management strategies can be considered when attempting to resolve a conflict situation:

- Integrating – exchanging information, examining differences and exploring alternatives to satisfy the parties involved.
- Obliging – minimising differences and examining commonalities to satisfy parties concerned.
- Dominating – at the expense of ignoring the needs of one party involved, the other party sets out to win over the situation and emerge with satisfaction.
- Avoiding – one party not only fails to satisfy their own needs, but also fails to show any concern for the needs of the other party; a lose-lose situation.
- Compromising – both parties agree to give and take and resolve the issue so that there is a win-win situation.

Rahim claims there isn't a best-fit approach to manage conflict but that the five strategies listed above give possibilities for parties to consider either concern for themselves, concern for others or perhaps a combination of both (compromising).

Team members' personality traits

In the 1970s psychologists working in the area of stress and conflict reached a conclusion that generally, people will fall into one of two personality traits as described below.

1. Type A personality – this person is prone to anxiety and is easily stressed by situations that occur. Being very restless, this person can easily become involved in conflict situations.
2. Type B personality – this person is generally more laid back and relaxed. Being easy going this person is less prone to stress and less likely to enter into conflict situations.

Your awareness of these two personality traits may lead you to identify which of your team members are most likely to become involved in conflict situations. This may help you to monitor team members in given situations, possibly enabling you to prevent conflict situations before they actually happen.

You may have heard of the 'fight or flight' syndrome. This suggests that in a stressful situation, people are likely to either stand their ground and fight back or they will choose to walk (or run) away from the situation. Those that select the option to stand their ground are more likely to create or fuel conflict in the workplace.

Think of the saying 'seeing red'. It is interesting to note that when stressed a person's brain receives a rush of additional chemicals as the body tries to deal with the stressful situation. As these chemicals reach the brain, a person may very quickly say something which is later regretted or even become aggressive. However, after about six seconds experts suggest the chemicals settle and the person calms down.

Key Term

Rivalry – competition between individuals or teams.

Take a close look at how your team members operate. Can you identify **rivalry** in any form? This could be between individual team members, or perhaps between two teams in your organisation. While competition can be healthy and productive, resentment can easily build up between competing teams or individuals, when reward or praise reaches some, but not all. Watch out, too, for acts of discrimination. Some team members may be on the receiving end of discriminatory practices and may initially try to ignore what is happening to them. Over time they can become more and more frustrated until they eventually retaliate leading to a conflict situation.

Given that conflict can lead to lowered morale, motivation and performance, taking action to avoid it can be particularly beneficial. When conflict occurs, workers may not have such an enthusiastic approach towards their work because the atmosphere is tense. This can prevent important and relevant information being passed from team member to team member, ultimately affecting the completion of tasks and the achievement of goals.

All of this can result in higher stress levels, leading to:

- more absenteeism (for example, people don't enjoy work and take unofficial days off)
- a higher sickness rate (for example, stress-related illnesses)
- increased staff turnover (for example, people leave to find a more relaxed working environment).

Bad publicity travels fast! Friends and family of your team members may tell other people outside of your organisation of the perceived poor working atmosphere. This, in turn, can damage the image and reputation of your whole organisation, potentially affecting future business opportunities and the job security of everyone.

Taking action to avoid conflict becomes increasingly important if the working relations of the team and indeed the reputation of the whole organisation are to be protected and safeguarded.

Avoiding, managing and resolving conflict

Back in 1976, management theorist Kenneth W. Thomas developed five approaches to managing conflict. It will be beneficial to analyse each of these approaches and consider which you believe is the best one!

- Forcing – you intend to get your own way at any cost and defeat the parties involved.
- Avoiding – you decide to wait and see what will happen and you don't address the reasons for the conflict.
- Compromising – your aim is to get things back to how they were, as quickly as possible. You may do this by moving things forward through bargaining and negotiation.
- Accommodating – you worry about upsetting anyone, so you simply accept what is being said to you and go along with what the other parties want.
- Collaborating – you aim to resolve problems so that all parties concerned feel they've been treated fairly. You aim to do this by discussing ideas together.

Now consider, if you:

- avoid dealing with conflict or are too accommodating, your behaviour may be considered to be passive by nature
- compromise or collaborate when dealing with conflict, then your behaviour may be considered to be assertive. This is because you are not being passive by not reacting, but neither are you being aggressive by using actions that will make sure you win at any cost.

When you are dealing with situations in the workplace that you think may lead to conflict if not resolved, structure a discussion with the parties involved (in a suitable quiet and private environment), that enables you to:

- obtain relevant information from the parties concerned
- identify exactly what the dispute is about
- get the parties involved to agree there will be different views

- aim for a win-win situation (all parties have a positive outcome)
- negotiate a fair outcome for all.

Remember

Being aggressive is unacceptable behaviour and will never resolve a conflict situation.

Activity 30 minutes

If one of your team members approached you to complain that a colleague is leaving early at the end of his/her shift, what actions would you take?
How would your responses differ if:

1. the team member leaving early is generally a very good worker

2. initially you have no proof that the team member has been leaving early, but you later find out that it is true and others have been covering for them.

It is worth noting that negotiation is a particularly useful strategy for resolving conflict. For this process to work, be clear in your own mind exactly what you want to achieve. Run through your mind, or write down on paper, what the best possible outcome might be and what the worst possible outcome might be. Do this before your discussions with the parties concerned. When negotiating to achieve a fair outcome, be open, honest and ask for explanations of anything you're not sure of. It's very important to listen well, be assertive and have relevant information to hand.

To avoid conflict escalating, this simple measure of calming the affected person or persons down can help. To calm someone, you should:

- find somewhere private and quiet to take them – invite them to sit down
- reassure the other person that their concerns will be addressed
- give them time to tell you their problem (get it off their chest)
- not interrupt – let them finish, but show you've listened
- be aware of your body language and don't appear threatening
- speak slowly and softly when you do respond.

Remember

Sometimes conflict can actually be good! There may be slight disagreement over the way a task is being carried out, or perhaps the writing of new procedures. Providing the process is carefully managed, everyone's views can be accepted and agreed upon, actually improving the way things are done.

It is important to consider that the way you and your team members respond to situations can seriously affect your working life. As a team, you may feel from time to time that you have unreasonable demands placed upon you when, for example, objectives and targets from others are not SMART. Your external customers may make your life difficult too, if they are constantly changing their mind or perhaps complaining. Remember that family and friends may unwittingly place pressure upon you to do things and eventually you may become too busy both in and out of work unless you monitor situations carefully.

You may become stressed and frustrated in these circumstances and so can your team members if the wellbeing of your team is overlooked, perhaps even the person passive by nature can be prone to conflict.

Activity ⏱ 30 minutes

The table below offers examples of causes of conflict and suggested remedies. Note that the awareness of remedies and implementing them promptly can be sufficient to avoid conflict happening in the first place!

The causes and remedies in the table have been mixed up. Your task is to examine each cause and then decide which remedy should sit in the table alongside it. Re-write the table correctly with the causes and their remedies and give a brief reason why the remedy is appropriate.

Cause of conflict	Suggested remedy
Personality clashes in the team	Ensure team members are involved in the process and offer clear reasons why the change will happen as early as possible before it actually does. Provide regular communication updates to the team.
Competition for resources between team members	Ensure all team members are aware of your organisational structure (show them the organisational chart). Is everyone clear of the chain of command, reporting remedies and accountability?
Issues over authority	Examine communication methods used. Where and when are discussions between you and team members held (e.g. team meetings)? Ensure procedures are easy to follow and regularly reviewed.
Misunderstandings between team members	Investigate your budget allowance for purchasing adequate resources with your manager. Examine procedures and rotas to examine how resources can be shared out and their use monitored effectively.
Change in the workplace	Consider separating team members from each other and examine the possibility of job rotation. Offer assertiveness training to team members involved in the conflict.

PLTS

This task will give you the opportunity to reflect on how you have managed a conflict situation and to evaluate what you have learnt from the experience to inform future progress (RL2, 3, 5; EP2, 3, 4).

Functional Skills

By preparing a 500-word document you will be practising your Level 2 Functional Skills in English: Writing. You will practise your grammar and punctuation skills, and structuring of your sentences.

Portfolio Task 4 ⏱ 45 minutes

Links to LO2: Assessment criteria 2.2, 2.3

1. Give examples to your assessor of potential conflict between your team members.

2. Explain the strategies you agreed with your manager or team members to resolve the potential conflict.

3. If you were to manage this situation again, would you do anything differently?

4. Reflect, in a maximum of 500 words, on the actions you undertook to try and avoid this potential conflict.

Advisory, Conciliation and Arbitration Service (ACAS)

There is also help outside your organisation to resolve conflict. The Advisory, Conciliation and Arbitration Service (ACAS) offers support to organisations in industrial relations. With regard to conflict, it advises that the actions in the table below can be of benefit.

Type of conflict	How it can be addressed
A personality clash or one-off minor disagreement	The manager or team leader has a one-to-one discussion in an informal manner
A persistent and ongoing situation	The team leader/manager has informal discussions with those involved to identify the root cause of the conflict
An employee uses the organisation's grievance policy to take action against another employee	This is a more formal case. The team leader/manager should follow the internal procedures to deal with this and make sure that human resources is notified
An employee wishes to pursue a claim and take the case to an employment tribunal	The team leader/manager and human resources should suggest mediation with ACAS wherever possible before action for a tribunal case goes ahead

Table D10.1 How to address conflicts.

Activity
20 minutes

Think of an example when your line manager encouraged you to resolve a problem or potential conflict that you had identified. Write down what the issue was, how you resolved it and how your line manager monitored your actions and evaluated the outcome.

Remember

Rather than spending time trying to resolve a problem or conflict situation, it's better to take steps to make sure difficult situations don't happen in the first place.

Be able to understand how to encourage team members to resolve their own conflicts

Involving your team in the identification and resolution of their own conflicts empowers them and gives them input into their own situation. It may not always be appropriate for team members to solve their own conflicts, but making it known that they are encouraged to take responsibility for them can have a very positive effect on morale and ultimately the success and effectiveness of the team.

Team members identifying potential problems

There may be occasions when your team members identify potential problems or conflicts and report them to you. If this happens, you must act quickly to resolve any issues before they become more serious.

The difficult situations and sources of current or potential conflict that team members may identify could be due to a variety of causes, for instance human error, a system failure or faulty equipment, unacceptable behaviour or simply a shortage of resources that are needed. It may be that procedures to address the way work is done need to be updated, additional training is required, and the way resources are allocated needs to be reviewed.

Whatever the cause, there is a knock-on effect to these problems, because they can lead to:

- increased conflict, absenteeism and perhaps good people leaving the organisation
- increased risk of accidents and incidents
- backlog of work and therefore unhappy customers as deadlines are not met
- more complaints from internal/external customers
- quality standards not being met and projects/tasks taking longer to complete
- equipment and machines not used effectively due to more downtime.

All of the above can lead to additional costs for the department/organisation, but can also greatly increase the risk of conflict between team members.

Identifying potential conflict areas or problems before they occur or when they are still at the early stages is obviously desirable. It is therefore prudent to encourage your team to be aware of potential problem areas and nurture a culture where they are encouraged to come to you as soon as possible if they foresee a problem.

Team members resolving their own difficulties

In some instances it may be better for you to encourage your team members to resolve their own problems or conflicts. This will depend on your team members and how serious the situation is or could become. You must use your judgement to decide whether to empower your colleagues to resolve the issue themselves, or whether you intervene.

Remember that encouraging your team members to resolve their own difficulties, within reason, can motivate them as they will recognise that you trust them and respect their judgement. You can encourage your team to take the initiative in this way in team briefings, through other public channels such as notice boards, or even specially timetabled meetings or workshops where you discuss with your team how problems can be resolved.

Consider this process that you can share with your team.

- Decide exactly what the problem or difficulty is.
- Collect information about the difficulty to understand why its happening.
- Think about how many alternative solutions there may be.
- Evaluate how effective each alternative solution might be (for example, costs, health and safety impact, customer service impact, impact on colleagues).
- Choose the best solution and implement it.

- Evaluate the outcomes to see whether your chosen solution worked.

You can reinforce this step-by-step approach to resolving difficulties by making reference to it in the PDRs/staff appraisals you conduct with your team.

> **Remember**
>
> Always examine the risks to the organisation of implementing your chosen solution in terms of cost, images and reputation.

To resolve problems, inform your team that there needs to be a balance between the needs of the organisation, the team members and ultimately the customers.

Make your team members aware that when resolving difficulties between themselves they need to listen to each other and respect each other's views and opinions. Failure to do this can result in additional conflict situations arising.

Your team should be encouraged to:

- avoid arguments between themselves and others in the organisation
- be assertive, but not aggressive
- be flexible in their approach
- acknowledge how others are feeling and include everyone in the problem-solving process
- avoid negative criticism
- use voice control (soft and quiet tone, no shouting)
- avoid sarcasm
- be aware of their own body language
- be aware of their own behaviour patterns (for example, don't intimidate others in the team).

The team must fully understand what it is that needs to be resolved and the consequences of not resolving it. There may well be obstacles to prevent them resolving a situation in the way they would like to, such as costs or perhaps new laws, such as health and safety regulations.

As team leader, you should monitor the actions your team members are taking to resolve their difficulties. Having empowered them, you still need to be mindful that time taken to resolve something means they may be distracted from their day-to-day tasks affecting the achievement of your targets. You could help avoid this by issuing a deadline for them to resolve the difficult situation.

Through training demonstrations, or team briefing opportunities, you may wish to familiarise your team members with the following conflict resolution tools.

Fishbone diagram

This tool is also known as an Ishikiwa diagram or Cause and Effect diagram. An example is shown in Figure D10.5.

> **Key Term**
>
> **Fishbone Diagram** – Tool used to help with brainstorming reasons for the cause of a problem.

Using the diagram, the team can brainstorm ideas, working backwards through the bones of the fish. Suitable headings can be placed on the main bones and responses written in as the discussion progresses.

Five whys model

Another useful tool is the five whys model, which aims to find the root cause of a problem. This is done verbally by asking 'Why?' five times.

Consider the example below:

Q: Why has the customer complained?
A: Because her delivery wasn't made as promised.

Q: Why wasn't the delivery made?
A: Because the order wasn't picked in the warehouse.

Q: Why wasn't it picked in the warehouse?
A: Because the new member of staff didn't follow procedures.

Q: Why didn't the new member of staff follow procedures?
A: Because she didn't receive the correct training to do her job.

Q: Why didn't she receive the correct training to do her new job?
A: Because her induction process was insufficient.

Root cause is that the induction process needs reviewing to incorporate sufficient training to do work effectively and efficiently.

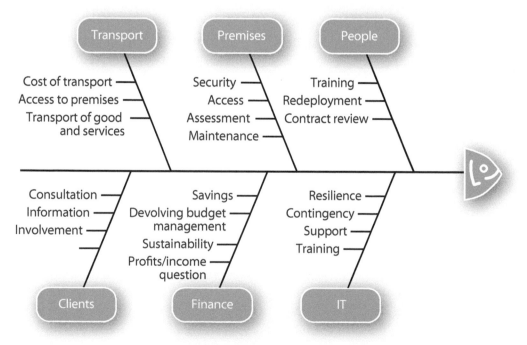

Figure D10.5 An example of a fishbone diagram

Helping your team resolve conflict

Reinforce with your team members that when resolving difficult situations themselves, they should:

- pool their expertise, recognising each other's strengths and weaknesses
- discuss ideas with someone else, perhaps in another team, who has had similar difficult situations to deal with
- explore how useful an action plan will be so everyone knows who is doing what and by when
- obtain permission from you before making any major decisions
- communicate with each other effectively, and you as team leader, so that everyone is kept up to date at all times.

Portfolio Task 5 — 30 minutes

Links to LO3: Assessment criterion 3.1

Using examples you currently use in your department, explain to your assessor how you encourage your team members to identify and resolve their own problems and conflicts. Explain any techniques you find successful and any that you find are unsuccessful. Give reasons for your comments. Your assessor will record this discussion as evidence for your portfolio.

Remember

Any task or actions your team members carry out should be in line with your organisation's policies and procedures.

Checklist

Remind your team members to try to resolve their own difficult situations by:

- sharing each other's knowledge and skills
- discussing and sharing ideas
- setting out an action plan if suitable
- seeking permission if making changes
- communicating and sharing the changes with everyone involved.

Developing respect within your team

Respect emerges from a process of understanding. In other words, respect has to be earned. Mutual respect between team members can minimise the risk of conflict situations arising and solidify the team's approach to fulfilling its obligations and meeting its objectives.

Key Term

Respect – listening and valuing other people's views and opinions.

By politely and promptly challenging each other's inappropriate behaviour when and as necessary, and by talking through difficult situations calmly, rapport can be built and maintained. This largely depends upon the culture that the team works within. You might imagine that a blame culture, for example, would not easily lend itself to a culture of support, rapport and respect.

Given that respect must be earned, examine whether team members have:

- full commitment to business objectives
- open and effective communication
- a reliable approach
- honesty, transparency and openness
- trust.

Activity — 15 minutes

Think about someone you respect in or out of your workplace. Why is it that you respect them? Is it because they are always helpful or polite or constantly supportive for example? Discuss your reasons with your assessor.

Keeping promises, promoting fairness and taking a genuine interest in others can lead to respect. Showing concern firstly, keeping confidence and admitting to mistakes can further develop respect.

When you respect someone it can result in a feel-good factor, for both you and the person to whom you show respect. This improves morale and motivation, and ultimately performance.

The feel-good factor will sooner or later ripple throughout the team helping to minimise the risk of conflict.

It may be useful to share some or all of the points in the checklist with your team, perhaps in a team meeting, explaining the importance of these for a good team spirit.

Remember

To be respected you have to respect others!

Portfolio Task 6 ⏱ 10 minutes

Links to LO3: Assessment criterion 3.2
Explain to your assessor what techniques you currently use to develop and maintain respect between team members. You should produce a personal statement that will provide product evidence for your portfolio.

Checklist

You should lead by example and if you want your team members to respect you, you should:

- be consistently polite and courteous
- never make promises, unless you know you can keep them
- involve your team in decision making
- always be fair when allocating work
- show genuine concern for the well-being of the team
- always try to be positive – even when things appear difficult (this can rub off on your team)
- be honest in your approach (it's no good saying yes just to keep someone happy when you should be saying no)
- be reliable and dependable and keep to your word
- keep up to date with latest trends and techniques – the team will look to you to share best practice
- show your team that you are content to receive negative criticism – as long as it is constructive. That's how everyone learns!
- conduct yourself with professionalism – don't swear, keep to the company dress code etc.
- not be afraid to express your own opinions – don't just agree with others to keep the peace.

Be able to understand legal and organisational requirements concerning conflict

Rights and obligations with regard to conflict

In any organisation both rights and obligations have to be considered. You could say that the organisation has obligations placed upon it and that employees have rights. But also, there are certain obligations placed upon the employees, and organisations too have rights.

For example, an organisation has an obligation to pay wages on time for services and skills provided by the employee. The employee has the right to work in safe conditions. Similarly, the organisation has the right to dismiss an employee for serious misdemeanours, such as **gross misconduct**, while the employee has an obligation to turn up for work on time.

Key Term

Gross misconduct – serious act by an employee, such as theft or fraud, leading to instant dismissal.

When dealing with conflict, there are obligations and rights for both managers and team members to consider, as detailed in Table D10.2.

With rights and obligations in place and clearly understood, conflict situations can be reduced.

The organisation's obligations (examples)	The employee's rights (examples)
– To provide a safe and healthy working environment – To provide adequate working conditions – Not to allow bullying and harassment – Not to allow discriminatory practices – To ensure everyone knows what's required of them	– To be free from victimisation – To be treated equally and fairly – To be free from unsafe and hazardous working practice – To receive written details of the contract of employment – To have sufficient facilities
The employees obligations (examples)	**The organisation's rights (examples)**
– To exercise appropriate behaviour – To give a fair day's work for a fair day's pay – To meet the organisation's SMART objectives – To use resources and share fairly with each other – To carry out reasonable requests – To respect colleagues and customers	– To control staff behaviour – To receive work of a good standard – To have its plans, mission and goals met – To expect employees to use resources sensibly – To have reasonable requests carried out – To expect employees to attend training to raise standards

Table D10.2 Conflict management.

Organisational policies and procedures to deal with conflict

Your workplace is likely to have policies, procedures or codes of conduct in place that can deal with conflict in your team. These will describe what to do or what should happen when conflict situations arise. These might include:

- bullying and harassment policy – this policy will explain what rights employees have and the obligations placed upon the organisation if employees claim they are being victimised in some way

- grievance procedures – this informs employees of their rights should they wish to complain about inappropriate behaviour of a manager or colleague or have any other grievance

- disciplinary procedure – if employees are deemed guilty of misconduct, then this will outline what action the organisation can take

- capability policy – This will suggest actions that can be taken with regard to an employee's capability to carry out tasks allocated to them. Are they not pulling their weight or do they need support guidance and training to help them?

ACAS can advise on disciplinary and grievance procedures and the government recommends that organisations adhere to the code of practice that ACAS has in place for following these procedures.

> **Key Term**
>
> **ACAS** – Advisory, Conciliation and Arbitration Service – an independent organisation who will provide advice and support on a number of employment issues such as disciplinaries and grievances.

Maintaining records

If situations of conflict are allowed to continue over time and perhaps an employee feels they have to leave their employment or is dismissed as a consequence, they may take action against the organisation, even after they have left. For example, they may claim wrongful or constructive dismissal and at a tribunal hearing the organisation will be asked to demonstrate what support was given to employees to prevent or minimise the risk of conflict. Also, once conflict has been identified, what actions were taken to support those involved. In order to be able to do this, the organisation must have full and accurate records of what took place.

It is therefore important to keep records of discussions, responses and actions put in place when conflict situations have arisen. For example dates, times and details of any incidents of conflict, records of verbal and written warnings and evidence that appropriate support was provided.

Examples of support might be:

- counselling – referring of parties involved, particularly victims of conflict, to a professional counsellor to assist them
- health and safety – involvement of the health and safety officer and application of the organisation's health and safety policy if accidents or incidents occurred as a result of a conflict situation.

Remember that if there is a prolonged situation of conflict, someone's health may suffer. They may feel stressed, leading to illness, absenteeism and further problems between the employees, the organisation, and perhaps yourself as a team leader. There may be a case for your team member in such circumstances, to bring a claim that your organisation has been in breach of the Health and Safety Act 1974 or associated regulations. Further, there is a possibility that a civil claim may be made against the organisation for negligence.

For a negligence case to be proved, the employee would have to demonstrate:

- a duty of care was owed by the organisation
- there was a breach of the duty of care owed by the organisation
- injury or damage occurred as a result of that breach of duty.

If these can be demonstrated then there can be a successful claim for negligence and the organisation may be sued for compensation.

Activity ⏱ 60 minutes

Talk to your manager or your human resources department to find out what legal and organisational policies or procedures are in place to deal with conflict in your organisation.
Then consider what external sources of help exist that can advise both employees and organisations when situations of conflict arise.

Portfolio Task 7 ⏱ 30 minutes

Links to LO4: Assessment criterion 4.1
Provide a 500-word document that outlines the legal and organisational requirements in relation to conflict in your team.

Functional Skills

By preparing a word-processed 500-word document you will be practising your Level 2 Functional Skills in ICT and English. You will practise entering, developing and refining information for your ICT Functional Skills and presenting information in a logical sequence using appropriate language, format and structure for your English Functional Skills.

An example would be that a conflict situation was allowed to persist without intervention or support from the organisation leading to stress related illnesses, which in the eyes of the law may be referred to as injury. It is vital, therefore, to keep accurate records so that the claim can be accurately judged.

Maintaining accurate and confidential conflict records

It is very important that records of discussions, actions taken and support given in relation to conflict are **confidential** and kept safely and securely.

Key Term

Confidential – kept secret, or shared only among a limited number of people on a need-to-know basis.

When you record details of conflict situations, make sure you don't miss out any information, no matter how trivial it may seem at the time. The records you keep should be accurate and complete. They should relay exactly what has happened and what action has been taken.

Confidentiality of records

Be aware of the **Data Protection Act (DPA) 1998,** and make sure all records you keep are stored safely and securely. The DPA ensures that individuals are protected from their confidential details being shared with others without their knowledge or permission.

> **Key Term**
>
> **Data Protection Act (DPA) 1998** – an act that specifies how personal information should be gathered, used, stored and shared.

As with any type of record held about an individual in the workplace, any discussions you have with a colleague regarding a conflict situation must be kept confidential with records stored securely and safely. There are eight principles to consider. Records should be:

- processed fairly and lawfully
- obtained for specified and lawful purposes
- adequate, relevant and not excessive
- accurate and up to date
- not kept any longer than necessary
- processed in accordance with the data subject's (the individual's) rights
- securely kept
- not transferred to any other country without adequate protection in situ.

> **Remember**
>
> Any reports or documents you have produced when dealing with your team members should be labelled 'CONFIDENTIAL' before you file them away.

> **Remember**
>
> You should make a note of any discussions you have with team members. You should record the date, who was involved and exactly what the problem was. You should also record what was agreed and what you advised should happen next.

Some records you should complete as evidence of support given in times of conflict include:

- reflective accounts you may have written up after informal discussions with the parties involved (including a date)
- more formal reports produced by you when conflict situations are more serious, which must be signed and dated by everyone involved, including management if you have had to consult them
- staff appraisal (PDR) records that show when you have discussed conflict situations with team members and actions you have agreed
- entries in accident books
- revised risk assessments and other relevant health and safety documentation
- copies of communications with ACAS when, for example, you have sought up-to-date advice
- copies of action plans developed to resolve conflict situations with your team members
- weekly target-setting documents used to improve and record team member's actions
- documentation leading up to and including disciplinary action such as warnings.

It is important to record the outcomes of your discussions with parties involved. For example, you may have agreed an action plan with a team member. This will show that as a result of your intervention, appropriate action has been taken.

> **Portfolio Task 8** ⏱ 30 minutes
>
> **Links to LO4: Assessment criterion 4.2**
> Discuss with your assessor the importance of maintaining complete, accurate and confidential records of conflict and the outcome of the conflict situation. Describe what types of records you would keep and how you would store them to ensure you comply with the Data Protection Act and your organisation's confidentiality policy.
> Your assessor will record this discussion to act as evidence for your portfolio.

Team talk

David's story

Hi, my name is David and I have been a team leader at a supermarket for five years. I have a good relationship with my team and I believe that all of them can come and talk to me about anything at any time. I have an open-door policy and I remind them of this during our team meetings. Generally, every team member has been working hard to meet our objectives, but recently I have noticed that Jim, an older member of the team, has been a lot quieter than usual. He doesn't contribute as much in meetings and he doesn't turn up to after-work team bonding nights any more. But his standard of work is still high and he meets all of his deadlines. I was concerned to find out what was upsetting Jim, so reminded the team again during our weekly team meeting that my door is always open and if any of them have any problems or concerns, that they should come and speak to me. Eventually Jim came to talk to me and confided that he was being bullied and harassed by a new, younger team member.

Top tips

David should take time to discuss the situation with Jim in more detail to find out exactly what has been happening and for how long. David will need to take detailed notes of the discussion and should, in confidence, inform his own line manager and/or his human resources manager of the situation. He should reassure Jim that he will investigate the situation thoroughly without attracting too much attention, which could, of course, make things worse.

David should offer as much support as possible to Jim and keep him fully informed of the outcomes. David will then need to speak to the younger member of staff on an informal basis initially, to make sure he finds out both sides of the story.

In consultation with his line manager, David should make both parties in the conflict situation aware that the organisation's bullying and harassment policy will be referred to for guidance. If it is the case that Jim is being bullied, then David will need to advise Jim that he may need to revert to the organisation's grievance procedures.

Ask the expert	
Q	How would you deal with a situation where a team member tells you they are being bullied by another team colleague?
A	You should treat any claims in confidence and make sure that you: ■ inform your line manager of the situation as soon as possible ■ keep detailed records of everything you discuss with both parties involved

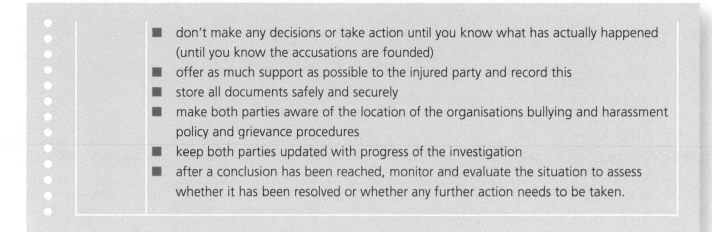

- don't make any decisions or take action until you know what has actually happened (until you know the accusations are founded)
- offer as much support as possible to the injured party and record this
- store all documents safely and securely
- make both parties aware of the location of the organisations bullying and harassment policy and grievance procedures
- keep both parties updated with progress of the investigation
- after a conclusion has been reached, monitor and evaluate the situation to assess whether it has been resolved or whether any further action needs to be taken.

What your assessor is looking for

In order to demonstrate your competency within this unit, you will need to provide sufficient evidence to your assessor. You will need to provide a short written narrative or personal statement, explaining how you meet the assessment criteria. In addition, your assessor may need to ask you questions to test your knowledge of the topics identified in this unit.

Below is a list of suggested documentation that will provide evidence to help you to prove your competency in this unit.

Work products for this unit could include:

- minutes of meetings with your team where you highlight support available
- examples of emails/minutes of meetings where you remind your team of the standards of work and behaviour expected of them
- organisational charts showing reporting and communication lines
- your organisation's bullying and harassment policy
- your organisation's grievance and disciplinary procedures
- records of informal notes taken during initial discussions when there is a claim of a conflict situation.

Your assessor will guide you through the assessment process as detailed in the candidate logbook. The detailed assessment criteria are shown in the logbook and by working through these questions, combined with providing the relevant evidence, you will meet the learning outcomes required to complete this unit

Task and page reference	Assessment criteria
1 (page 102)	1.1
2 (page 105)	1.2
3 (page 108)	2.1
4 (page 113)	2.2, 2.3
5 (page 117)	3.1
6 (page 118)	3.2
7 (page 120)	4.1
8 (page 121)	4.2

Unit D11 Lead and manage meetings

This unit covers how to lead and manage meetings in the workplace. It also explains how to prepare for meetings and how to communicate information effectively.

Preparing for meetings is important because you will need to understand the purpose and objectives of the meeting and the anticipated outcomes. There are no specialist skills or knowledge required to prepare for and attend meetings, you just need to adopt a methodical approach and be open to learning new skills.

Leading and managing meetings can be daunting, especially if it is something that you are doing for the first time. However, by being well prepared for the meeting you should be able to enjoy it and gain additional skills and knowledge along the way.

What you will learn

- Be able to prepare to lead a meeting
- Be able to manage meeting procedures
- Be able to chair a meeting
- Be able to undertake post-meeting tasks

Be able to prepare to lead a meeting

Perform activities needed to be carried out in preparation for leading a meeting

Before your meeting you must perform a number of preparatory activities. Different types of meetings will have different purposes and objectives. First, you should consider the purpose and the format of the meeting and have some clear objectives on what you want it to achieve.

If, for instance, the purpose of your meeting is to issue instructions on a new procedure, then your objective will be to ensure that the new procedures are communicated to your team clearly. The outcome will be that your team has fully understood what has been communicated to them so they are able to implement the new procedure.

Different meetings need to be set-up in different ways. For instance in a creative-type meeting you may need to organise flip charts, marker pens and sticky notes to facilitate creative thinking and participation by all attendees. The way that you plan this type of meeting will be different from a meeting where you are just communicating information, but you will still need to have a detailed plan of your purpose and objectives. However, try not to restrain the meeting as all good ideas should be explored.

Regular meetings, such as team meetings will need less planning as a standard process is likely to be in place, but your objectives and outcomes should be very clear.

Booking a meeting room or venue

When you are booking a meeting venue, you will need to consider a number of elements to ensure that the meeting is accessible to all and that the specific needs of those people attending are met.

You will know where the meeting rooms and the car parking is at your own organisation, but what if one or more of your meeting attendees are visitors to your organisation? Will a visitor who has never attended your office before know this information?

Make sure that you send detailed instructions to everyone when you send out the agenda.

Housekeeping issues are critical to the success of a meeting. By planning the meeting and venue well and by making everyone comfortable in a pleasant, well-ventilated room with adequate lighting, you will stand the best chance of everyone enjoying the meeting and it being a success. Always remember that the detail is important and make sure that you know all the information required. For example, someone is bound to ask you where the toilets are or if smoking is allowed on site or what time the lunch break will be.

Key Term

Housekeeping – making sure the meeting room is safe and tidy, all the equipment is working and in place and that the refreshments have been ordered.

Activity 60 minutes

Explain what activities you need to carry out in order to plan for a meeting, including each thing you need to consider before sending out the agenda.

Explain what documentation you need to be able to prepare if you are planning to lead a meeting.

For the practical elements of booking a meeting venue, you can use the following checklists to help you. You will need to check different things for internal meetings and external venues.

Checklist

For internal meetings, always check:

- which meetings rooms you can use
- that the room is the right size for the number of people attending the meeting
- that there is adequate access for all attendees
- how to book the room correctly (there may be a central booking system)
- any additional costs (e.g. lunch) and agree these costs with the relevant person in advance of the meeting
- that all the resources you need are booked.

Checklist

For external venues, always check:

- that the budget for the event has been agreed with the relevant person
- the correct procedure for booking the event; you may need to place an official order and get it signed
- what size of room(s) you need
- that the room is well lit and adequately ventilated
- that you can have the room layout that you want
- the catering and refreshment arrangements, ensuring that the venue can cater for any special dietary needs
- what resources are available and what elements need to be taken to the meeting, for example whether there is a laptop, screen and projector available
- car parking arrangements
- directions to the venue, for instance from the railway station or main road routes.

Take a common sense approach and again check each element in detail. It may even be worth you visiting the venue to check the suitability, especially if it is nearby. Always get written confirmation from the venue of the booking.

Pre-meeting information

When you are arranging a meeting, make sure that you plan it well in advance and inform everyone of the key information. Essential requirements for all attendees to know about are:

- the date, venue and time
- car parking arrangements, access facilities
- length of meeting
- whether refreshments or lunch will be provided
- when to RSVP by and to whom.

Resources that will be required at the meeting

If you are leading and managing meetings, it is likely that you will also be arranging them. Think of all of the different types of resources required for your meeting and ask yourself the following questions.

- Does everyone know about the meeting?

- Have the agenda and reports been sent out?
- Does any other paperwork need to be taken to the meeting, such as copies of the previous minutes?
- Is the right equipment in place e.g. laptop, flip chart, projector?
- What else might I need to take – spare copies of the agenda and reports?
- Are there adequate pens, paper, sticky notes and water?
- Does the venue meet the relevant health and safety requirements?
- Are access facilities adequate?

If you are unsure, but think that you might need something for the meeting, take it with you. If you have the information to hand at the meeting, it will save a lot of time.

Checklist

In preparation for your meeting you will need to:

- think about the objectives you want the meeting to achieve
- understand the format that the meeting should take
- prepare an agenda
- think about who will chair the meeting
- think about who will take minutes
- read the agenda and previous minutes before the meeting.

Planning meetings to meet the agreed aims and objectives

Some formal meetings can have written terms of reference. These explain the committee's purpose and state the frequency of the meetings and details of the chairperson. For informal meetings a process and frequency of meetings may be agreed in advance and a schedule of forthcoming meetings drawn up. It is also common to rotate duties. For example, the minute taker and chairperson might change from meeting to meeting. You may want to adopt this approach in your team as it provides opportunities for team members to acquire additional skills and experience.

Meetings can use considerable resources and can be costly so before arranging a new meeting do think about whether it is actually necessary. Consult with your colleagues and manager to check if there are any alternative ways to resolve the issue, for instance by email, or a ten-minute **stand-up meeting**.

Key Term

Stand-up meeting – where a group of people meet to discuss issues standing up. Useful for short meetings and can often focus people's attention better than a meeting where people sit down around a table.

All meetings should have a specific purpose and the meeting should link into the formal performance management systems that may be in place within your organisation. When you arrange, attend or manage meetings, be clear what the purpose of the meeting is and always challenge yourself and consider the following questions.

- Why is this meeting taking place?
- What are the objectives of this meeting?
- How are we going to meet those objectives?
- How do we agree and clarify the outcomes?
- After the meeting, what is the next stage in the process?

The importance of communication

Consider your own organisation and think about what would happen if each employee planned their own meetings, but did not record the dates and times and did not inform other people where the meetings would take place. The situation would be chaotic and it is likely that:

- meetings would be impossible to plan and organise
- staff would not know where meetings were being held or what time
- resources would not be able to be shared effectively.

When you are planning and organising meetings, it's important to know how your organisation books meetings and rooms. Many organisations have a diary system in place. This may be a manual diary usually held in the reception area, or a central electronic diary system.

An effective diary system can ensure that:

- activities can be planned and managed effectively
- resources are properly shared, for example the booking of rooms, using equipment, such as laptops or projectors, and utilising catering facilities.

Remember

There are no specialist skills or knowledge required when organising meetings. It is important to undertake a logical approach and consider the implications of any actions that you take. By being organised you can plan meetings successfully.

Activity 60 minutes

List what resources would be required for a meeting to take place in your team.

Portfolio Task 1 60 minutes

Links to LO1: Assessment criterion 1.1

Imagine that you are arranging a team meeting in your business area to explain about a new process, for example the implementation of a new computer system. It is important to ensure that you communicate this proposed change effectively.

Consider what you would want to achieve from the meeting – what are your objectives and what outcomes do you want to achieve? You may want write this up as a personal statement or record this as part of a professional discussion with your assessor.

PLTS

By arranging a team meeting, you will be ensuring that you involve your team in the decision making process and also keep them informed of any relevant issues (TW, CT, IE, SM).

Produce documentation in support of activities

The success of a meeting is often determined by the way in which it has been organised.

There are two main items to consider prior to a meeting taking place: the meeting brief and the agenda.

A meeting brief

A meeting brief sets out the purpose of the meeting and what issues need to be discussed. The meeting brief will vary in format, for example it may be a report or the terms of reference. Preparing the brief for a meeting forms part of the overall planning process for organising, leading and managing meetings. If you are arranging a meeting, you will need to speak with the meeting **originator** and check:

- the purpose of the meeting
- who should be invited to attend
- where the meeting will take place
- what reports need to be prepared, who is preparing them and who is presenting them.

The agenda

An agenda is the key document that structures the meeting, providing a framework to ensure that the meeting is undertaken in a methodical and structured way. Agendas follow a fairly standard format and an example is shown in Figure D11.1.

XYZ HEALTHCARE TRUST
HEALTH AND SAFETY COMMITTEE
16th JULY 2012 – 9.30am COMMITTEE ROOM 1

AGENDA

1. Apologies for absence
2. Minutes from the last meeting held on 24th May 2012
3. Matters arising from the minutes
4. Report from the health and safety officer
5. Verbal update from the health and safety representatives
6. Health and safety training plan
7. Any other business
8. Date of the next meeting

Figure D11.1 A typical agenda.

Key Term

Originator – the person who has decided the meeting is necessary (this may be you).

Certain terms and phrases often used in agendas are defined in Tables D11.1 and D11.2.

Phrases used in an agenda	Definition
Apologies for absence	A note of those people who have informed the originator that they cannot attend the meeting
Matters arising	Review of the previous meeting's minutes to check for accuracy and for the chairperson to give any relevant updates
Reports	Make up the main business of the meeting
Regular items	Any items that always appear on the agenda, for example, health and safety
Any other business	The chance for anyone to raise a new issue not already covered rather than wait for the next meeting

Table D11.1 Descriptions of phrases used in an agenda.

Other phrases associated with meetings	
Quorum	The minimum number of people required for the meeting to take place. If the number falls below this amount, then the meeting is postponed
Ultra vires	From the Latin 'beyond or outside the powers of'. It is used if a committee has to refer a decision to a different committee because the decision is beyond their own remit.

Table D11.2 Other phrases associated with meetings.

How to write an agenda

When preparing an agenda, follow the following guidelines:

- Use the standard house format.
- Check the minutes from the last meeting for anything from that meeting that needs to be included on this agenda.

- Contact the people who normally attend the meeting and ask them whether there are any items that they want included on the agenda.

- Make sure that the items run in a logical sequence, for example, if there are items that will affect another item make sure that they are sequenced in the correct order as the earlier decision may have an impact on a later item.

- Deal with the simple items first before you get onto the main business.

- Deal with the main business that involves more people next, to get all attendees engaged in the discussion.

- Deal with business that only involves one or two people nearer the end of the meeting.

- If the meeting is likely to be very long, consider the possibility of deferring some of the final items to the next meeting so that they are given the time and discussion they need.

- Ensure that you are aware of all of the items for the meeting including any reports, budgets, performance information or hand-outs that will be presented.

- Agree the final agenda with your manager and circulate it and all the relevant paperwork well in advance of the meeting date.

Portfolio Task 2 ⏱ 60 minutes

Links to LO1: Assessment criteria 1.1, 1.2
With the agreement of your manager, prepare the agenda for your next team meeting and book the room. This will provide useful evidence for your portfolio.

Functional Skills

You may be able to use this activity as evidence towards Functional Skills English Level 2: Reading and Writing. You need to demonstrate that you have read and understood the process involved in the preparation of agendas within your organisation. Then you will need to ensure that you have formulated the agenda in a logical sequence and that the spelling and punctuation is correct.

Checklist

When organising a meeting, remember to:

- apply a logical and systematic approach
- plan well ahead of the meeting date
- draw up an agenda
- communicate the relevant information to all of the people who are due to attend
- book the room, refreshments and other resources e.g. laptop or flipchart, well in advance of the meeting date.

Be able to manage meeting procedures

In order to manage meetings successfully, you will need to make yourself familiar with the procedures in place in your own organisation. Consider:

- the frequency of meetings
- any house styles that may exist e.g. format of the agenda or minutes
- how information about meetings is communicated – this may be verbally or by email
- how you gather the information from other parties who are attending the meeting.

Identify any formal procedures that apply in own organisation

Formal meeting procedures are likely to be dependent on the type of meeting that is being held. Examples of the various meetings that you may come across in a business environment include:

- team meeting – this could be held on a regular basis, say once a each week
- health and safety committee – this could be held each month or each quarter
- annual general meeting of a company or organisation – takes place once a year
- ad-hoc meeting – might be arranged to discuss a specific issue, for example, a budget overspend or a new product
- working group or progress meeting – can be regular or one-off events

- training session or creative meetings – can be regular or one-off events.

The type of meeting will also affect how details of the meeting are communicated. If the meeting is to be attended by a large number of people who have the same email system, the meeting could be arranged using Microsoft Outlook®, but an ad-hoc meeting could be arranged verbally between the attendees.

Meeting structures

Some large organisations, such as local councils, will have a formal structured meeting process in place. The way that these meetings operate will be detailed in their written constitution, which will also set out how frequently they will meet, what powers and responsibilities they have and how the decision-making process is undertaken. Some committees, often referred to as sub-committees, will have only specific, limited powers and may have to refer decisions upwards to another committee. An example of a structure in a large company with many sub-committees is shown in Figure D11.2. Other committees may have delegated powers, which enable them to make decisions within their remit. Limited companies will detail their committee structures within their 'Articles of Association' legal document.

> **Remember**
>
> In large organisations, sub-committees will report to main committees, which will in turn report to the overarching committee in the organisation, for example, the main board.

Smaller organisations may not have a formal structure, but meetings will still take place. Most meetings will normally have the following features:

- At least two people will be in attendance.
- Someone will be manage the meeting – the **chairperson**.
- There will be an agenda to discuss the items – this may be unwritten.
- Someone will take notes or minutes of the meeting.
- There will be an **outcome** from the meeting – e.g. a decision taken.
- There will be a record of what was said and any action points arising (e.g. minutes).

> **Key Terms**
>
> **Chairperson** – the person leading the meeting.
> **Outcome** – the decision decided upon and the understanding of that decision by all.

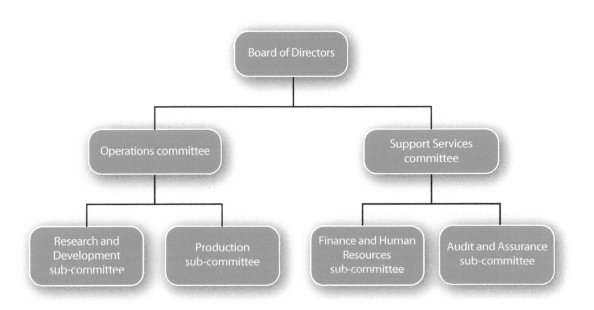

Figure D11.2 How a large organisation might arrange its committee structure.

Formal procedures in your organisation

If you work in a large or medium-sized organisation, there will be certain protocols in relation to meetings and minutes. These will probably cover the frequency of meetings, who the chairperson is, who takes the minutes and what powers that committee or group has. You may also have a standard house style agenda and minutes that are used across the organisation. If you plan and attend meetings, this will help you understand how they work as the structure will enable you to check previous agendas and minutes and understand the process more thoroughly. In smaller organisations, there may not be the relevant systems and processes in place, but you can implement a standard approach in your own team, perhaps by using the examples of the minutes and agendas shown in this unit.

Portfolio Task 3 🕐 60 minutes

Links to LO2: Assessment criterion 2.1

Explain any relevant formal procedures that apply in your organisation. This could include any room booking procedures, any standard house style documents that you should use and the agreed frequency of meetings. Write this up as a personal statement or undertake a professional discussion with your assessor.

PLTS

When explaining the formal procedures you will show that you are an independent enquirer and self-manager.

Be able to chair a meeting

The chairperson leads, co-ordinates and manages the meeting. Their competence in how to run a meeting is essential if the meeting is to be structured and successful. As a team leader, you may be asked to chair meetings on a regular basis. Key duties of a chairperson are:

- making sure the meeting starts on time
- being well prepared and understanding the purpose of the meeting and the anticipated outcomes
- introducing any new members of staff to the rest of the group
- only allowing only one person to speak at a time
- encouraging input from all the people attending the meeting
- being able to summarise the discussion at the end of each item
- reaching a decision and agreeing an action point or outcome.

Attributes of a successful chairperson

A successful chairperson needs to be well prepared, diplomatic, assertive and an effective communicator. They will be:

- well prepared before the meeting and be able clarify the exact purpose of the meeting
- organised in terms of booking the room and managing the housekeeping issues
- comfortable that there is adequate business for the meeting to take place and that the key people will be in attendance
- able to manage the meeting effectively including encouraging discussion, challenging people, confirming actions and summarising information including the agreed decisions and responsibilities
- able to review the meeting, evaluate progress and check if the outcomes have been achieved.

If the meeting is going to be structured and successful, it is essential that during the meeting the chairperson:

- summarises the discussion at the end of each item and agrees an action point or outcome that is acceptable to all
- links back the decision on the item to the initial problem or issue. This is important because if the decision made at the meeting does not address a way forward from the status quo, it will not resolve the issue which was being discussed.

Manage the agenda in co-operation with participants to ensure meeting objectives are met

In order to manage the agenda effectively ensure that you understand:

- the purpose of the meeting
- the format of the meeting
- how information will be communicated at the meeting
- the content of the meeting – look at previous agendas or minutes and familiarise yourself with the content and how the discussion took place
- the style of the meeting – speak to other people who are attending. If it is your first attendance, ask about the format, length and style
- how to plan the agenda and gather any other relevant information from colleagues contributing to it.

Secondly, you need to consider your own role at the meeting for instance you might be:

- the chairperson
- a participant, i.e. attending but not having a specific role
- an expert if you have a specific knowledge or skill and attend different types of meetings, e.g. health and safety adviser.

Finally, confirm what you want to get out of the meeting. This will help you to plan what you are going to say at the meeting to ensure that you can

get the right outcome for you and your team. Plan the specific detail of the points that you want to make and write them down to jog your memory during the meeting.

Remember

Remember that during a meeting you are likely to undertake many different roles including observing, collecting data and information, presenting information, asking questions and actively participating.

The meeting room or venue

If you are managing a meeting, get to the room early. Check that:

- the room is clean and tidy and free from any hazards, e.g. trailing cables
- the lighting is adequate and the room is well ventilated and at an acceptable temperature
- the furniture layout is correct
- there is adequate access to the room and other parts of the building if required, e.g. toilets or evacuation
- there is adequate signage for the meeting attendees to find their way to the meeting room
- resources and equipment are in place and work correctly
- catering arrangements are in place.

Don't leave things to chance. Finding out information at the last minute can be stressful; a successful meeting is more likely when everyone feels comfortable and relaxed.

Finally, find out if there is anything else that you need to be aware of, for example, if the meeting is being held at an external venue, they may be planning a fire drill for that day – it is important to know this type of information.

Computerised presentations

Check before the meeting who is responsible for setting up any computerised presentations and making sure that they are working properly. This could involve checking a computer or projector and uploading some files for a presentation. Make sure that the files are in the correct format, that

It is important that you check that the room is suitable for your needs, particularly if electronic equipment is being used.

the disc or memory stick has been virus checked and that the files are not password protected. Allow plenty of time for this as it is quite common to have a few minor problems when setting up presentations, particularly if you are away from your main office. Keep the contact details of your in house IT specialist to hand so they can help you if you have any difficulties.

Final preparation

The final stage, before the meeting commences, is to review the agenda and plan how you will manage the meeting. Try to allow ten minutes before the meeting to familiarise yourself with the following issues:

- Apologies for absence (people who are unable to attend).
- An update on any new information or issues that have recently arisen.
- A note of any new attendees who you can introduce.

- What you will say/how you will introduce each item on the agenda.
- Any information relating to the next proposed meeting, e.g. agenda items or the date.
- Any specific things that you want to mention which are not on the agenda.

You can make any relevant notes on your copy of the agenda to assist you as you work through the meeting to make sure that everything runs smoothly. You should also try to allow a provisional time allocation for each item.

> **Activity** ⏱ 60 minutes
>
> Collect examples of any objectives that you and your team need to achieve. Explain the purpose and benefits of managing performance through discussion in a meeting environment.

Once you have checked that all of the housekeeping issues are in place, you can then concentrate on making sure that you are well prepared. Decide where you are going to sit; this may be at the head of the table. Put all of your paperwork into a logical order.

- Have a couple of sets of spare agendas and reports. By doing this, if someone arrives without their agenda, you can quickly pass them a copy.
- Put the files that you have brought with you next to where you are going to be seated.
- Put any paperwork or other information in a logical order so that you can quickly refer to it if required If anyone wants some information during the meeting, perhaps relating to the minutes from a previous meeting, you will be able to quickly find it.

Commencing the meeting

Once everyone has arrived, you should open the meeting and announce any general housekeeping issues first, for instance, requesting that mobile phones be switched off, explaining any fire drill/ evacuation procedures and when refreshment/ lunch breaks are.

You may also need to agree who will take the minutes. For formal meetings at a large organisation, it is normal for the same person to always take the minutes – this could be the company secretary.

Lead and manage meetings Unit D11

Checklist

To ensure the meeting is structured and successful, it is essential if you are leading the meeting that you:

- ensure that the meeting starts on time
- are well prepared and understand the purpose of the meeting and the anticipated outcomes
- introduce new members to the rest of the group
- allow only one person to speak at a time
- encourage input from all the people attending the meeting
- summarise the discussion at the end of each item and agree an action point or outcome that is acceptable.

Your audience

Always consider your audience when participating in meetings. You may have an in-depth knowledge of the subject that you are talking about, but other people may not be as familiar with the issues as you. Think about how you will manage this as you introduce your items consider the detail that you will need to go into.

In terms of the level of detail that you go into, you should take a common sense approach. For example if you are presenting some information at one of your own team meetings, you will probably take an informal approach. An example could be as follows:

'*As you all know the sales figures have dropped over the last 6 months and we need to agree a plan to try and increase sales, so I have prepared some information for us to discuss to then hopefully agree some actions to resolve the issues*'.

It is likely that the ensuing discussion will be informal and at quite a detailed level. You will need to manage this discussion effectively and be able to summarise all of the points at the end and agree some kind of action (the outcomes).

A second example could be as follows. Imagine that you are attending a meeting for the first time involving other people from outside of your team. It may be necessary to take a slightly more formal approach and introduce the item in a bit more detail:

'*As you are probably all aware, I manage the sales team for the Eastern region. The report that I'm presenting today details our sales figures for the last quarter. Hopefully you've all had chance to have a look at it, so I'll just talk you through the main points and then I'm happy to take any questions*'.

It is likely that once you have given an overview of the main issues, there will be some specific questions for you to answer. You will need to be well prepared for these questions and be confident in your response. At the end of the discussion you will then need to be clear what the actions or outcomes are. If this is not clear, you need to clarify with the chairperson what was specifically agreed etc. Bear in mind though that there are not always further actions as you may have been presenting the report for information purposes only.

You will soon get the idea of how to present information and the level of detail that you need to go into. Remember if you are the chairperson, you will also be presenting information as well as managing the meeting.

Problems that may occur during the meeting and tips on how to solve them

Most meetings run very smoothly, however, you do need to be prepared to expect the unexpected. Here are some examples of what can go wrong and tips on how you could resolve difficulties.

- *Certain participants are regularly late for meetings causing frustration among the other attendees.* Make sure that you phone these people the day or even an hour or so before and remind them of the meeting and reiterate the importance of everyone being there on time and starting the meeting promptly. Let them know that it is not acceptable to regularly turn up late for meetings.

- *Part way through the meeting, people start to wander into the room and look surprised that your meeting is taking place.* It is possible that the room has been double booked and you will need to check if any other rooms are available for you. The worst-case scenario is that you would need to adjourn the meeting for a short while or postpone until another day. The double booking may not have been your fault, but it is always worth checking that the booking is in the diary either the day before or on the morning of the meeting.

- *Someone in the meeting is insisting on repeating old arguments relating to a decision that was made months ago. They are also jumping to conclusions and interrupting everyone.* Try to remain calm and keep the meeting flowing by working to give the rest of the attendees a chance to participate. It is your responsibility to keep control of the meeting. You should tackle this person during the meeting and you should also speak to the person after the meeting and ask them to be more professional in their conduct at future meetings.

Other issues that you will need to be aware of and manage effectively include:

- the silent participant – involve those who are reluctant to speak as much as possible – for instance by actively inviting their contribution

- the attention seeker – try to focus their resources and thank them for contributing, but don't allow them to dominate the meeting. Make it clear that everyone needs to make an equal contribution and it is now someone else's turn to make their point.

- the joker – don't allow anyone to 'make light' of every item. A friendly joke on a particular item to lighten up the meeting can be useful, but this can't get out of hand. The meeting needs to be treated seriously by all.

Acknowledge other viewpoints presented at the meeting

You will not be the only person with information and viewpoints to put across at meetings. If you

are the chairperson you will need to manage this process of ensuring everyone gets their say, and do not let one person or issue hijack the meeting.

When you attend meetings, be open-minded and not opinionated. Everyone has a right to their own opinion and while one individual's communication style or skill may not be as good as another person's, they may still have useful information and valid points to contribute to the meeting. Listen actively to what is being said, do not interrupt, let the speaker finish and do not jump to conclusions. You may have reservations about their ideas, but you must listen to their suggestions and then respond if appropriate in a balanced way, agreeing, disagreeing or challenging, taking everything into account. Remember, some people are experts in their own field, so give them credit for knowing what they are talking about.

It will be up to you as the chairperson to summarise the discussion at the end of each item and to then formulate the specific outcome that all parties are agreed upon.

Remember

You do not have to formally agree or disagree with each issue at each stage of the meeting. It is often sufficient to just acknowledge that a viewpoint has been heard.

Contribute to meeting discussions

Most meetings within your organisation will provide you with the opportunity to share relevant information to other interested parties. Many regular meetings are between managers or team leaders where all attendees' feedback on their team's current performance.

Meetings will provide you with an effective method to communicate information and assist in managing the performance of your team. In order to contribute effectively you should familiarise yourself with relevant documentation and have information relevant to the meeting at hand. You may have to summarise this information at the meeting and also be able to be challenged on it and answer relevant questions.

How to participate effectively during a meeting.

- Be well prepared before the meeting, understand the purpose of the meeting and identify what you want to achieve.

- Be organised with the meeting paperwork and prepare in advance what you are going to say and any papers that you want to circulate.

- Make yourself familiar with the agenda, any relevant protocols and the running order of the items.

- Be aware of the other people attending the meeting and be clear about the level of detail that you will need to cover etc.

- Look the part – be smartly presented and confident. Remember first impressions count.

- Be aware of your tone of voice. It is important to vary the tone and have a warm non-aggressive style.

- Be aware of your body language. Maintain good eye contact, do not slouch and be alert at all times.

- Look confident and interested and ask constructive questions.

- Take a deep breath before you start, smile and speak in a clear, fluent and confident manner.

Portfolio Task 4 ⏱ 60 minutes

Links to LO3: Assessment criterion 3.1

Collect examples of meetings that you have attended recently and explain how you contributed and, if leading the meeting, acknowledged different viewpoints and give specific examples. If possible, ask a colleague to complete a witness statement of how you contributed to and/or dealt with a difference of viewpoints at a meeting. This will provide useful evidence for your portfolio.

PLTS

By working in a collaborative way with your team, you should be able to reach agreements by managing discussions to achieve an outcome that everyone is agreed upon (TW, CT, IE, SM).

Seek clarification or confirmation of own understanding of outcomes

Be very clear in your own mind what was agreed at the meetings that you attend. Always clarify exactly what was meant and check specifically what actions you are required to undertake as a result of the meeting. As a general rule, unless a different deadline is given, it is usually assumed that action points should be completed before the next meeting.

Activity ⏱ 15 minutes

Once you have led and managed a couple of meetings, have a go at the self-assessment checklist detailed below. This asks a series of questions relating to your behaviour at the meetings and it will give you some pointers on how to improve in the future.

My behaviour	Agree	Disagree
I'm always well prepared for the meetings that I attend and I understand the purpose and objectives of those meetings		
I understand the meeting structures in my own organisation and I understand the authority that I and others have to make decisions		
I dress appropriately for the meeting and I'm always pleasant and confident		
I'm confident when presenting information and I'm able to state my own point of view in a clear and concise way		
I listen carefully to what other people are saying and I always allow speakers to finish what they are saying and I do not interrupt them		
I respect other people's views, I value different opinions and I'm happy to concede when I'm wrong. I always understand what actions I need to take for the next meeting		

Remember

Meetings can fail if the objective/s are unclear, if they are not managed effectively, if the wrong people are in attendance and if attendees do not have the relevant knowledge or **authority** to take decisions.

Key Term

Authority – the power or right to make a decision.

Portfolio Task 5  45 minutes

Links to LO3: Assessment criterion 3.1
Explain in your own words how you contribute to meeting discussions, how you acknowledge other viewpoints presented at meetings and how you clarify your understanding of the meeting outcomes. Use recent examples to demonstrate your understanding.

PLTS

By reflecting on your performance and identifying any learning points, you will be able improve your performance in the future TW, CT, IE, SM).

Produce minutes of the meeting and allocate action points after discussions

It is likely that as a team leader you will sometimes be expected to take the minutes of meetings. There are two main types of minutes:

- verbatim – this means a 'word for word' account of the meeting
- narrative – these are a detailed summary of the discussions that took place.

Minutes give an account of what was discussed and the action points arising from the meeting. What was agreed is often recorded as 'agreed by' and any relevant action is normally recorded stating who should perform the action.

Minutes of a meeting should always include the date and time of the meeting, who attended, who sent their apologies, a record of items discussed and the date and time of the next meeting. Minutes do vary a little and it is likely that your organisation or team will have a house style.

It is important to write up minutes for all meetings, even if they are informal. The benefits of doing this are to:

- act as an accurate record of what was discussed
- track progress on particular issues
- help to demonstrate how you and your team manage and improve performance by recording what was agreed or what action has been undertaken
- ensure that the team are kept informed.

In addition, written minutes can be passed on to team members who were unable to attend the meeting.

The minutes shown in Figure D11.3 follow a straightforward format, which is easy to follow. They are easy to read and it is clear what the action points were. If you don't already produce minutes for your team meetings, you could adopt these types of minutes.

However you present your minutes, you will find the following guidelines useful for compiling them.

- Be prepared – have plenty of paper to hand, understand what is on the agenda and the types of things that will be discussed. Put sub-headings on your notes of all of the agenda items and leave plenty of space to record the discussion.
- Listen carefully – this sounds straightforward, but it is not always easy to follow exactly what is being said. You will need to concentrate and be objective in your summary of the discussion – state what was said and not your interpretation or own viewpoint. Work with the chairperson to get the group to agree a summary of the discussion and any decision or actions agreed.

Team meeting minutes - 27 January 2012

PRESENT:

John Staunton (Chairman)

Janet James, Elaine Brown, Nigel Dawson and Celine Stevens

1. Apologies were received from Jolene Hart

2. New sales leads

The number of new sales leads was noted as follows:

- Jolene 9 + 2 new leads pending
- John 18
- Nigel 21
- Celine 18

John explained an issue with a sales lead in Stoke whom he had difficulty in contacting. It was agreed that Nigel would attempt to contact her in the next few days.

Agreed:

It was agreed that Elaine would countersign all of the new confirmed sales and pass them through to head office.

3. New brochure

Celine gave an update on the new sales brochure and handed round a draft version. The team discussed the brochure and passed comments back to Celine.

Agreed:

It was agreed that Celine would take on board all of the comments received and would incorporate them into the final brochure.

4. Sales targets for 2012/13

Each member of the team gave a verbal update on their progress to date.

Agreed:

It was agreed that Elaine would formalise the targets and agree them with each team member at the forthcoming appraisal meetings.

5. Interviews for new sales representatives

Janet explained that the proposed interviews had been delayed, but they would now take place in mid-February.

Date of next meeting – 24 February 2012

Figure D11.3 An example set of team meeting minutes.

- Summarise the main points of the discussion and get used to writing abbreviations for names and main points. For example if you're constantly referring to the chairperson, you could use the abbreviation 'ch sd' for chairperson said.

- Always write minutes in the past tense as you are referring to something that has already happened. Use words like 'said', 'explained', 'gave', 'discussed' etc. An example would be 'David explained how the system worked'.

- Write the minutes up as soon as possible after the meeting has taken place as all the information will be fresh in your mind.

- Use sentences and bullet points and use clear, plain English that can be understood by all.

- Don't worry if you miss something out. There are other people at the meeting who you can speak to afterwards. Either leave a gap in your minutes or maybe use a highlighter to remind you to clarify what was said at the end of the meeting. The chairperson will also be able to assist you with any issues of this nature.

Portfolio Task 6   ⏱ 2 hours

Links to LO3: Assessment criterion 3.2
Ask your manager if you can sit in on a meeting and record the minutes or maybe ask if you can take the minutes at your next team meeting. Ensure that you allocate action points from each of the discussion items and explain how you will follow up these actions.

PLTS

By trying out relevant new tasks and identifying any learning points, you will be able improve your performance in the future (TW, CT, IE, SM).

Be able to undertake post-meeting tasks

Meetings are not an end in themselves. They will invariably generate tasks to be actioned by the next meeting or a given deadline. Their purpose is to exchange information and drive things forward, so it is important to understand what is expected of you after the meeting has taken place.

Explain that the minutes of the meeting provide an accurate record of proceedings

If you were the minute taker you will need to finalise the minutes as soon as possible after the meeting while the information is still fresh in your mind. Minutes are the formal record of the meeting and describe what was discussed and agreed and what the action points are. It is essential for everyone to know, understand and be clear about what the meeting outcomes were. You should send the draft minutes to the chairperson for their comments. If there are any complicated or controversial parts of the minutes they should be able to help you in providing a diplomatic phrase or wording. You can then circulate the draft minutes to the other attendees for comment.

Once you have received any comments back, you can make the relevant changes. It is also a good idea to then let the chairperson have a brief final check to confirm that they are happy that the minutes reflect a true and accurate record of the meeting. You can then circulate the final minutes to all of the people who attended the meeting and to anyone who sent their apologies. It might be easiest to do this by email and you can remind people of the date of the next meeting at the same time and also ask them to forward any agenda items that they may have for the next meeting.

Finally, evaluate any problems from the meeting and consider any improvements that you may want to make for future meetings.

Communicate and follow up meeting outcomes to relevant individuals

When you attend meetings, you are representing your team or section and it is likely that any outcomes and actions will involve not just you but the team as a whole. Communicating information links directly with managing performance and you will need to be able to communicate effectively to your team members any relevant information gathered at meetings.

You must also be able to motivate your team to support you with any required actions. You may need to negotiate with your team and admit defeat where you are out-voted. Collective decisions that the whole team is committed to with are more powerful and more likely to work than those decisions imposed by the team leader. Be careful though, as if you agree something at a meeting and then deliver something different or nothing at all, things could get difficult. If you can't deliver what was agreed at the meeting, for whatever reason, you need to communicate this back to the relevant people.

As your skills and knowledge develop, you should become good at negotiating at meetings. Feed information back to your team on a regular basis and try to get into the habit of agreeing a set time to feedback information from any meetings that you have attended.

Confidentiality

Some meetings will discuss confidential and sensitive information, which may or may not directly affect your team. You will need to keep confidential information to yourself and you should be sensitive and respectful towards your colleagues. If you are trustworthy, you will soon gain the trust and respect of your peers and the senior managers in the organisation.

If you do have some important or sensitive information that needs to be communicated to your team, you should do this as soon as practicably possible and by a face-to-face method if possible. This will avoid any uncertainty and should ensure clarity.

Follow-up actions

At the meeting it would be agreed who would undertake the relevant actions. It is normal for the person who is nominated as the secretary for the meeting to manage this process – this could be part of your role. You should always try to ensure that these actions are completed within the timescales agreed. You could ask your colleagues to email you once they have completed their action. If it gets near to the next meeting you may need to chase them up to find out what is happening.

> **Activity** ⏱ 15 minutes
>
> Find a copy of some minutes from a past meeting in your organisation that you have attended. Write on the minutes to explain any relevant updates. For example if you were asked to undertake an action or follow up an item from the meeting, state what you did. This will provide useful evidence for your portfolio.

Evaluate whether the meeting's objectives were met and identify potential improvements

In order to constantly improve, it is important to reflect on your experiences and think about what you can do better next time. By improving your performance, you should become more efficient in your role. Always recap on what the purpose of the meeting was and challenge yourself to ask if the objectives were met.

Remember that not everything is within your control. For example if you booked a buffet lunch for a training event and had written confirmation of the booking, but it still did not turn up, then this is not your fault – the error lies with the catering company. In this situation it is impossible to make alternative arrangements and all you can do is apologise to the people at the training event. However, you can reflect on whether you should use a different catering service in the future.

Improvements and reflections

For any activity that you undertake in an office environment, it is a good idea to reflect on your experiences and try to improve for next time. Take time after the meeting to consider what went well and what needs improving for next time. Ask your colleagues for feedback.

You don't need any specific skills or knowledge to be able to plan and run meetings, you only need to be well organised, have a methodical approach and plan all the elements well in advance. If you do this, things should run smoothly.

Figure D11.4 provides a brief checklist to ensure that any problems can be resolved for all future meetings.

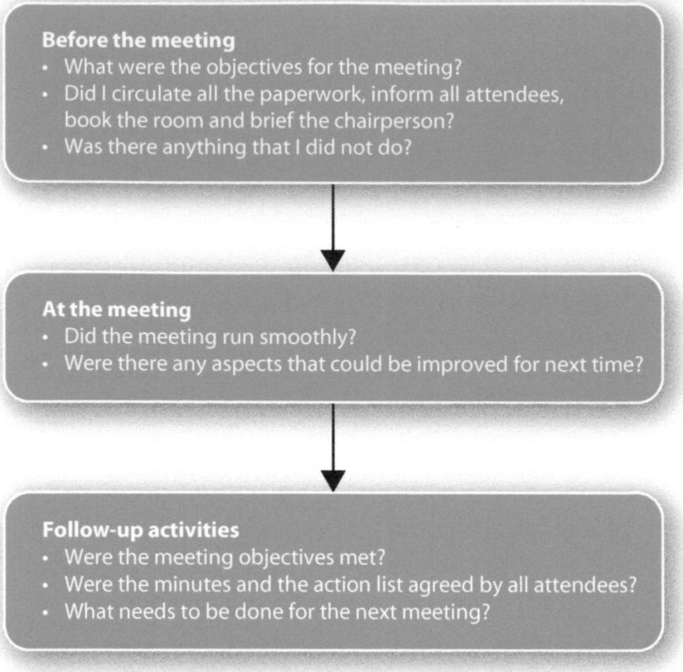

Before the meeting
- What were the objectives for the meeting?
- Did I circulate all the paperwork, inform all attendees, book the room and brief the chairperson?
- Was there anything that I did not do?

At the meeting
- Did the meeting run smoothly?
- Were there any aspects that could be improved for next time?

Follow-up activities
- Were the meeting objectives met?
- Were the minutes and the action list agreed by all attendees?
- What needs to be done for the next meeting?

Figure D11.4 Planning a meeting.

Portfolio Task 7   90 minutes

Links to LO4: Assessment criteria 4.1, 4.2, 4.3

Using some minutes that you have taken, or for a meeting you have attended, explain how they provide an accurate record of the proceedings.

Explain how you have followed up and communicated meeting outcomes to relevant individuals.

Think back to a meeting you have attended recently and evaluate whether the meeting's objectives were met and identify any potential improvements. You can use the following pointers to help.

- What were the objectives of the meeting and were they achieved?
- How well did I manage/contribute to the meeting?
- Did I communicate effectively during the meeting?
- What were the best and worst aspects of the meeting?
- Overall, was the meeting successful?
- What can I do better next time?

By working through these questions, you will quickly establish your overall experience and be able to identify any areas for improvement. If you have some areas for improvement, you might want to include them in your personal development plan, which is a key part of this qualification and is covered in more detail in the mandatory Unit A2: Manage own professional development within an organisation.

Functional Skills

You may be able to use this personal statement as evidence towards Level 2 Functional Skills in English: Reading and Writing. You need to demonstrate that you have understood the process involved in how meetings are conducted in your organisation and also be able to reflect on the issues in an objective way and link them into your personal development plan.

Team talk

Peter's story

My name is Peter. I'm 28 years old and employed as a team leader in a medium-sized manufacturing company. Our organisation has decided to introduce team meetings for all teams. These need to be held monthly and a standard house style agenda has been circulated for me to use.

I have only been a team leader for a few months and I'm finding difficult to communicate issues to all of my team members as many of them work part-time and I can never seem to get everyone together at once. I also get the feeling that the team think that meetings are a waste of time. I spoke to my manager, Susan, to ask for some help in sorting out how I could organise the meetings. I decided that I would write a list of the main issues that were causing me concern and I arranged a quick chat with Susan.

Susan was pleased that I had spoken to her and asked for her support. She was also impressed that I had taken time to write down a list of the main issues and we talked through them. I was concerned about how I could get everyone together at one time and I was also worried about gaining the respect of the team as I found the thought of managing a team meeting a bit daunting. Susan talked through the issues with me and gave me a few pointers. She also agreed to attend the first meeting to provide me with some support.

For the first meeting I wrote out a list of things that I wanted to do as follows.

- Remember to use the standard agenda and give enough notice to staff to ensure they are all available to attend the meeting.
- Check if there is a meeting room that I can use and book it.
- Finalise the date and time of the first meeting with all of the team and Susan.
- Prepare the agenda well in advance and circulate it to all of the team members.
- A couple of days before the meeting check with everyone that they are still OK to attend.

I also spent some time preparing what I was going to say on each agenda item.

The meeting went really well and we now have a process in place to make sure that we hold regular meetings.

Top tips

Peter put a process in place to arrange the meeting, circulate the agenda and prepare the meeting. Peter did well to write down a checklist of the things he wanted to do. This demonstrated that he had thought about everything and by preparing a list, he had started a structured process to try and put in place a system for regular team meetings.

Can you think of anything else that Peter could have done better?

Ask the expert

Q I have to organise a team meeting to take place next month. What do I need to do?

A Prepare a quick checklist of the things you need to do and then action each item in turn. You will need to consider the following things.

Before the meeting
- Consider what the agenda will be like – do we have a standard format or can I pull together my own agenda.
- Ensure that all team members can attend and that we have a room/area for the meeting to take place.
- Ask your team members if they want to put any items on the agenda.
- Be well prepared before the meeting, understand the purpose of the meeting and identify what you want to achieve.
- Be organised with the meeting paperwork and prepare in advance what you are going to say and circulate the agenda and any other relevant paperwork.

During the meeting
- Look the part – be smartly presented and confident.
- Be aware of your tone of voice. It is important to vary the tone and have a warm non-aggressive style.
- Be aware of your body language. Maintain good eye contact, do not slouch and be alert at all times.
- Look confident and interested.
- Listen carefully to what other people have to say and respect their views and opinions.

After the meeting
- If you have taken the minutes for the meeting, prepare the minutes and then circulate them to the rest of the team.
- Communicate any relevant information from the meeting to relevant colleagues and stakeholders.
- Complete any actions points that you agreed to undertake within the agreed timeframe.
- Prepare and plan for the next meeting in good time.

What your assessor is looking for

In order to prepare for and succeed in completing this unit, your assessor will require you to be able to demonstrate competence in:

- planning, organising and preparing for meetings
- leading and managing meetings effectively
- participating in meetings
- being able to communicate information effectively.

You will demonstrate your skills, knowledge and competence through the four learning outcomes in this unit. Evidence generated in this unit will also cross reference to the other units in this qualification.

Please bear in mind that there are significant cross-referencing opportunities throughout this qualification and you may have already generated some relevant work to meet certain criteria in this unit. Your assessor will provide you with the exact requirements to meet the standards of this unit. However, as a guide it is likely that for this unit you will need to be assessed through the following methods:

- An observation of relevant workplace activities or a witness testimony.
- A written report or reflective account.
- A professional discussion could be undertaken.
- Any relevant work products to be produced as evidence.

The work products for this unit could include:

- the preparation undertaken by you for a meeting
- a copy of the agenda and minutes from a meeting that you attended and participated in
- any written communications in relation to the meeting; this could include emails that you have sent to confirm or arranging a meeting or perhaps an email to clarify a point discussed at a meeting
- a copy of any agenda's or minutes that you have produced.

Your assessor will guide you through the assessment process as detailed in the candidate logbook. The portfolio tasks will provide relevant opportunities to meet certain elements of the learning outcomes.

Task and page reference	Assessment criteria
1 (page 128)	1.1
2 (page 130)	1.1, 1.2
3 (page 132)	2.1
4 (page 137)	3.1
5 (page 138)	3.1
6 (page 140)	3.2
7 (page 142)	4.1, 4.2, 4.3

£10

Unit E10 Make effective decisions

As in life generally, people in your workplace will have different interests, views and opinions. These differences can make the decision-making process difficult. This unit will introduce you to a variety of decision-making techniques that will enable you to bring your team together in making decisions, involving them so that everyone feels part of the process.

You will learn how different types of decisions are made at different levels and how these influence the planning, objective setting and success of your organisation. It is important for you to know how decision making affects your stakeholders and that communicating with them effectively is part of this process.

Understanding that the objectives of a decision must link to the criteria you use and that the right type of information influences the success of your decisions, will help you to develop your skills as an effective decision-maker.

Business organisations operate in a constantly changing environment and tools to address the internal and external factors that influence your decision making will be explored, giving you the opportunity to learn how and when agreements must be reached to make effective decisions.

What you will learn:

- Be able to identify circumstances that require a decision to be made
- Be able to collect information to inform decision making
- Be able to analyse information to inform decision making
- Be able to make a decision

Links to the Technical Certificate

If you are completing your NVQ as part of an Apprenticeship Framework, you will find the following topics are also covered in your Technical Certificate:

- Analysis of how to use information to make effective decisions
- Explanation of decision-making and problem-solving techniques
- The importance of communicating decisions made

Be able to identify circumstances that require a decision to be made

Imagine what would happen if your organisation paid little attention to decision making. How would things get done and how would your customers' expectations be met? Someone has to be responsible for making important decisions if successful outcomes are to be achieved.

Sometimes a wrong decision can be made and when this happens it can be costly and even lead to the loss of an important contract! To minimise the risk of making a poor decision, the right information must be gathered so that choices of actions can be considered. This means there is a difference between making a quick decision on impulse and working through the process of making an informed decision.

> **Activity** 🕑 30 minutes
>
> Think about an important decision you have made recently in your personal or work life. What information did you gather beforehand? When you look back, did you make the right or wrong decision? Why?
> Write down your views and share these with your assessor.

Circumstances requiring decisions to be made

In your department, circumstances requiring a decision to be made might include:

- staffing problems such as **absenteeism**, key team members leaving, conflict between team members, equality and diversity issues, health and safety concerns, or poor performance
- customer problems such as complaints about poor quality of work or missed deadlines
- production/output problems such as increased downtime, quality control, increased costs or a backlog of work
- supplier problems such as not receiving deliveries on time, stock control procedures not being effective, or wrong items being ordered.

> **Key Term**
>
> **Absenteeism** – a member of staff away from work sometimes long term, usually on sick leave.

Making decisions for planning activities

To put the decision-making process into context, consider the planning activities that take place in your organisation. They may use:

- long-term planning, 5–10 years ahead
- medium-term planning, 1–5 years ahead
- short-term planning, up to 1 year ahead.

The model in Figure E10.1 illustrates the levels of planning.

Figure E10.1 Levels of planning in an organisation.

Strategic decisions

Directors or senior managers will be concerned with the long-term mission and objectives of your organisation. Some decisions at this level can mean the difference between success or failure of the organisation and be considered risky, such as moving to new premises to expand the business. Other decisions at this level will be the creation of new policies. Decisions which affect or alter the direction of the business are known as strategic decisions.

Tactical decisions

Middle managers need to make sure that strategic decisions made by senior managers are put into practice. Tactical decisions are made to help implement those strategic decisions. Middle managers are concerned with medium-term decisions. If, for example, senior managers make a decision to merge with another organisation, middle managers will make decisions about staffing requirements and resource allocation.

Operational decisions

As a team leader you might be **empowered** to make operational decisions. If not, you will very likely be involved in decision making with your line manager. These types of decisions will be made on a day-to-day basis, such as drawing up staff rotas or job rotation for your team members.

> **Key Term**
>
> **Empowered** – when an individual or a team is given the authority to do something, such as make their own decisions.

Routine and non-routine decisions

You need to be aware that in some organisations different terminology is applied to the decision-making process. For example, strategic and tactical decisions might be referred to as non-routine decisions and operational decisions might be referred to as routine decisions.

- Non-routine decisions are associated with the long-term direction and aims of your organisation, for example to merge with another organisation.
- Routine decisions are short-term decisions relating to your operational duties, such as allocating work or job scheduling.

> **Checklist**
>
> Decisions can be separated into three categories:
> - Strategic – long-term decisions.
> - Tactical – medium-term decisions.
> - Operational – short-term decisions.

Bounded and unbounded problems

Decision makers sometimes refer to bounded problems or unbounded problems.

- Bounded problems are those that can quite easily be put right and the decisions made to resolve these types of problems allow lessons to be learnt to avoid them happening again.
- Unbounded problems need more input and require more research to be carried out before a solution can be found and a final decision made.

> **Activity** ⏱ 45 minutes
>
> Identify a workplace problem that has:
> 1. been easily put right by making a decision quickly (a bounded problem)
> 2. been more difficult to resolve and decisions have taken longer (an unbounded problem).
> Show your responses to your assessor.

Decision making and problems

Decisions are often made in response to:

- internal affairs (for example, new procedures or policies are introduced)
- external affairs (for example, new environmental laws).

In addition, problems that need to be resolved or decisions that need to be made can generally be placed into the following three categories.

1. **Crisis problems** – these need urgent responses. Major equipment breakdowns, financial difficulties or key suppliers going out of business would be examples.

2. **Non-crisis problems** – although urgent action is not needed, these types of problems will need to be resolved reasonably quickly to prevent them turning into crisis problems. Examples would be a complaint about a product or services from a major customer or actions to respond to a visit from an environmental health officer.

3. **Opportunity problems** – these are nice problems to have, but decisions still have to be made! If for example a competitor has closed down and all of its customers want to transfer their business to you, decisions will have to be made about how you will cope with the extra demand.

> **Activity** 🕐 30 minutes
>
> Think about your career to date or reflect on events at work when you have been involved with crisis, non-crisis or opportunity decisions. Record your responses and share them with your assessor.

In some cases, decisions made can have long-lasting and not necessarily desirable consequences. These are sometimes referred to as messy decisions. For example, a decision to expand a chemical factory may have long-term consequences for the organisation. There is likely to be a lot of resistance from groups of stakeholders, particularly the local community. In such circumstances, organisations may devise a decision strategy, which means they will make a sequence of smaller decisions over time, minimising the impact one major decision would have on its stakeholders.

You should also consider the opportunity cost of deciding to do something. In other words what other opportunities have you missed by deciding to go ahead with a particular action?

Imagine if you went to your local shop and bought a large bar of chocolate instead of buying some lottery tickets. You may have just missed out on the opportunity to become a millionaire! Some decisions can be of a rational or irrational nature.

> **Remember**
>
> Often when someone is extremely stressed or tired they can make an impulse decision based on the easiest and quickest solution, without thinking things through. This can have dire effects for the organisation or in some cases for the safety of individuals.

Dependent and independent decisions

You may also notice some managers using the following terminology.

- **Dependent decisions** – these are made at strategic and tactical levels. Final decisions made will be dependent on information gathered so that managers have many options to consider. The **consequence** of each option will be carefully explored and decisions will be made against the **norm** in the organisation. In other words, past decisions will influence the outcome of future decisions.

- **Independent decisions** – these are made at operational level by first-line managers or team leaders. They are short term and independent of other decisions made.

> **Key Terms**
>
> **Consequence** – the effect or result of something taking place.
>
> **Norm** – the standards set within the organisation that everybody follows.

The desired objectives for making a decision

Whether you work in the public, private or voluntary sector, as a team leader you will need to make informed decisions if your team is to meet its targets effectively. You will need to be clear about what you want to achieve and this means you should put together objectives so that you know exactly what you want to make an informed decision about.

Figure E10.2 Cascading decision-making objectives throughout the organisation.

> ### Checklist
>
> There are three sectors in the British economy:
>
> - public sector – offers a service to the public and is funded mainly by the government, e.g. NHS
> - private sector – aims to make a profit and provide a high-quality service to their customers, e.g. Sainsbury's
> - voluntary sector – made up of charities and non-profit making organisations who work to educate the public or raise awareness, while making enough funds to continue their work, e.g. NSPCC.

Group decision making

Group decision making is popular in public sector and voluntary (or third) sector organisations. This is mainly because there are committees where members vote on the final decision. This means that important decisions are made collectively and no one person has ultimate power.

Even in the private sector, senior management team meetings or board of director meetings may be used as a platform for group decision making that affects the whole of the organisation.

The decision-making process

Achieving your organisation's objectives will be easier if informed decisions are made at the right time. Planning and research can assist this process. In other words the decision-making process must involve the use of relevant and accurate information.

The objectives you use for your decision making activities will, in some way, link to the business objectives your managers have agreed at strategic and tactical levels. Look at the example in Figure E10.2.

To be able to make each decision at each level, important information needs to be collected. For example, you will need to gather information to make informed decisions about reducing your staffing costs.

You know what you want to achieve (your objective) and now you must take steps to:

- decide on the best way to make your decision
- decide who you would like to involve in the process
- decide who you need to consult with (internally or externally)
- find out exactly what resources you have (or will have) to work with
- understand the risk involved with each option you consider
- understand the criteria you will use to select the best option.

Your objective will inform you of what you want to achieve and what you need to make a decision about. Your objective should be based on the acronym SMART. For instance, assume you must reduce staffing costs in your department by 10 per cent by a given date.

- Specific – what specifically are you trying to achieve? What exactly are your intentions? (Reduce staffing costs.)

- Measurable – how can you measure the outcome of your intentions? How will you know whether you've achieved what you wanted? (Staffing costs have or have not been reduced by the required percentage by the date you selected.)

- Achievable – is your intention really feasible? (Can you really reduce staffing costs by 10 per cent without affecting staff morale, current levels of output and customer satisfaction?)

- Realistic – is your intention realistic? (Will your 10 per cent cut in staffing allow you to continue to meet orders and will you manage to obtain the reduction by the date selected?)

- Time-bound – is your objective time specific? (Do you have a clear date by which the reduction in costs must have been found?)

Other operational decisions you may have to make could include:

- reducing waste in your department
- improving the quality of your product or service
- reviewing your team's targets, levels of output and allocation of work
- increasing levels of morale in your team
- enhancing the skills and knowledge of your team members
- reducing conflict in the team and reducing incidents and accidents
- establishing a strategy for diversity, equality and inclusion
- establishing effective methods of communication to use with your team
- adhering to existing and new laws (for example, health and safety).

Activity 🕐 30 minutes

Based upon what you wanted to achieve for your team over the last six months, list the operational decisions you have had to make. Share your responses with your assessor.

Establishing decision-making criteria

When you make your decisions you have to be clear about the principles or standards by which you will make your judgements. These criteria can be affected by many things.

Internal and external constraints

Your decision-making process can be hampered by internal and external **constraints**.

Key Term

Constraint – something that gets in the way of what you are trying to achieve (i.e. your objective).

Internal constraints might be:

- insufficient skills or knowledge in the team to achieve your SMART objective
- attitudes of people in your workplace may be negative
- insufficient funds to do what you want to do
- your organisation's policies preventing you from taking certain actions
- insufficient room, equipment or training to achieve what you want
- your own limits of authority.

External constraints may be:

- new or existing laws or regulations preventing you achieving what you want
- the demand from the marketplace in your industry falling
- competitors' performance being better than yours
- your suppliers being unreliable
- the economic climate preventing customers from spending.

Remember

Some of the decisions you and your managers make can have a direct effect on the success of your organisation and therefore job security. This is why it is so important to take decision making very seriously!

Activity ⏱ 45 minutes

Think of a recent decision you have made. What did you have to spend time thinking about before you could make a final decision?

The things you thought about would have been the criteria you used to make a judgement towards your final decision. It would have been difficult for you to do this without knowing the objective of your decision in the first place (i.e. what you actually want to achieve).

Write down what you thought about your criteria and share your responses with your assessor.

Your decision-making criteria

Changes in the economy and your industry's requirements will often force you to amend your decisions or make new or different decisions.

Choosing and evaluating different courses of action is a very important part of your decision-making process and will help your organisation to remain competitive.

With a clear objective of your decision in mind, it is important that you think about using the right criteria to help you to make the most appropriate, relevant and well-informed decision.

Your manager may ask you to justify the reasons for your final decision and discussing the criteria you used can help you to do this.

You might find suitable criteria to help you reach a decision contained in the list below. You can answer 'yes' or 'no' to some of these or alternatively establish to what degree they affect your decision-making process.

- Is training or retraining required?
- Are new risk assessments needed?
- Can current staff do what is expected?
- Will there be a disruption to everyday tasks?
- Will new laws have to be adhered to?
- Will there be health and safety implications?
- Will the current quality of the service/product be affected?
- Will customers' expectations be met?

- Will it take long to do?
- Will it help the organisation to meet its business objectives?
- Will it require large expenditure?
- Will waste be reduced?
- Can current equipment and materials be used?
- Will costs be reduced?
- Will staff be required to work overtime?
- Will staff hours be reduced?
- Will staff morale be affected?

Programmed and non-programmed decisions

- Programmed decisions – structured decisions made on a day-to-day basis at operational level. As team leader, these types of decisions would relate to your repetitive tasks in line with your procedures, such as drawing up staff rotas.
- Non-programmed decisions – unstructured decisions made in response to unexpected or out of the ordinary situations. These types of decisions would ideally involve your team members to establish the best way to react. As team leader, you would make non-programmed decisions in response to unusual problems that occur.

In any organisation there will be:

- decision makers – people involved in the decision-making process, who work through options to arrive at a final decision
- decision takers – everyone who works in the organisation! Staff members working at different levels will learn about decisions made that affect them and the way they do their jobs. They will be expected to accept these decisions, whether involved in the decision-making process or not.

Experts suggest that successful organisations are the ones that value their employees' opinions and involve them in making decisions rather than expecting them to take decisions after they have been made.

Portfolio Task 1 ⏱ 45 minutes

Links to LO1, LO2: Assessment criteria 1.1, 1.2, 1.3, 2.1

As a team leader you make decisions regularly. Use the table below to make a list of the decisions you make on a daily, weekly and monthly basis.

	Decisions made	Information needed	Reasons for the decision
Daily	e.g. allocating work to team members at morning briefings	e.g. job lists	e.g. ensure your team's and organisation's objectives are achieved
Weekly	e.g. allocating holidays	e.g. holiday timetable	e.g. meeting legal obligations
Monthly	e.g. setting team objectives during monthly team meetings	e.g. your plan of objectives and strategies (your team strategic plan)	e.g. to ensure organisational objectives are met in time

PLTS

By completing this task, you will be analysing and evaluating the importance of information and making informed decisions (IE4).

Remember

Programmed decisions are also known as structured decisions. Non-programmed decisions are also known as unstructured decisions.

Be able to collect information to inform decision making

Accurate information is needed if sound decisions are to be made. You need to understand what information really is and where it comes from. The model below illustrates that there is a process to analyse raw data that has been collected and turn it into useful information.

Figure E10.3 Information transformation process model.

- Raw data (or facts) are collected from reliable sources.
- The data (or facts) are **processed** in some way perhaps through analysis, assessment or judgements.

- The data (or facts), once processed, will become meaningful and useful sources of information for decision-making purposes.

To illustrate this, think about a decision you have made recently. In particular, think about how the information you used to make a decision made you feel good because you were able to help someone or resolve a problem. It's all about finding the right information!

Remember

Carrying out research to help you make a decision can be very interesting – the process doesn't have to be as boring and tedious as some people think.

Key Term

Processed – inputs are changed or altered in some way resulting in outputs.

Identify the information needed

There are many ways to identify the information you need. You can gather raw data from questionnaires, speak to people, look up information and so on.

A step-by-step approach

There is a useful step-by-step process that can be used when faced with an issue or problem that needs to be resolved.

1. Define exactly what the problem is.
2. Collect appropriate and relevant data to help resolve the problem.
3. Develop alternative solutions for resolving the problem.
4. Assess the consequences of using each solution.
5. Select the best solution.
6. Implement the best solution.
7. Measure and evaluate the results to see if the solution is working.

Each step is examined in further detail below.

Define the problem

First of all you should establish and agree (perhaps with your team members or managers) exactly what the problem is, who it is affecting and in what way. Decide who is equipped to help you to find solutions. This may be one person who is very knowledgeable about the issue or it could be your whole team.

Then you should devise SMART objectives (what you want to achieve or happen) to help you to prioritise how you intend to approach the problem.

Collect relevant data

Be sure about what data you need and what you need it for; your time can be wasted researching and sourcing data that won't actually assist your decision-making process. You might also waste other people's time by consulting them when you don't really need to.

Have decisions been made in the past in your organisation that will help your process now? Talk to your managers and team members to find out.

Also be aware that data might be out of date or inaccurate, depending on where you get it from.

Finally, decide what methods you will use to collect your data (for example, staff questionnaires or internet research).

Develop alternative solutions

Depending on how quickly you need to find a solution, you could spend time obtaining the views and ideas of other people and incorporate these into a list of possible solutions for your problem.

Assessing the consequences

You should consider what will happen if you choose one solution over another. Why should one solution be chosen and the other not? Factors to consider are the cost of each solution and how it will be accepted by those it affects, for example, your customer. The benefits and risks (including health and safety) of each solution should be carefully analysed.

Select the optimum solution

The most favourable solution must be selected. You should consult with others to find out who supports your choice and who is against it. It is important to find out why they support your choice or otherwise.

Once a final agreement is reached, decide who will be involved in the implementation of the solution and how quickly it must be done. At this stage in the process, you could consider producing an action plan (a plan of who will do what, by when, and what resources will be needed).

Implement the solution

Once the solution is chosen and an action plan has been drawn up, the process of **implementation** must be monitored carefully.

> **Key Term**
>
> **Implementation** – putting your plan into practice and making it happen.

Effective communication is vital so that everyone involved knows what is expected of them, what they must do and by when. In other words, have those involved with the production of your action plan been issued with a final copy of it? You must then monitor how well the plan is being followed by getting regular feedback, perhaps through regular team meetings.

Measure the results

Your action plan should have a review date column included. This will prompt further meetings to assess how effective the chosen solution has been. The feedback obtained should be recorded (for example, minutes or notes) and used to write up a report on the whole process. You may wish to arrange future meetings so that the chosen solution to your problem is monitored and evaluated over a future period of time.

It is important that you ask yourself whether:

- the right data has been gathered
- the data gathered has been processed effectively and converted into meaningful information.

Remember

You can enhance morale by involving your team members in your decision-making process whenever possible.

Gathering research for making decisions

It has already been established that you need to collect data to be processed into useful information to help you make decisions. You can collect data by carrying out primary research, secondary research or sometimes both.

Primary research

Collecting primary research means finding something out for the first time ever. This will be something that nobody has ever found out before and can be quite satisfying.

Methods you can use to carry out primary research include:

- questionnaires (for example, staff or customer surveys)
- observations (you could record how many

people you see using the photocopier in one day for example)
- interviewing (you could interview people to obtain their views).

The data you collect from your primary research can be processed into graphs, tables, charts or text to give you information that has never been found out before.

Secondary research

Secondary research means taking steps to collect data that already exists. In other words, someone else has already carried out primary research and has made their findings available for other people to see.

Items you could use to find secondary research include:

- newspapers and magazines
- textbooks and journals
- manuals and reports
- newsletters and leaflets
- intranet and internet.

You now need to think about the type of data you have collected. There are two main categories:

- quantitative data – raw facts relating to numbers or quantities. Think about sales figures, hours worked, average spends per customer or the costs of producing something.
- qualitative data – raw facts relating to people's views, opinions or attitudes about something. For example, someone's views about a training course.

Sometimes a mixture of quantitative and qualitative data will be required to enable you to make an informed decision.

Workplace systems and procedures

Decisions have to be made regularly so that everyone knows who should be doing what and how they should do it. A procedure for processing a sales order will have relied on the input of many people to agree on the best way to write it, meaning many decisions will have been made. Similarly when devising a system, many decisions

Converting inputs into outputs.

will need to be made to establish the best way to convert inputs into outputs. Think of raw materials in a factory (inputs) being processed on the production line to make finished products (outputs).

A hairdryer is a good analogy here:

1. Cold air is sucked in (input).
2. It is heated in the dryer (a process).
3. Warm air is blown out (output).

Checklist

Systems can be described as:
- inputs
- a process
- outputs.

Systems and procedures should be reviewed regularly to:

- improve efficiency and output
- ensure customers' expectations are met
- help the team to achieve its targets
- ensure everyone works to the same standard of quality
- ensure that everyone is safe from harm or abuse in the workplace.

The UK government regularly makes decisions that will affect you, your team and your organisation. Similarly, changes higher up in your own industry may prompt a review of the way you do things. This will result in decisions being made at strategic, tactical and operational levels, if you are to remain competitive.

In any organisation there will always be:

- risk – situations where outcomes are unknown
- uncertainty – where outcomes can only be estimated or forecasted.

Stakeholders and decision making

What do you think about the following quote from an anonymous senior manager?

'We make the decision and then we tell them!'

Perhaps not the best approach, but it is what some managers do. It's worth thinking about who is affected by a decision and who should be involved in the decision-making process.

Now look at another quote:

'Managers should make decisions that take account of the interests of all the stakeholders.'

R.E. Freeman (1984)

This suggests that building strong positive relationships with **stakeholders** is very important. All organisations have stakeholders, but the nature and size of the business will dictate how many and how powerful they are.

> **Key Term**
>
> **Stakeholders** – any individual or group of individuals who has an interest in what the organisation is doing.

Often, stakeholders will be involved in decision making that affects the culture of your organisation. Workplace culture can be described as 'the way in which things are done'. Naturally, the way things are done will vary from organisation to organisation and your culture may be quite different from that of your competitors.

> **Remember**
>
> The success of your organisation depends on the support you get from your stakeholders.

You should be aware that your culture is as it is because decisions have been made about:

- policies and procedures to influence people's behaviour
- leadership styles and their influence
- the way people's beliefs, attitudes and views are dealt with
- your organisation's approach to planning
- your organisation's customs (for example, are people greeted with handshakes?)
- the values your organisation holds
- the methods of communication that are used.

> **Remember**
>
> Communication is about getting the right message to the right people at the right time and then obtaining feedback.

> **PLTS**
>
> This activity gives you the opportunity to carry out research, analyse the importance of the information and put forward reasoned arguments (IE2, 4, 6; CT1).

Portfolio Task 2

 60 minutes

Links to LO2, LO4: Assessment criteria 2.2, 2.3, 4.1, 4.2, 4.3

Provide examples to your assessor of techniques you use to communicate with your stakeholders. You should consider obtaining evidence such as examples of:

- emails sent informing stakeholders of decisions made
- witness testimonies from your managers explaining your ability to communicate face to face with stakeholders
- minutes of meetings where you have discussed decisions made and how you update your stakeholders.

Discuss the evidence with your assessor, explaining why you used the techniques you did to communicate your decisions.

It may be necessary for your assessor to observe you communicating with your stakeholders perhaps on the telephone or face to face. Your assessor will discuss this further with you if required.

Your organisation may or may not have shareholders as a group of stakeholders. This depends on whether you trade as a business or have been approved by Companies House to trade as a company. If you have shareholders they must be involved with strategic decisions.

Communicate decisions to stakeholders

Your stakeholders should receive regular updates about decisions made or changed. Your customers are one of your most important groups of stakeholders. Without your customers you will have no business! The decisions you and your managers make can affect how your customers' perceive you.

If you have attended a customer service training course you will have learnt about the importance of listening carefully without interruption as well as that you can tell a lot from reading your customer's body language. You will need to apply the same thinking when communicating with all of the stakeholders affected by your decision-making.

Don't forget that the feedback you get from stakeholders can help you to make informed decisions. You must listen carefully to what they tell you as this can help you to establish their needs and help work towards building a successful relationship. In face-to-face situations their body language can communicate their approval or disapproval of the decisions that have been made.

Top-down and bottom-up communication

When you communicate, you must select the most appropriate method to suit the circumstance you find yourself in. Another very important group of stakeholders is the employees of an organisation. Without these, the organisation couldn't function.

When managers communicate with employees they can use a top-down approach or a bottom-up approach.

Top-down communication is the most commonly used approach in organisations. Managers make decisions and pass instructions down the hierarchy to employees below.

Bottom-up communication is more or less the opposite. Employees are encouraged to get involved with the decision-making process to enhance morale and motivation. This is often referred to as employee involvement (EI).

Activity 🕒 30 minutes

Write down the advantages and disadvantages of top-down and bottom-up communication. Discuss your responses with your assessor.

Effect of leadership styles on communication with stakeholders

Successful decision-making often depends on the leadership styles that are used in an organisation. Kurt Lewin, a management theorist, identified three styles:

1. Autocratic – managers make decisions without consulting staff members and then tell them what they should do and how they should do it.
2. Democratic – managers involve their staff members in the decision-making process and ask them for their ideas.
3. Laissez-faire – managers allow staff members to make their own decisions. This style usually applies to people working in specialist roles who need little management support.

You may have noticed that the autocratic leadership style is linked to top-down communication whilst the democratic leadership style is linked to bottom-up communication.

How to inform stakeholders

When communicating decisions to your internal stakeholder (your team, colleagues, and managers), think about methods such as:

*   notice boards in staff rooms and corridors
*   notices in reception and warehouse areas
*   group emails
*   reports
*   your organisation's intranet
*   presentations or discussions in meetings
*   leaflets or newsletters.

When communicating decisions to your external stakeholders (your local community, suppliers, customers and creditors) think about methods such as:

- press releases
- focus group meetings
- open days
- exhibitions
- magazine articles
- fliers or information leaflets
- emails
- letters
- websites
- e-newsletters and hard-copy newsletters.

Both internal and external stakeholders will benefit from knowing and understanding the process used for decision making. You will get their commitment and support if the reasons for the decision made are clearly communicated.

Trying to get stakeholders onside when making difficult decisions is a strategy many organisations use. Imagine if you were in charge of an organisation that wanted to develop a privately-run landfill site on the outskirts of a pretty village.

You need to think about potential conflict caused by your decision. Shareholders in your company who will profit from their investments will support your decision whereas the local community may object to your decision. Your stakeholders' views of your decision will differ because of:

- social costs (the negative aspects such as noisy lorries and pollution)
- social benefits (the positive aspects such as new jobs for local people and workers spending in local businesses)
- private costs (investors will need to fund and run the project)
- private benefits (shareholders and other investors will want to make a profit).

Initially, you could expect to be challenged by groups of stakeholders who object to your decision. These groups might include:

- the local community
- the county or district council (if there are no other options, the council may support your decision however)
- competing organisations
- the local parish council
- other businesses in the locality
- the police.

Over time, you may be able to convince your stakeholders that you will be sympathetic to the local landscape and will make promises to minimise pollution and make the area safe.

Here is another example. Think about the decisions that had to be made before the Channel Tunnel was finally built. The social costs and benefits and the private costs and benefits were carefully considered and a cost-benefit analysis showed that the benefits outweighed the costs, which is why a decision was made to go ahead and build it.

Remember

In terms of your organisation's image and reputation it is often a good idea to consult with your stakeholders to get their views before making a major decision.

Stakeholder map

Some organisations use a stakeholder map to help identify who holds power to help with decision making.

A matrix similar to the one in Figure E10.4 will help you to understand who will have a high or low level of interest in your decision, who has high or low power over your decision, who you must keep satisfied and who should be monitored for their reactions to your decisions.

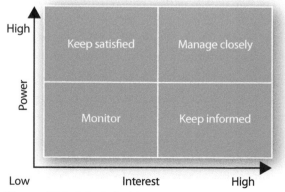

Figure E10.4 Stakeholder map.

Your stakeholder map can help you to analyse who holds:

- high power and high interest in what you do – you must make efforts to communicate regularly with these groups and keep them satisfied
- high power but less interest – you still need to communicate often here but perhaps not as regularly
- low power but high interest – due to their interest, feedback from these groups can be useful, but you only need to communicate periodically to get their views and to keep them informed
- low power and low interest – these groups will not expect or indeed want to receive regular communications from you. You need to keep in touch every so often however to monitor their views and actions.

Knowing how to manage your stakeholders is just as important as managing your processes in the workplace. Very often if you engage with the right people, your decision-making process can become a lot easier to manage too.

This means you have to know who you should seek support from. Another way to look at this is to think about who has power, influence or who will be interested in the particular decision you are making.

Activity 🕐 30 minutes

Think back to the landfill decision example above. Draw up a stakeholder map to analyse which groups of stakeholders you would insert into each box. Once you have written in the appropriate groups of stakeholders into each box, show your completed map to your assessor.

Portfolio Task 3 🕐 30 minutes

Links to LO3: Assessment criteria 3.1, 3.2

When making decisions, how do you check that the information you use is valid and relevant? Discuss your responses with your assessor. Your assessor will record this discussion in order to generate evidence for your portfolio.

Be able to analyse information to inform decision making

Often, by reflecting on your decision-making process, you may question how relevant the information you used was. You may also question its validity in terms of its honesty and accuracy and whether from a legal point of view you were allowed to use the information at all!

Activity 🕐 30 minutes

Write down your views of whether you would prefer to make a decision based purely on your own views and information or based on the views and information put forward by a group of people. Discuss your responses with your assessor.

Identifying valid and relevant information

The information gathered to help you make the right decisions may come from a variety of primary or secondary sources.

Identifying the information you need to help to make a particular decision can be tricky, because people you consult with may offer subjective rather than objective views, which can colour the validity and relevance of the information being used to make final decisions.

Continuum of empowerment and leadership and its effect on the decision-making process

Some years ago, theorists Tannenbaum and Schmidt devised a continuum of empowerment and leadership model. This explores to what extent managers involve their employees in the decision making process, see Figure E10.5.

Depending on the complexity of a decision it may be possible for you to obtain all the information you need from your own team members or in some cases you may need to consult with other key members of staff.

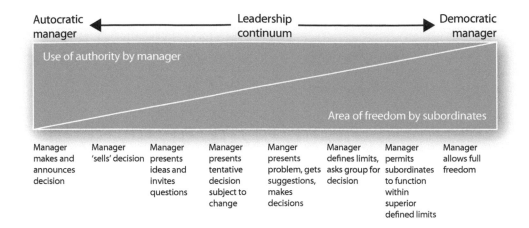

Figure E10.5 Continuum of leadership behaviour.

Examine the following examples of obtaining relevant information.

- You seek the views of your team members because they have sound working knowledge of the product or service you offer. This would be useful if you need to make a decision about updating a procedure that your team uses.

- You seek the views of your line manager and others such as your finance/human resources managers if you need to make a decision about acquiring a new machine or additional staff to enable your team to function effectively.

Remember

Generally, the role of a manager is to plan, co-ordinate, control and organise the work of a department or organisation. To do this successfully, decisions will have to be made regularly!

Remember

If you work in a large company, you will have directors who are likely to involve shareholders in their major decision-making processes.

From time to time, your managers are likely to seek your views and involve you in decisions they must make.

Very often, managers need to look at a variety of solutions to a problem and then implement the best one. Different courses of action can be taken and the final decision will dictate the choice of action to be taken.

When making decisions, the information you identify to help you must be:

- current – is it up to date? Is it the latest available?

- sufficient – is it of enough substance and detailed enough?

- accurate – is it from a reliable source and correct in nature?

Once you have identified valid and relevant information, the decision you make should:

- provide a quick solution to your problem or situation

- involve all concerned parties

- not be in breach of your organisation's policies, rules or regulations.

Remember

There is a difference between making a decision and making an informed decision. It is important to collect the right information for each decision such as trends, statistics, qualitative and quantitative information.

Analyse information against established criteria

The criteria you select to help you make a decision could include making sure that:

- the costs of the solution don't exceed the budget
- the solution will be made in a given time frame
- the solution improves customer satisfaction.

These are only examples and the criteria you set will depend upon the nature of the problem you are trying to put right.

Once you have set your criteria you should examine the information you have collected and analyse how it will help you to make a decision to fulfil that criteria.

For example, if your criteria was to improve customer satisfaction, you might use primary data, secondary data or a combination of both.

Imagine that the decision you want to make is about customer delivery times. Perhaps there are many complaints about late deliveries. You can use customer survey questionnaires (primary data), which you could analyse to establish what the main complaint is, or you could compare your organisation to other similar organisations by questioning sales representatives or customers to find out what their delivery times are and how reliable they are.

You could read trade magazines, company reports, consumer magazines such as *Which?* and advertising material to get some idea of what other organisations promise their customers (this would be your secondary data). Of course, you could use both sources to give you a deeper understanding of how you will fulfil your criteria.

Think about the criteria you have established and whether they:

- enable your organisation's policies, rules and regulations to be adhered to
- will help to meet your business objectives
- enable you to prioritise your team's objectives
- will be agreed and accepted by everyone concerned with or affected by your decision.

Your organisation's values

When you analyse your information against your criteria you should think about your organisation's **values**. These are what an organisation considers important and how they want their staff to behave. Often an organisation's culture will reflect its values and attitudes and beliefs of employees will be influenced by them.

> **Key Term**
>
> **Values** – principles and beliefs of an organisation or individual.

The criteria you set for your decisions should ideally consider your organisation's values, which may be listed in your staff handbook or on your intranet.

The cereals giant Kellogg's takes pride in its values and in 2002 produced a *Little Book of Kellogg's Values*. Some of its reported values are as follows:

- We act with integrity and respect.
- We are all accountable.
- We are passionate about our businesses, our brands and our food.
- We speak positively and supportively about team members when apart.
- We involve others in decisions and plans that affect them.
- We serve our customers and delight our consumers through the quality of our products and services.
- We admit our mistakes and learn from them.

> **Remember**
>
> The values of an organisation often influence its strategic planning decisions.

> **Activity** 🕐 30 minutes
>
> Find out whether your organisation has written values and if so, make a record of them. Write a paragraph on how you think an organisation's values can influence its decision making. Show your work to your assessor.

Be able to make a decision

To recap, making a well-informed decision depends upon the selected criteria used, careful analysis of the information used and an evaluation of options or choices available. It is important to examine whether the final decision made will help meet the objectives you have set.

Decision-making techniques

There are many techniques that you can use to evaluate whether you are making the right decision and communicate your final decision to stakeholders.

Often, tools such as a SWOT or a PESTLE analysis can identify the need to make decisions.

The acronym SWOT stands for:

- Strengths
- Weaknesses
- Opportunities
- Threats.

This tool helps you to identify what are your team's current strengths and weaknesses, but it also enables you to think about what opportunities you have to improve things and what obstacles (threats) may get in the way of your progress. It's helpful to write down each of the four headings and then make bullet-points list underneath each of those headings.

Your SWOT analysis can help you to make decisions to minimise any threats and address your weaknesses, hopefully turning them into strengths. You can also make decisions to maximise your potential for new opportunities.

The acronym PESTLE stands for:

- Political
- Economical
- Social
- Technological
- Legal
- Environmental.

A PESTLE analysis can be used to identify areas of concern that are outside the control of your

organisation but still affect it, such as economic problems. As with a SWOT analysis, bullet-point lists of ideas should be written down beneath the PESTLE headings listed above.

Portfolio Task 4 — 30 minutes

Links to LO4: Assessment criteria 4.1
Produce a SWOT analysis for your team and its work. Once completed, show it to your assessor. You could use the template below.

Strengths	Weaknesses
e.g. Expertise of team members	e.g. Too many customer complaints
Opportunities	**Threats**
e.g. New equipment to speed up process	e.g. Competitors delivery times are quicker

PLTS

This portfolio task will give you the opportunity to engage with issues that affect your work and the work of your team and organisation. By producing your SWOT analysis you will be presenting a case for persuasive action through encouraging your team and your managers to reflect on the analysis you have undertaken (CT1, 3; EP2).

Functional Skills

By completing your SWOT analysis in word processing software, you will be practising your Functional Skills in ICT at Level 2.

Activity — 45 minutes

Talk to your managers to find out whether a PESTLE analysis is carried out in your organisation. Ask to see what has been listed underneath each heading and what decisions were made in relation to each factor listed. Alternatively, carry out some research to find an example of a completed PESTLE analysis and write down your views about its content and how the tool can help an organisation to make decisions.

The decision-making cycle

Often, a visual representation of decision making is easier to understand. Below is a decision-making cycle you can show to your team.

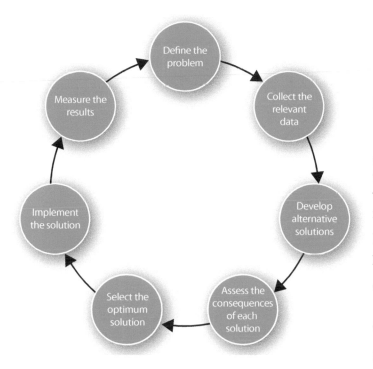

Figure E10.6 The decision-making cycle.

Management theories on decision-making techniques

Management theorist Kurt Lewin devised a useful tool called a Force Field Analysis to assist with the

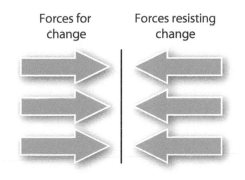

Figure E10.7 Kurt Lewin's Force Field Analysis diagram.

decision-making process (see Figure E10.7). The tool will enable you and your team to establish valid reasons for or against doing something and reach a final decision.

For example, when making a decision to change a procedure affecting your team's work there are:

- driving forces – changes to government legislation
- restraining forces – staff fear of change.

Some people score each response listed, for example between 1–10 with 1 being a weak force and 10 being the highest force. When totalled up, if the driving force scores are higher than the restraining force scores, then a decision should be made to go ahead with the change.

Perhaps the most commonly used technique in organisations is the decision list. This tool is used most effectively when:

- all identified criteria are listed
- each option identified to resolve a problem is evaluated against the criteria (look back at the decision-making cycle)
- a tick or cross is placed in appropriate boxes to show whether each alternative option meets the criteria or not.

Examine the example on the following page.

The decision list shows that in this case option 4 is the one that satisfies all of the criteria and a decision should be made to go with this option.

Criteria for selection	Options			
	1	**2**	**3**	**4**
Essential criteria				
Costs within budget of £1000	✓	✗	✗	✓
Changes can be made within a 6 month time limit	✗	✓	✓	✓
Changes won't disrupt workflow	✗	✓	✗	✓
Desirable criteria				
No need for additional staff training	✗	✗	✓	✓

Table E10.1 A decision list.

Coming to a team decision

Sometimes, team members are reluctant or too shy to express their views. If this is the case you could consider trying the nominal group technique, which promotes a more relaxed setting where team members are encouraged to share their thoughts.

With this technique, you encourage team members to write down their views on paper without anyone else seeing them. Then one by one, team members will briefly describe their views to the rest of the team, in a relaxed environment. All views will be recorded on a chart/board and each person's views will be evaluated jointly. The team will vote to reach a final decision on which view or idea should be put into practice.

Other useful techniques that could help you and your team to determine a decision include:

- quality circles – for example, you may allow your team to get together on a Wednesday morning for half an hour every other week. They will discuss any issues that will lead to improved quality of the product or service you provide. You and your team can then agree on a final decision to improve quality.
- scenario planning – through discussions with your team you can estimate what might happen in the future. In other words, you try to forecast what positive or negative scenarios may occur in the future and what decisions could be made

should they happen (for example, a scenario where suppliers are on strike and can't get materials to you).

- analogies – it's often useful to examine past experiences to help resolve a current problem. Your final decision may be influenced by the actions of someone else in your organisation (or externally) who has experienced the same problem.

Explain how decisions are made in line with objectives

It may be necessary for you to prepare a report for your line manager to explain how you arrived at the decision you made. Whether your report is formal or informal in format will depend upon how serious the issue you were addressing was. Other groups of stakeholders may also want to see a copy of your report.

Your actions, and to some extent the content of your report, may help you to gain the support of your stakeholders for future decisions too.

Earlier action planning was briefly referred to. It's often helpful to create an action plan to explain to others how the decisions you have made are in line with your objectives. You could use headings that explain who did/will do what, by when and what resources were used, as in the example in Table E10.2.

Actions/Tasks	By whom	By when	Resources needed	Completion date	Evaluation date
To ensure sufficient stock control system is in place	JE	31 Oct 2012	Time/ Stock control manual		
To ensure order processing system is reviewed	BJ	31 Oct 2012	Time/ Customer order procedures file		
To examine reasons for downtime	FG	31 Oct 2012	Time/Production schedule reports		

Table E10.2 Action plan to resolve backlog of work.

For example, if you have a team objective to improve delivery time for your customers then you could use the information you have collected to make decisions to offer training on service improvement techniques.

Any organisation will need to evaluate its overall performance and it can do this by reviewing its objectives and decisions it has made in the past.

Consider the example of a company hierachy:

- Board of Directors – devise corporate objectives
- Senior managers – devise strategies (strategic decisions)
- Middle managers – devise tactics (tactical decisions)
- First-line managers – ensure tasks are carried out (operative decisions)
- Team workers/operatives – carry out tasks.

A series of decisions must be made in order to achieve the overall corporate objectives. Without action to make decisions at each layer of the hierarchy then it is unlikely that a company will be successful.

Objectives, strategies and tactics should be regularly reviewed as part of the monitoring and evaluation process; have they worked or do they need changing? Your SWOT and PESTLE analysis may also prompt objectives and therefore offer strategies and tactics to be changed from time to time.

Remember

The same process above will apply to an organisation trading as a 'business' rather than a 'company', with the difference being there will not be a board of directors!

Team talk

Tony's story

Hi, my name is Tony and I am 34 years old. I have been a team leader for a leading fast-food chain for two months now. I enjoy my job as it gives me the opportunity to lead a team of youngsters keen to learn and I get to talk to customers all the time.

Over the last few weeks I have noticed that the customers seem to be moaning a lot more than they used to. They are not happy with the service they get and have started going to our major competitor up the road. I have asked some of them what they don't like and they say it's all due to poor customer service due to lack of staff training. I know my staff are fully trained as I keep detailed records of who attends what training. I asked the team if they have any problems, but they all seem quite happy with the way things are going. I just don't know what to do.

My line manager is eager for me to resolve this problem as our area manager is due to visit in the next couple of months. I need to get this problem sorted out as soon as possible to avoid the situation escalating to the next level.

Top tips

Tony needs to find out what the actual problem is. The only way to do this is to do a bit of research. Firstly Tony needs to speak to his team again to identify whether they have any issues. This could be done either as a brainstorming session or during team meetings. Also, Tony will need to do more research into what the customers want. This needs to be done through either face-to-face questioning or customer comments cards (i.e. questionnaires). Tony could also carry out some secondary research to see how the major competitor up the road is running its business differently.

Ask the expert	
Q	How can Tony deal with this problem? What decisions does he need to make?
A	In order to deal with the problem, Tony should follow the decision-making cycle shown on page 165. The cycle will take Tony through the main stages to manage this problem and make an effective decision. It's also important to remember that once the decision has been made, Tony evaluates its effectiveness. He may find that the first decision he makes to manage the problem does not actually resolve the issue and therefore the decision-making cycle starts again (i.e. define the problem). The cycle will be continuous until the problem has been resolved.

What your assessor is looking for

In order to demonstrate your competency within this unit, you must provide sufficient evidence to your assessor. You will need to provide a short written narrative or personal statement, explaining how you meet the assessment criteria. In addition, your assessor may ask you questions to test your knowledge of the topics identified in this unit.

Below is a list of suggested documentation that will provide evidence to help you to prove your competency in this unit.

Work products for this unit could include:

- minutes of team meetings when decisions have been made
- emails, letters or reports negotiating decisions
- emails, letters or reports to stakeholders communicating the decisions made
- decision-making tools e.g. SWOT analyses

- examples of objectives and decision-making criteria you have used.

Your assessor will guide you through the assessment process as detailed in the candidate logbook. The detailed assessment criteria are shown in the logbook and by working through these questions, combined with providing the relevant evidence, you will meet the learning outcomes required to complete this unit.

Task and page reference	Assessment criteria
1 (page 154)	1.1, 1.2, 1.3, 2.1
2 (page 159)	2.2, 2.3, 4.1, 4.2, 4.3
3 (page 161)	3.1, 3.2
4 (page 164)	4.1

Unit B6 Provide leadership and direction for own area of responsibility

Leadership is the ability to inspire and motivate others. With a little hard work and a lot of determination, anyone with the drive to do so can learn to become an inspirational leader.

In this unit you will look at models of leadership and use these to examine your own individual leadership qualities and strengths. You will look at ways in which you can provide leadership by outlining the direction and vision for your team. You will also investigate objective setting aligned to organisational goals.

Good communication is an essential leadership quality and you will examine ways in which you can develop effective communication to inform your team of the direction they are to follow. This helps them to understand how their day-to-day tasks are important to the wider goals of the business.

Feedback is an essential element of performance assessment and you will investigate ways in which you can collect and assess feedback from others in order to bring about improvements to your leadership skills and abilities.

What you will learn:

- Be able to lead in own area of responsibility
- Be able to provide direction and set objectives in own area of responsibility
- Be able to communicate the direction for own area of responsibility and collect feedback to inform improvement
- Be able to assess own leadership performance

Links to Technical Certificate

If you are completing your NVQ as part of an Apprenticeship Framework, you will find the following topic is also covered in your Technical Certificate:

- Communicate knowledge and information to team members

Be able to lead in own area of responsibility

In this section, you will investigate some of the defining qualities of effective leaders, as well as assessing and evaluating your own leadership skills. This is an important activity for you to undertake at this stage in your career, and one that will help you to identify how you can capitalise on your existing strengths, as well as looking at ways of developing other skill areas.

Identifying own strengths and ability to lead in a leadership role

In this section you will review some of the key models and principles of leadership. You can then apply these ideas to your own role as a basis for identifying your own particular leadership strengths. This will also be useful in identifying areas that you need to develop in the future.

Defining leadership

Leadership includes the ability to persuade, motivate, inspire and influence people to do something. It also includes having vision, as well as the determination and tenacity to see that vision through. Leaders are admired because of their strength of character and personality, rather than because they occupy a particular position within an organisation.

Leadership qualities

You have probably seen many examples in the press of high profile industry figures, who are variously described as visionaries, pioneers and gurus in their fields of endeavour.

Examples include Steve Jobs, former CEO of Apple, Bill Gates, Chairman of Microsoft, Richard Branson, founder of the Virgin Group and Winston Churchill, the former prime minister who led the country through the Second World War.

These people achieved greatness in their endeavours as leaders in their respective fields. But what is it that specifically defines a good leader?

Some key leadership qualities include:

- integrity and honesty
- the ability to lead by example
- determination
- creativity and innovation
- a vision for the future
- the ability to inspire respect and trust
- knowledge of the organisation and the industry
- excellent communication skills.

Leadership behaviours

Leadership experts Warren Bennis and Burt Nanus state that there are four key leadership behaviours, or strategies, that enable inspirational leadership.

1. Attention through vision – focusing your attention closely on your goals, to keep sight of what you are ultimately aiming to achieve and ensure that all subsequent actions are aligned to the overall vision of the organisation.

2. Meaning through communication – communicating regularly and clearly with your team to influence them and to get them to share your goals.

3. Trust through positioning – demonstrating integrity by saying what you mean and sticking to it.

4. Deployment of self – having a strong sense of self-awareness, being socially skilled in your actions and communications, having confidence in your skills and abilities and a focus on continuous self-improvement and development.

Activity ⏱ 10 minutes

If you look back over the four key leadership behaviours above, you will be able to see certain underlying skills for each behaviour. Identify the key skill for each one and think of how you could demonstrate that skill in your current position.

PLTS

When you are connecting your own and others' ideas and experiences in inventive ways, you are practising your skills as a creative thinker (CT).

Leadership and management

Leadership is closely linked to the concept of management. Both are necessary for an organisation to run smoothly and the terms are often even used interchangeably. However, it is important to differentiate leadership from management.

- Leadership comes first and involves setting the overall direction of the business, so that the correct processes can be established to take the business in the right direction.
- Management follows logically on from leadership and involves overseeing the processes, procedures and day-to-day tasks needed to achieve goals.

Another good way to differentiate leadership from management is to remember that leadership is associated with effectiveness, whereas management is more aligned with efficiency. Good leaders effectively map out where the organisation needs to be in the next year and good managers devise efficient processes to achieve this.

> **Activity** 🕐 15 minutes
>
> Think of a situation where you have experienced first-hand ineffective leadership. This does not have to be a work-related experience, it may be something that occurred in your personal or social life, or even something you saw discussed in the media.
>
> Write a very short paragraph saying what the situation was and why, in your opinion, the leadership was ineffective, what was going wrong and what you would have done differently in that situation.

> **PLTS**
>
> When you are identifying improvements, you are practising your skills as an effective participator (EP).

Leadership styles

Autocratic leaders are **authoritarian**, do not listen to the views of their subordinates and make decisions based on the needs of the task, not the people. They expect staff to obey rules and do not seek their views. Autocratic leadership styles can be suitable in situations where team members are inexperienced, unskilled or need close monitoring. However, as team members become more experienced and develop higher skill levels, this type of leadership is inappropriate. It is also a suitable leadership style in a crisis situation, where every action can be critical. Over-use of this style of leadership, however, can understandably lead to low morale among the team.

Democratic leaders, on the other hand, are more **consultative** in their leadership style. They engage in two-way communication with their staff and ask their opinions, rather than simply imposing decisions upon them. Democratic leaders are concerned with relationship building and with encouraging their team to discuss their ideas and suggestions.

Laissez-faire styles of leadership leave the majority of decision-making and work processes to the team to decide and to implement. Laisscz-fare leaders have minimal input and involvement with their team. This type of leadership works well where a team is highly expert and experienced. However, it is unsuitable for unskilled or unmotivated team members.

> **Key Terms**
>
> **Authoritarian** – strict and controlling.
> **Consultative** – discussing issues with those affected before making a decision.
> **Laissez-faire** – a hands-off approach, leaving actions and responsibility to others.

Managerial grid

The Managerial Grid, shown in Figure B6.1 and created by Robert R. Blake and Jane Mouton, shows leadership style as being comprised of two elements:

- concern for people
- concern for production.

This model demonstrates the organisational requirement for looking after the interests of both the human and task elements of work, which must both function smoothly for an organisation to prosper. The model shows the likely problems that may arise as a result of focusing on only one of these elements; neglecting either the task or the people who perform them is inevitably going to lead to problems. Work targets or employee relations will suffer as a result. The model also shows the grave effects of neglecting both tasks and people. Interestingly, the approach that caters equally highly for production and people is referred to as the team management approach, which achieves its goals by careful integration of the production and human elements.

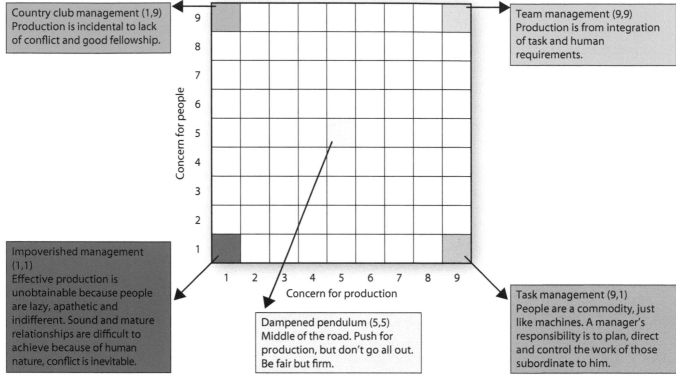

Country club management (1,9) Production is incidental to lack of conflict and good fellowship.

Team management (9,9) Production is from integration of task and human requirements.

Impoverished management (1,1) Effective production is unobtainable because people are lazy, apathetic and indifferent. Sound and mature relationships are difficult to achieve because of human nature, conflict is inevitable.

Dampened pendulum (5,5) Middle of the road. Push for production, but don't go all out. Be fair but firm.

Task management (9,1) People are a commodity, just like machines. A manager's responsibility is to plan, direct and control the work of those subordinate to him.

Figure B6.1 Managerial grid.

Management approach	Description
Country club management	A high concern for people but minimal concern for tasks. The thinking behind this approach is that by looking after your staff well, they will get the work done because they are happy.
Impoverished management	A neglectful type of management which focuses neither on tasks nor on people. This type of management occurs where people do just the minimum needed to get by. This approach will inevitably lead to major problems with both tasks and people.
Dampened pendulum	Adopts a middle of the road approach and, although there is a fair concern for both tasks and people, team performance will never be more than average.
Task management	A high concern for tasks ensures that performance targets are met and may even be exceeded. However, this approach entirely neglects the human factor and, as such, puts the team at risk of severe interpersonal problems and hence, low morale.
Team management	The ideal type of approach, as it shows equally high levels of concern for both the task and the human elements of the team. This ensures that people and processes are integrated for optimum performance and with the greatest degree of thought and consideration – which will go a very long way towards creating a good working environment and a climate of trust.

Table B6.1 Different management approaches.

Activity 🕐 15 minutes

Take another look at the diagram of the managerial grid and put a cross in the box that you think corresponds with where your production and people focus currently lies. Provide evidence from your work that backs up your answer. Write a short paragraph explaining what you have learned from this about your future leadership skills development.

PLTS

When you are adapting your behaviour to suit a leadership role, you are practising your skills as a team worker (TW).

Action Centred Leadership Model

The Action Centred Leadership Model, developed by the renowned leadership expert John Adair, is a very useful model for analysing leadership activities in terms of three elements – task, team and individual. The basic framework of this model is:

- build the team
- achieve the task
- empower the individual.

This model looks at leadership as an integrated activity, where you often need to combine two, or even all three of the elements, in order to resolve a problem.

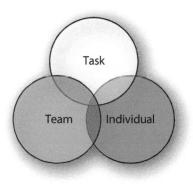

Figure B6.2 Action Centred Leadership Model
http://www.johnadair.co.uk, © John Adair.

Identifying leadership skills relevant to your career

You do not have to excel in all leadership skills we have looked at so far. Some of them may not even be relevant to you or to your role. The important thing for you at the moment is to identify those specific leadership skills, behaviours and abilities that will make you a more effective leader in your current position – and maybe those that will help propel you to your next position.

Activity 🕐 20 minutes

Take a look at the leadership skills checklist below and identify those specific skills relevant to your current role. For each one, explain why this skill is necessary. Next, rate yourself for each skill on a scale of 1–10, 1 being completely inexperienced and 10 being fully proficient.

Make sure you keep a copy of your notes as they will be very useful for completing Portfolio task 1 at the end of this section.

- Communication skills (written, verbal, presentation ability)
- Drive and motivation
- Dependability
- Persistence
- Ability to motivate others
- Vision
- Honesty and integrity
- Self confidence
- Ability to inspire trust
- Knowledge of the business and the industry in which it operates

PLTS

When you are assessing yourself, identifying opportunities and achievements, you are practising your skills as a reflective learner (RL).

You do not have to become expert in every possible leadership skill, concentrate on the areas that are central to the achievement of goals in your current role and prioritise your skills development needs by putting together a plan listing areas for current and future development. This will help you to avoid feeling overloaded.

Evaluate strengths within own area of responsibility

Evaluating your strengths is an important step in beginning the process of managing your own development. Effective managers need to accept responsibility for developing their leadership skills. This involves answering questions such as these.

- Where am I now?
- Where do I want to be?
- How do I get there?
- What help and resources will I need?

Appraisals

Appraisals are an essential tool for conducting a detailed evaluation of your current strengths in relation to your role and to discover which key areas need focus and development over the coming year.

Appraisals have many other benefits too. They are a valuable – and often rare – opportunity for employees to have one-to-one time with their manager, to review progress over the last year, to set goals and targets for the coming year and to discuss hopes, fears, ambitions and future career development opportunities.

When conducted well, the appraisal process can be a very positive experience, motivating employees and allowing them to reflect on their past performance, as well as considering their ambitions for the future. It can also be a great opportunity for managers to praise good performance and to offer assistance with areas that need development. This could take the form of in-house or external training courses or self-study opportunities.

Activity 🕐 30 minutes

Answer the questions below. This exercise will help you to evaluate your leadership skills.

1. What are your key job requirements?
2. List the key skills needed to perform these job requirements effectively.
3. How do you match up these skills requirements?
4. What skills do you posses that make you a good leader?
5. How can you capitalise on these skills?
6. What areas do you need to work on and develop?
7. How can you achieve this?
8. Which of these skills are priorities for you?
9. Are there any priority leadership skills in which you are not yet proficient?

Discuss your answers with your tutor.

Checklist

Your appraisal is your opportunity to:
- receive feedback on your current role
- let your manager know both the good and bad points of your current role
- discuss your career aspirations
- ask for support and training if required.

Good communications

A key requirement for effective appraisals, however, is to have good two-way communications between the manager and appraisee, based on genuine openness and honesty. Good communications may be difficult to establish where there is normally infrequent face-to-face contact between manager and employee during the course of the year. This often happens where, for example, each works from a different office, or where one or both parties are usually travelling, or even working remotely. Managers should attempt to remedy this lack of face-to-face contact by establishing regular, periodic meetings throughout the year, maybe monthly, or quarterly, for informal updates. This will help to build closer, more open relationships with staff, which will make the prospect of a face-to-face annual appraisal not seem so overbearing or unnatural for either party.

Formal and informal appraisals

Smaller organisations may have informal appraisals, or none at all. Larger companies usually have formal appraisal processes and associated paperwork. Although sometimes perceived as an administrative chore by both manager and employee, documenting the appraisal process in this way provides a formal record of the objectives and targets which have been set, along with a record of achievements that have been acknowledged. This information helps managers plan staffing issues for the year ahead, such as recruitment, promotion and succession planning, as well as sometimes being linked to pay awards and bonuses. Some organisations, however, keep appraisals and pay reviews separate from each other.

Most appraisals are carried out annually by line managers. However, sometimes they can be carried out more frequently than this. Also, there are other methods of carrying out appraisals, which involve people such as:

- colleagues
- subordinates
- other managers
- clients/customers
- other stakeholders.

Whatever the format, the normal procedure involves the completion of an appraisal form, which outlines the main skills areas of the employee, along with some form of scoring or judgement on performance achieved over the review period. A typical performance appraisal form is shown in Figure B6.3.

Self-appraisal

Self-appraisal is a surprisingly effective method of evaluating your strengths and weaknesses. In fact, most employees are tougher on themselves than their line manager would be. Self-appraisal can, however, seem awkward or uncomfortable, as many people are used to their line manager being responsible for scoring their performance and perhaps do not feel qualified to make such judgements.

Peer appraisal

Peer appraisal involves being appraised by your colleagues. You can either approach colleagues directly or else your line manager can approach your colleagues and incorporate this feedback into their own appraisal of your performance.

This system can work well where there are good working relationships between all parties. However, the peer appraisal process can be skewed by over- or under-scoring. This means that colleagues may give either too high or too low scores on the appraisal form due to inexperience or personal bias. This can be minimised by using feedback from as many peers as possible, as having more feedback to review reduces the impact of one or two skewed results.

PERFORMANCE APPRAISAL

Name:	Department:

Job title		Date of review	
Reviewer		Date started in role	

Objective #1	Rating:
	Comments:
Objective #2	Rating:
	Comments:
Objective #3	Rating:
	Comments:
Objective #4	Rating:
	Comments:

Employee statement:

Employer statement:

Signed (employee):	Date:
Signed (employer):	Date:

Figure B6.3 A typical performance appraisal form.

360 degree appraisal

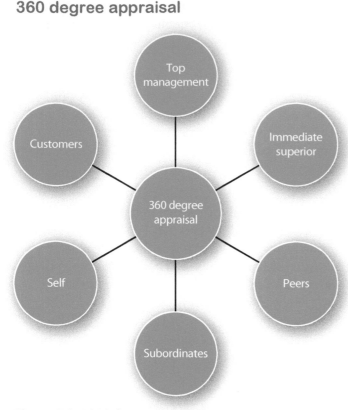

Figure B6.4 360 degree appraisal.

A 360 degree appraisal, as the name suggests, involves the collection of performance feedback from the full circle of those with whom you work – your superiors, subordinates and peers. It can also include feedback from external customers. The idea is that the appraisee benefits from these multiple perspectives on their performance and gains more valuable feedback on their role than would be received from the traditional method conducted solely by their line manager. Again, however, results can be skewed due to inexperience on the part of those providing feedback, as well as how well the parties get along. Overly critical comments can arise from parties who have a particular grudge, for example.

There are some clear benefits to the idea of collecting a wider range of feedback on employee performance. It takes into account the importance of a wider circle of work relationships. However, this method of appraisal is not widely used in organisations as it requires a large amount of input for each individual employee appraisal. It is therefore seen as expensive and time-consuming.

Action planning

Following your annual performance appraisal review, the next step is usually to create an action plan covering the next twelve months, which sets out the objectives/activities that you will undertake to further your personal development.

Action/objective	Resources	Due date
Improve time management	Read a time management text book	By the end of July
Improve skills in conducting performance appraisal reviews for my team	Appraisal skills training course	By the end of September
Improve knowledge of the industry and competitors	Attend conferences and seminars	By the end of the year
Develop assertiveness skills	Attend assertiveness training workshops	By the end of August

Table B6.2 An example of an action plan.

Remember

Where possible, your action plan objectives should be SMART – specific, measurable, achievable, realistic and time-bound.

Activity ⏱ 30 minutes

Have a go at completing an appraisal form for your current position. It does not matter if you have not yet done this at work. In fact it will be good experience for you. If you do not have an appraisal form at work, you can easily download a standard performance appraisal form from the internet and complete this.

PLTS

When you are assessing yourself and others, identifying opportunities and achievements, you are practising your skills as a reflective learner (RL).

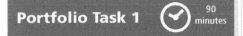

Portfolio Task 1 ⏱ 90 minutes

Links to LO1: Assessment criteria 1.1, 1.2

1. (a) Summarise the key leadership qualities you think are important in an effective leader. You may like to use examples of real leaders to illustrate your answer.

(b) Identify your own strengths and abilities as a leader.

2. Carry out an evaluation of your strengths within your own area of responsibility. It may help you to consider the strengths you already possess at the moment, as well as those skills you consider important to develop in the near future. You may like to use one or more of the management models discussed in this section to demonstrate where your skills currently lie.

Your assessment could take the form of a written narrative or a professional discussion with your assessor. It could also include the production of workplace evidence, work-based observations or the use of witness testimonies, as appropriate.

Functional Skills

If you take part in a professional discussion with your assessor as part of the assessment for this learning outcome, you will be practising your Level 2 Functional Skills in English: Speaking and Listening.

Be able to provide direction and set objectives in own area of responsibility

Providing overall direction and guidance to your team and being able to influence, persuade and motivate them to follow this, is one of the single most critical leadership qualities. Leaders who are able to achieve this will benefit from having a high-performing team whose work is aligned to the strategic vision of the business. In this section, you will investigate ways of setting the direction for your team so that their work supports the goals of the business. You will also look at ways of setting objectives with colleagues that are aligned to those of the organisation.

Outline direction for own area of responsibility

Have you ever stopped to think about the overall purpose of your job? Why does your role exist in the business? What exactly do you contribute to the business as a whole? By considering the bigger picture in this way, and by stopping to consider these questions, you can gain a better understanding of the way in which your team or department fits into the organisation. This will help you to effectively communicate this direction to your team.

Looking at the organisational structure chart for your business (if there is one) will also be useful in this respect, as it gives you a clear illustration of the position of your department and shows how it relates to other areas of the business.

Setting a clear direction

Providing clear direction helps your team understand the reason why they do what they do – and why their role is important. This reinforces a sense of self-worth and value among employees within the team. If people cannot see a reason for having to complete certain tasks, this can be a cause of frustration and resentment, which can lead to performance issues in the future.

Establishing a common purpose

Clear direction also provides the basis for establishing a common purpose and understanding, which are essential for good team morale and a co-operative team working spirit. It is also the basis for inspiring and motivating your team. All of these factors ultimately contribute to getting tasks completed on time and to a high standard because people understand their importance, are motivated to achieve and are inspired by feeling that their hard work is valued.

Motivated people make a tremendous difference to the performance of your team, as they will always go that extra mile and pull together at critical times. Unmotivated people, on the other hand, will not. They may not even care if a critical deadline is missed or that the quality of goods sent out to a customer is unsatisfactory.

> **Activity** 🕒 15 minutes
>
> Give a brief summary of the overall direction of your team covering the next twelve to twenty-four months. Include the long-term team goals that you are aware of and relate these to the organisation's goals.

Leading by example

Leading by example means behaving in ways that you expect your team to also behave. This is a key method of bringing about desired behaviour in your team, especially in relation to demonstrating ethical standards of behaviour. These standards could relate to direct customer contact, as well as liaison with contractors, suppliers and any other key business stakeholders.

By being seen to demonstrate high standards of behaviour yourself, your team will see that you have integrity, and they will follow your lead. You need to understand that your actions and behaviour have a profound effect on the working ethos of your team. Imagine, for example, that you had asked your team to work late one night this week to complete an order for a key client, but that you had gone home on time that particular night. You could rightly expect resentment from your team and a loss of trust and respect for expecting something from them which you were not yourself prepared to do.

Reinforcing team identity

Setting direction and focus for your team will serve to reinforce **team identity**, which is a distinguishing feature of high performing teams. Teams with a clearly communicated direction and focus have a strong sense of shared values and a common purpose – and this is what defines them and their work. Team identity is not only felt among team members themselves; it is also visible from the outside. If you have ever worked in an organisation where a particular team or

department were well known for their consistent brilliance, then you can be sure that this team has a strong sense of team identity and a very clear direction and focus.

If you work in a larger organisation with a suitable budget for such items, themes, branding and even slogans could also be used to reinforce company or team identity. They could be a highly innovative way of building up a shared identity among team members. Giveaways, such as branded laptop bags, baseball caps, T-shirts and mugs can also be effective in spreading the identity of the team.

> **Key Term**
>
> **Team identity** – commitment to shared values, behaviours and goals.

> **PLTS**
>
> When you are assessing yourself, identifying opportunities and achievements, you are practising your skills as a reflective learner (RL).

> **Activity** 🕒 15 minutes
>
> Review your skills in setting direction for your team by completing the following checklist. Tick one of the boxes below where 1 is no experience, 2 is fair and 3 is fully competent.
>
> | Skill area | Score | | |
> |---|---|---|---|
> | | 1 | 2 | 3 |
> | I clearly communicate to my team our required direction and focus | | | |
> | I support my team to provide direction for them by regular objective setting | | | |
> | I check to see how well my team understand the team direction | | | |
> | I take action to state and clarify direction to my team regularly | | | |
> | I take action to build team identity and shared values | | | |
>
> Review the results of your checklist and identify any areas in which you would like training or support to develop your skills.

Implement objectives with colleagues that align with those of the organisation

The overall mission, goals and targets of the organisation ultimately have to be cascaded through the departments and broken down into objectives, which are then set for individuals and teams to achieve. This process ensures that the tasks everyone works on are relevant to, and supportive of, the wider aims of the business.

Aligning objectives with organisational goals

It is essential that individual and team work objectives have a good fit with the goals of the organisation for the simple reason that it prevents wasted time and effort being spent on activities that do not support the organisation.

Strategic fit

When objectives are aligned to the wider goals of the organisation, they are said to have a good strategic fit. So, how can you establish whether your work objectives – and those of your team – have a good strategic fit? Remember how important this is in ensuring all activities are relevant to the wider goals of the business. The following is an example of how objectives can be developed based on the wider goals of the organisation.

The objective setting process

The first stage in the objective setting process is to identify the organisational goal from which the objective will be created. Figure B6.5 shows how this could work in practice.

We have arrived at an objective that each of the individual sales people needs to meet. This objective, if achieved by each of the outlets, will bring in an overall revenue for the business of nine million pounds.

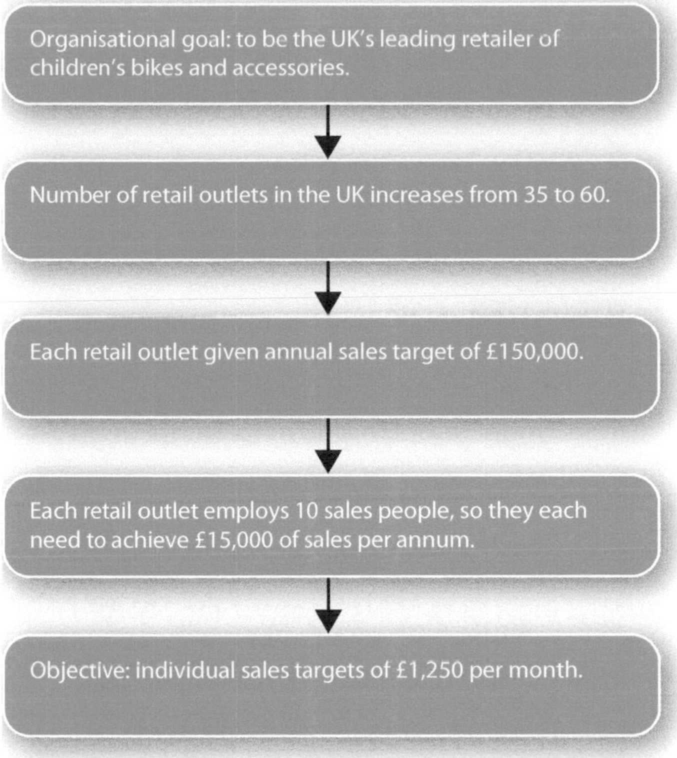

Organisational goal: to be the UK's leading retailer of children's bikes and accessories.

Number of retail outlets in the UK increases from 35 to 60.

Each retail outlet given annual sales target of £150,000.

Each retail outlet employs 10 sales people, so they each need to achieve £15,000 of sales per annum.

Objective: individual sales targets of £1,250 per month.

Figure B6.5 The process for breaking down organisational goals into work objectives.

This objective also satisfies the SMART criteria, which have been mentioned in units A2, B5 and D5 – it is specific, measurable, achievable, realistic and time-bound.

This objective is derived directly from the goal of the organisation by being broken down from a strategic, to a functional and then to an individual level. Team objectives could also be set by using this process. The way in which broad organisational goals can be broken down like this is to repeatedly ask the question 'How?' for each stage.

A final point to note from the example above is that there are potentially many more business objectives that could have been derived from this strategic goal. Think about the other functions of the business, such as marketing, human resources, IT and accounts, for example. Each of these will be able to derive their own departmental objectives from the overall business goal, according to what they specifically need to achieve.

Select a business goal relevant to your organisation. Then go back to the list used to arrive at a sales objective and use this same process to break down your organisational goal into a team or individual work objective, or set of objectives, that are relevant to your team.

When you are trying out alternatives or new solutions and following ideas through, you are practising your skills as a creative thinker (CT).

Make sure that the objectives you set for your team are generally achievable by the majority, not just the most talented (remember the SMART acronym). Failing to do this will ultimately cause feelings of resentment among team members, especially if achievements are linked to bonuses or other rewards.

If you use word processing software to produce a report for the assessment of this learning outcome, you will be practising your Level 2 Functional Skills in ICT: Developing, presenting and communicating information.

Be able to communicate the direction for own area of responsibility and collect feedback to inform improvement

In the previous section, you looked at the importance of outlining the direction for your area of responsibility. Now you'll examine ways in which you can best communicate direction to your team and create a strong sense of focus and team cohesion. You'll also look at ways of collecting feedback from others and using this to plan future improvements.

Communicate the agreed direction to individuals within own area of responsibility

Good communication is an essential skill for anyone in a leadership position. It is necessary to have communication skills to keep your team, your colleagues and your own line manager informed on progress and to make them aware of any specific issues needing attention. Good communication also ensures good working relationships among your team and also between teams and departments, as it allows smooth information flow. These are all essential elements of a successful business.

Links to LO2: Assessment criteria 2.1, 2.2

1. **(a)** Explain what you understand by the term 'direction' and say why outlining direction for your area of responsibility is an important aspect of a leadership role.
   (b) Give examples of ways in which you could outline direction for your own area of responsibility.
2. **(a)** Explain why objectives must be aligned to the goals of the organisation.
   (b) Give three examples of objectives you could implement with colleagues and demonstrate how they are each aligned to those of the organisation.

Your assessment could take the form of a written narrative or a professional discussion with your assessor. It could also include the production of workplace evidence, work-based observations or the use of witness testimonies, as appropriate.

The direction of the team is linked with the long-term strategy of the organisation and the bigger picture of where the team and the organisation are going. As a manager, you are in the unique position of being involved with both the strategic, as well as the tactical level of the business. In fact, you are the essential link between the two. You need to be able to clearly communicate the direction of the team as a whole, and of your individual team members.

Inspiring and motivating your team

The direction setting process should be inspirational. When your team have a good understanding of their long-term direction, and where the team is going, this allows them to see the bigger picture and they are more likely to be motivated about their specific role. They are also more likely to develop a good team-working spirit, because they can see the inter-relationship between their own and others' jobs and the reasons why specific daily tasks are important. Providing people with direction increases their involvement and their commitment.

Without the hard work, determination and efforts of its staff, no business will ever survive, let alone achieve success. To this end, inspiring and motivating your team by explaining the direction the team is aiming for and how they are a key part of this, will reap enormous rewards in developing a committed, focused and high performing team.

Checklist

When communicating direction to your team, try to:
- be inspirational
- create a strong sense of shared values
- regularly restate your key messages.

The communication process

In order to be an effective communicator, you need to have an understanding of the communication process. This process consists of:

- a sender – who sends out the message
- encoding of the message to be sent – via choice of words used and, importantly, the tone of the message
- the message itself – which is sent using a particular medium, such as email, written report, fax, face-to-face discussion
- the receiver – who receives the message
- decoding of the message – where the receiver interprets the contents and meaning of the message
- the response – where the receiver responds to the message according to how they have interpreted its meaning.

Barriers to effective communication

The communication process can fail at any stage. For example, external factors may be present, referred to as noise in Figure B6.6 on the following page, which distort or reduce the impact of the message so that the receiver does not receive the message as intended.

Errors in the communication process can also occur at the encoding or decoding stages. For example, the sender could select inappropriate words or phrases, which block the processing of the message. They may inadvertently either cause offence or total misunderstanding. Using the wrong tone in a message can have a similar blocking effect. The receiver then interprets the tone in some unintended way, maybe as aggressive, condescending or sarcastic – and creates a response that is a reaction to this misinterpretation.

The medium selected by the sender can also be a source of communication failure. This is why it is so important to plan out your message and think especially about how you are going to get it over to your audience. To illustrate this point, imagine how you would feel if you had been informed of your impending redundancy via SMS text message. This is an extreme case of choosing the wrong medium for communication.

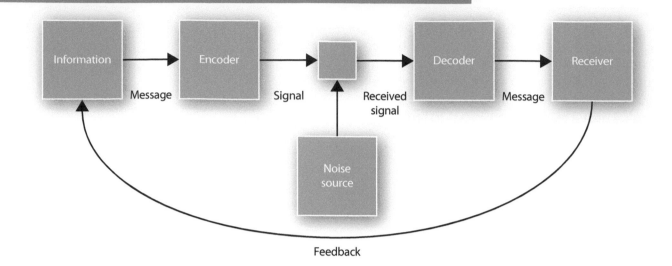

Figure B6.6 The communication process involves various stages.

Message characteristics

You need to get your message across to your team clearly, quickly and consistently so that everyone hears the same message – and hopefully remembers it – so you need to consider the tone of your communication. Remember that direction setting needs to be inspirational, so think about and rehearse the delivery of your communication if you are doing it as a presentation, so that it is uplifting and grabs the attention of your audience.

Good presentation skills also involve non-verbal elements, such as pace of speech, body language and mannerisms, good eye contact and facial expressions. Becoming practised in these skills will help to make your presentations lively, interesting and more likely to capture the attention of your audience.

Methods of communication

Next, we'll take a closer look at some of the different communication methods available to you, so that you can review the most appropriate methods for communicating direction to your own particular team.

Formal and informal communication

Communication can be formal or informal in nature. Formal communication methods include meetings and presentations, as well as one-to-one interviews and letters. Informal methods include emails, general discussions and conversations,

and newsletters. They could also include use of text messaging and other forms of social media networking, as well as internet messaging services, such as Windows Live® Messenger or Skype.

Formal communication methods are suitable for announcing important or business critical information, so as you can see, there is a case for using an element of formality in communicating direction to your team. However, one of the drawbacks of formal communication methods is that they do not always allow for much two-way exchange. Your team members may wish to ask questions to clarify meaning, so it could be advantageous to combine more than one method of communication, using a mixture of formal and informal techniques.

Verbal communication

Verbal or spoken communication includes face-to-face conversations, telephone calls and teleconferences. It can also include team or individual discussions (one-to-one or one-to-many communications). The key benefits of verbal forms of communication are that they allow free flowing two-way communication, as well as immediate checking of understanding and clarification. These types of communication are called **synchronous**.

Key Term

Synchronous – happening at the same time.

Activity   🕐   10 minutes

What do you think is the main disadvantage of using verbal communication methods, such as telephone calls? Think of a way to get around this disadvantage.

PLTS

When you are supporting conclusions using reasoned arguments and judgement, you are practising your skills as an independent enquirer (IE).

Written communication

Written communication methods in the workplace can include:

- letters
- emails
- faxes
- reports
- memos
- newsletters
- noticeboards
- intranet.

Information exchanges via written communications methods are said to be **asynchronous**, as they are all pre-prepared and then either sent or displayed. This has the benefit that the information contained within them is permanently available, so people can go back and re-read the information to check points of information, or take a copy of it and take it away for later reference.

Key Term

Asynchronous – where the sending and receiving of information do not happen at the same time, such as with a posted letter.

Visual and audiovisual communication

Visual and audiovisual communication methods can add an element of novelty and are good for capturing people's full attention. These types of communication can include:

- PowerPoint® presentations
- posters
- CDs and DVDs
- podcasts on the company intranet
- video presentations.

Planning your communication

Taking time out to plan your communication is the best way to make sure it achieves your aims. You need to consider factors such as:

- who your audience are (skilled, semi-skilled, old, young)
- how many of them there are (communicating to three people will require a different approach from communicating to a hundred, for example)
- their preferred methods of communication
- how they will best listen to – and remember – your message
- timing
- reinforcement of messages by regular reminders – never assume that everyone will remember all they have heard first time round.

Remember

Taking time out to plan your communication will ensure you produce the best results possible. It will also prevent blocks to your communication, which can ruin the impact of your key messages.

Communication plan for outlining direction to my team for the 12 month period from .... to			
Key objectives:			
1. To present the direction in which our team is headed, including our priorities, development plan and key target areas.			
2. To increase motivation and commitment by emphasising the importance of each individual team member's role in achieving our long-term goals.			
Audience	**Key messages**	**Communication method(s)**	**Timing**

Figure B6.7 A communication plan.

Using a communication-planning tool similar to the one above will help you to map out your communication plan prior to implementing it. Ask your assessor or a colleague at work to look over it for you and make any suggestions for improvements. Remember to think about the communication process you looked at earlier to make sure that you match your message to its medium and to your audience.

Collect feedback to inform improvement

We all rely on feedback to find out how well we are doing, to get positive reinforcement and to receive guidance on where we need to make changes. From learning to read to learning to manage a team, or even a company, feedback is what allows us to make progress, learn and achieve.

Types of feedback

Feedback can be given formally, as occurs in meetings and by completing official appraisal forms, or it can be provided informally, via email or even a brief chat. Formal feedback is likely to be more detailed and more time consuming to collect, whereas informal feedback is probably quicker and easier to obtain. Both types of feedback have value, however, and trying to obtain a mix of both formal and informal feedback will give you a good balance between the two.

Frequency of feedback

There is a simple rule of thumb for frequency of feedback and that is to obtain it as frequently as is practically possible. Monthly or quarterly feedback is a good idea, if you can find ways to keep to this schedule.

Ideally, feedback should be part of a continual process and not, as is sadly the case in so many organisations, an annual, box-ticking formality. The more frequently it occurs, the more natural the process becomes and it is also easier to then take on board negative feedback in the true spirit in which it was given – to help you improve. Formal annual appraisals can be overly procedural and can be uncomfortable for both the appraiser and appraisee. This means that nobody really benefits from using the time as an opportunity to discuss hopes, fears, ambitions and dreams – which is central to inspiring and motivating staff.

Feedback sources

Who should you ask to provide feedback to you on your performance? The simple answer to this is anyone who is well placed to give you useful and valid information, which you can use to make future improvements. It may be a useful starting point to use the 360 degree model of appraisal and, for each group represented within it, select individuals who you think could give you particularly insightful comments and advice.

Activity 20 minutes

Using the 360 degree model of appraisal, identify all of the potential people in your organisation who could provide valuable feedback to you. Give an example of the type of feedback each of these people could provide and say how this would be useful to you.

Be able to assess own leadership performance

Assessing your own leadership performance requires a certain amount of skill and objectivity on your part. You need to be able to review and analyse your past performance and use your experiences to decide what behaviours you would repeat, as well as what you would do differently in the future. We'll begin this section by looking at assessment of feedback on your leadership performance.

Assess feedback on own leadership performance

Once you have received feedback on your leadership performance, what do you do with it? How can you **assimilate** all of this information into a meaningful analysis? The first thing to do is to read over any paperwork and recount the main points raised in any verbal discussions. Next, make notes on the main themes that you noticed running through the feedback. Use headings and bullet points to keep the information as clear and as simple as possible. If a particular point was made on more than one occasion, this adds weight to its credibility.

Note down the most important points, paying special attention to areas where you were:

- excellent
- fair
- in need of improvement.

> **Key Term**
>
> **Assimilate** – to take in and understand fully.

What the feedback tells you

Go back to the leadership models that were discussed in the first section of this unit and see, based on your feedback, where you are in terms of:

- the managerial grid – concern for people/ concern for production
- the action centred leadership model – team, task, individual.

Portfolio Task 3 ⏱ 90 minutes

Links to LO3: Assessment criteria 3.1, 3.2

1. (a) Give reasons why providing direction to your team is a key leadership skill.

(b) Demonstrate ways in which you have, or could, communicate the agreed direction to individuals within your own area of responsibility.

2. (a) Explain the value of collecting feedback to inform improvement to your leadership performance. Give examples of people in your organisation from whom you might collect such feedback.

(b) Give examples of feedback you have obtained to inform improvement.

(c) Say in what way this feedback will help you to develop your leadership skills.

Your assessment could take the form of a written narrative or a professional discussion with your assessor. It could also include the production of workplace evidence, work-based observations or the use of witness testimonies, as appropriate.

> **PLTS**
>
> When you are generating ideas and exploring possibilities, you are practising your skills as a creative thinker (CT).

> **Remember**
>
> Try to find ways of obtaining feedback from others on a regular basis. The more frequent the feedback process, the better and more useful it will be for you.

> **Functional Skills**
>
> If you produce a written report as part of the assessment for this learning outcome, you will be practising your Level 2 Functional Skills in English Writing.

Is this a picture of you as a leader where you want to be? If not, you need to look into the areas where you should develop skills to enhance your profile to where you feel it needs to be. This could mean a move from concern for people, for example, to an equally strong concern for production. It could mean less telling and more selling. The type of leader you wish to become is an entirely personal decision and it is only you who can decide what is right for you.

Dealing with difficult feedback

If you receive feedback with which you disagree, do not discount it immediately. Review it and reflect on it for a while. If it initially leaves you feeling angry or upset, you need to create some distance by coming back to it the next day, or maybe a few days later, with a calmer, more considered and more reflective response. It is entirely possible that someone has misinterpreted some aspect of your behaviour and created a biased view of you on this basis. On the other hand, it could indicate an area for future development.

Remember that you do have the opportunity to respond to comments made about your performance as a part of the appraisal process. So if, after due consideration, you still disagree with a comment made, you can give your reply, but make sure to do so in a professional and courteous manner.

Evaluate own leadership performance

Now that you have gone through the process of receiving and assessing the feedback on your performance from your manager, and maybe also from colleagues and other relevant stakeholders, you will have a fairly good picture of how your skills rank according to the various aspects of your leadership performance. If your assessment consisted of feedback from more than one other person you will also have a good picture of the general trends that will have emerged.

Your next task is to evaluate this feedback. Evaluating comments received and identifying

common themes in the feedback will allow you to see at a glance the areas in which you are perceived to be strong, as well as those areas where you need to develop your leadership skills. It may well be that if you are a relatively new manager, you simply haven't yet had opportunities to carry out some leadership tasks. But don't worry, you have plenty of time to be able to acquire all of these skills in the future.

Identifying and building on your strengths

A good starting point is to list the common areas that have been noted as your key leadership qualities. These could include your excellent interpersonal skills, your ability to envisage the bigger picture of where your team or department is going (your vision), or it could be your tenacity and determination in seeing tasks through and motivating your team to perform – especially during the tough times.

Once you have compiled your list of strengths, you are now in a position to identify which of these you can capitalise upon and identify the help and resources you may need to achieve this. You should make time to speak to your line manager or HR department to establish specific developmental activities, training or learning which may be appropriate for you.

Activity — 15 minutes

Make a list of what you believe to be your key leadership strengths. For each strength discuss one possible method of building upon this over the next twelve months. Remember to also identify any additional resources or help that you will need to do this.

PLTS

When you are assessing your performance and identifying opportunities and achievements, you are practising your skills as a reflective learner (RL).

Key area for development	Resources or approval required	Activity to be undertaken	Time, venue and date	Review of developmental activity
Presentation skills		Present to the senior management team on my team's progress against targets	At the end of each operating quarter	
Report writing	Assistance from line manager	Produce month end reports for management	At the end of each month	
Knowledge of the industry	Line manager approval	Attend industry annual conference	Glasgow, 26–28 March	

Table B6.3 Leadership skills annual development plan.

Taking action to develop weaker areas

The next stage of evaluating the feedback on your leadership performance is to analyse the areas identified as either needing improvement or those in which you do not yet have any experience. You should set aside time to sit down with your line manager to review these areas for development.

One good approach is to formulate a personal development plan, either on your own, or in conjunction with your manager or assessor. For each key development area, plan activities, work experience or training initiatives specifically designed to allow you to develop your skills in these target areas. Table B6.3 is a basic example of how you could produce a development plan.

Remember

The secret to effective development is to keep activities regular and review progress often. You can do this by setting up monthly review meetings with either your line manager or your assessor.

Activity 20 minutes

Produce your own personalised development plan based on the key leadership skills you identified earlier as needing development. You can use the template provided in the illustration as a basis for completing this. Ask your assessor to help you if necessary.

Portfolio Task 4 90 minutes

Links to LO4: Assessment criteria 4.1, 4.2

1. **(a)** Describe the reasons why obtaining feedback on performance is beneficial. Give examples of some of the individuals who might be well placed to provide such feedback to you and why.
   (b) Provide examples of actual feedback you have received on your own leadership performance.
   (c) Give your own assessment of your leadership performance.

2. Carry out an evaluation of your own leadership performance. You can ask your line manager or your assessor to help you go through this process.

Your assessment could take the form of a written narrative or a professional discussion with your assessor. It should also include the production of workplace evidence, work-based observations or the use of witness testimonies, as appropriate.

PLTS

When you are evaluating experiences and learning to inform future progress, you are practising your skills as a reflective learner (RL).

Functional Skills

If you take part in a professional discussion with your assessor as part of the assessment for this learning outcome, you will be practising your Level 2 Functional Skills in English: Speaking and Listening.

Team talk

Kelly's story

My name is Kelly Bromwell and I am 32 years old. I have been a manager in a bar restaurant for five weeks and am responsible for six staff. It is my first experience of management so I have been slightly apprehensive. However, at the same time, I am also determined to make a good first impression on my boss in my new role. My team all get along with each other very well and even regularly socialise together outside of work.

I have begun to notice some issues, however. The staff do not seem to have a strong customer service ethic at all. They do not seem to notice when customers are kept waiting, nor do they seem overly concerned that customers are often served the wrong dishes.

They also happily chat with one another while customers are left waiting to be seated.

I know that the situation is unacceptable but I do not want to appear heavy handed and create an unpleasant working environment – especially as they all get on so well with one another. It seems to me that, although the people working here are happy, the jobs at hand are not being given the focus they require.

Top tips

Style of management needs to align with the staff and their tasks. A strong management focus on concern for task completion will ensure the customer service levels among the team are drastically improved. Combining this task focus with a concern for the staff will ensure that the working environment remains pleasant and that the staff remain happy in their jobs.

Ask the expert	
Q	My team does not have a very good attitude towards customer service. I need to do something to change this but am unsure of how to go about it – or which management style to adopt in this new role.
A	You need to take more of a task-based than a people-based approach to managing the team, as this is an area that has clearly not been very well handled by the previous manager. You also need to introduce customer service standards to the team that address all of your key performance areas. This will be an excellent method of underlining your task focus. The sooner you do this, the sooner your team will improve the level of service they provide.

What your assessor is looking for

In order to prepare for and to succeed in completing this unit, your assessor will require you to be able to demonstrate competence in:

- leading in your own area of responsibility
- providing direction and setting objectives in your own area of responsibility
- communicating the direction for your own area of responsibility and collecting feedback to inform improvement
- assessing your own leadership performance.

You will demonstrate your skills, knowledge and competence through the learning outcomes in this unit. Evidence generated in this unit will also cross reference to the other units in this qualification.

Please bear in mind that there are significant cross-referencing opportunities throughout this qualification and you may have already generated some relevant work to meet certain criteria in this unit. Your assessor will provide you with the exact requirements to meet the standards of this unit. However, as a guide it is likely that for this unit you will need to be assessed through the following methods:

- One observation of relevant workplace activities to cover the whole unit.
- One witness testimony may also be produced.
- A written narrative, reflective account or professional discussion.

- Any relevant work products to be produced as evidence.

The work products for this unit could include:

- your team's development plans and long-term goals
- communications between you and your team concerning direction and goals
- examples of feedback you have been given on your performance
- your own performance appraisal and personal development plans.

Your assessor will guide you through the assessment process as detailed in the candidate logbook. The detailed assessment criteria are shown in the logbook and by working through these questions, combined with providing the relevant evidence, you will meet the learning outcomes required to complete this unit.

Task and page reference	Assessment criteria
1 (page 179)	1.1, 1.2
2 (page 182)	2.1, 2.2
3 (page 187)	3.1, 3.2
4 (page 189)	4.1, 4.2

Unit C6 Implement change in own area of responsibility

Change is an inevitable factor that for many reasons organisations must take on board. For instance, new legislation may be introduced that affects the way your organisation has to do things or you may face competition from a new rival entering your market, putting extra strain on your resources.

Whatever the reason for change, it must be managed effectively to ensure that everybody involved is clear why the change is happening and what the benefits, if any, are likely to be. The reasons for change must be communicated effectively before rumours take hold, creating an atmosphere of insecurity. It is important to get everybody working together to ensure there is a smooth transition period as the change is introduced.

This unit will explore the planning and management of change helping you to understand some of the key problems associated with a change programme and the best practice that can be applied to the introduction of something new, be it large or small scale.

What you will learn

- Understand how to implement change in own area of responsibility
- Be able to involve and support others through the change process
- Be able to implement and monitor a plan for change in own area of responsibility

Links to the Technical Certificate

If you are completing your NVQ as part of an Apprenticeship Framework, you will find the following topics are also covered in your Technical Certificate:

- Understanding how to implement organisational change
- Understanding the need for organisational change
- Be able to plan for organisational change

Understand how to implement change in own area of responsibility

It is almost impossible to prevent changes from occurring in your workplace and often changes are necessary if an organisation is to survive. It is important for any changes to be implemented and managed carefully if the effects of the changes are to be accepted by everyone concerned. You should also be aware that changes made anywhere within your organisation may have a direct impact upon your own area of responsibility.

Often changes in a workplace occur because:

- costs need to be reduced
- restructuring is to take place (e.g. a merger process)
- flexible working patterns need to be accommodated
- **lean systems** and **continuous improvement strategies** are introduced
- customer response times need to be improved
- there is a crisis of some type.

Key Terms

Continuous improvement strategy – policy to improve the overall quality of the organisational process, for example, total quality management.

Lean systems – ways of working that simplify processes and organise the working environment to minimise waste, and keep people and equipment working adequately to meet demands.

Remember

Changes bring about new challenges, so it is necessary for staff to be both adaptable and flexible in the face of change.

Changes might need to take place in your organisation to ensure that it remains profitable or can maintain its ability to attract funds. There are several external and internal factors that your organisation may need to respond to, including:

- environmental factors – changes in the law or customers' tastes, trends or fashions, such as whether they choose to select and buy goods and services online
- organisational factors – changing corporate objectives, restructuring
- changes in the market place – decisions to increase market share, or introduce a new range to equal or better competitors; fluctuation in customer demand, for instance in response to the economic climate forcing changes to an organisation's range of products or services
- working processes – introducing multi-skilling or flexible working arrangements to satisfy staff while still meeting customer demand; new policies and procedures or new production lines
- technological factors – equipment might become obsolete or new systems introduced in order to remain competitive
- staffing considerations – training programmes for the latest procedures or equipment being introduced; new shift patterns such as flexible working
- industry changes – changing best practice within the industry requiring organisations to conform; scientific breakthroughs or new industry-led regulations encouraging change
- legislation – new laws requiring changes to the way things are done. This is seen particularly in health and safety, consumer protection and employment law.

Remember

Large scale changes that take place in larger organisations may result in managers involving and negotiating with trade unions at the planning stage.

Tesco plc recently made changes to the way in which it looks after its staff's welfare. Introducing a motto that Tesco is 'A great place to work', it aims to develop its staff by offering study leave, lifestyle breaks, time off for training to become foster parents and other ideas. At its head office, there is an Attendance and Flexibility Manager who oversees these initiatives.

Activity ⏰ 30 minutes

Think of some changes that you have made in your personal life. Consider what prompted you to identify that a change was needed and how you planned for it. Also think about how effective your plans were and whether upon evaluation, the change(s) you made have been successful.

Write down your responses and discuss them with your assessor.

How to plan for change

When planning change in your own area of responsibility, you should consider:

- how your team members will react
- how the culture may need to change
- how the change will be scheduled
- what resources you will need (time, money, equipment and so on)
- what training will be required
- what additional health and safety considerations you will have
- whether there will be major disruption to normal day to day activities during the change process.

Your team members are likely to ask the following:

- Why is this change taking place?
- What is wrong with the way we do things now?
- How will things be improved?
- Will the change(s) affect our job security?
- What will happen if we just carry on the way we are?

You must update the people you manage on a regular basis and be prepared to explain the reasons for the change that is taking place. You should do this as early as possible before starting to plan for the change as this will help to get people on board to work with you, rather than against you.

Change within an organisation can be:

- inevitable – for example, if environmental factors make it impossible not to change

- imposed – for example a change in government policy or legislation forcing you to change the way things are done
- initiated – your organisation chooses to make changes, for example in response to a threat from a competitor in the market place or introducing new working processes to become more competitive.

Intel undertook what it described as a major change, when it was faced with huge competition from other memory chip manufacturers. Top management responded by changing Intel's processes, which affected staff at all levels. This is a good example of a large organisation using a potential crisis as an opportunity to change things for the better.

You should be aware that it may not always be necessary, or appropriate, to make large scale changes that affect the whole of the organisation at the same time. Often incremental changes will be met with less resistance from employees.

Remember

Fear of the unknown is one of the biggest obstacles to the acceptance of change.

Resistance to change

When changes occur, people are often taken out of their **comfort zone** and may start to feel unhappy in the workplace. This can have a serious negative impact upon levels of morale and motivation, leading to underperformance. When managing a change process in your own area of responsibility, you should consider that your team members may experience:

- increased levels of stress, as they get used to doing things differently
- increased levels of conflict due to varying levels of confidence as they adapt to changes
- an overwhelming desire to go back and do things the old way.

Key Term

Comfort zone – where people feel at home and like to exist in the general conducting of their daily lives, carrying out tasks in a familiar, non-threatening way.

Models and methods for managing change

Approaches to managing change vary, depending on the type of changes that need to happen and the way your managers involve staff members in the decision-making process. Your senior managers may take various different approaches, such as:

- making major changes without consulting staff members
- calling meetings with staff members to obtain their views and opinions
- negotiating ways forward that will introduce changes while keeping everyone as content as possible.

Activity 45 minutes

Identify a change that has occurred in your own workplace (or something that you think should be changed in some way). Write down your views on whether managers approached, or would approach, the change in a way that 'told' staff what was happening, 'involved' staff to obtain their views or 'negotiated' a way forward with staff.

Which do you think is the best way to manage change?

Share your responses with your assessor.

Kurt Lewin model of change

In 1951, Kurt Lewin, a theorist who researched the concept of change in the workplace, developed a three-phrase model of change. Lewin suggested that the following steps should be undertaken if the change process is to be successful.

Figure C6.1 Kurt Lewin model of change.

Unfreeze

This step examines the unfreezing of current behaviour of employees. In other words, managers should involve employees from the outset and raise awareness of the need for change. It may be necessary to point out to employees that their current habits and attitudes towards their work may have to alter to accommodate the changes that need to be made. Communicating the reasons for the changes well in advance is very important, as this can help to get employees on board by understanding why the change process is necessary.

Change

The second step is to actually make the changes happen. This will include establishing new behaviours, systems and procedures and perhaps, in some cases, a restructure of the organisation, possibly leading to redundancies or changes to shift patterns.

Re-freezing

This final step involves stabilising the changes. At this stage, feedback from employees is crucial and top management support must be evident. New **values** and new lines of communication will help to stop the old ways of doing things from creeping back into the **culture** of the workplace. Employees should be re-frozen into the new practices and ways of doing things and prevented from reverting to the old ways of doing things.

Key Terms

Culture – written or unwritten code of an organisation that influences the staff attitudes, management decision-making and style. How things are done in an organisation.

Values – standards or principles of individuals or organisations.

Activity 45 minutes

Think of your own area of responsibility. Identify a change that has happened, or in your view needs to happen. Write down how you think the steps of Lewin's three-phase model could help the smooth transition of the change you have identified. Discuss your findings with your assessor.

The organisational development approach

Some organisations use an organisational development approach to change management. This requires support from senior managers so that everyone in the organisation is encouraged to play a part in driving the change process forward.

Generally the organisational development approach to change encourages:

- the inclusion of everyone in the decision making process
- the involvement of everyone concerned to make the change
- a change of the organisation's culture, so that a change programme is accepted by all
- the use of **change agents** to maximise the chance of success
- an effective process of regular communication
- teams or departments being part of the design and implementation of the change process.

Key Term

Change agent – someone appointed to oversee the process of change from start to finish and to work with everyone involved in the process, offering constructive advice to overcome any problems.

Change agents

Organisational development (OD) is concerned with the long-term views of how change needs to be implemented and then changing the attitudes of employees so that a new culture of mutual trust is created.

Change agents play an important part in the planning and implementation of change in the workplace and are therefore an important aspect of the OD approach.

Change agents can be:

- internal – someone with a vast knowledge of how the organisation works and very familiar with the existing culture, systems and procedures. A potential problem with an internal change agent is that through their experience of working in the organisation for a considerable period of time, they may have become stale in their working practices and ways of thinking, meaning they may not have sufficient vision to effectively see through the change.

- external – someone appointed (usually as a consultant) to oversee the change process. Being brought in from the outside means that the agent will have a fresh approach towards the organisation's circumstances and won't be influenced by current systems procedures or the culture of the organisation. Equally they might not understand the need to maintain certain fundamental aspects of work processes through the change.

An example of an organisational development model for change is shown below. The appointed change agent will be responsible for overseeing each stage of the model and keeping everyone involved.

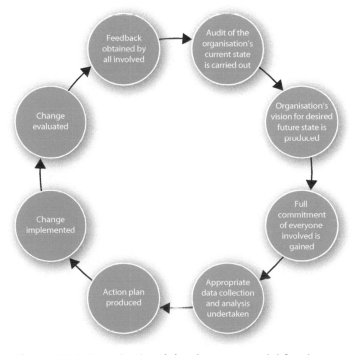

Figure C6.2 Organisational development model for change.

Organisational development is a suitable approach for planned or incremental change programmes. It is not ideally suited to rapid change, which may be required, for example in a time of crisis.

Strategic planning and change

Organisations often change the way things are done in response to their strategic planning activities. When creating a strategic plan, managers will often begin by asking three crucial questions:

- Where is the organisation now?
- Where does the organisation want to be?
- How will it get there?

SWOT analysis

To assist with the strategic planning process management tools, including SWOT analyses, can be used as seen in Tables C6.1 and C6.2. The acronym SWOT stands for:

- Strengths
- Weaknesses
- Opportunities
- Threats.

Strengths	Weaknesses
Good brand products	Product not profitable
Quality	Low budgets
Experienced management team	Poor labour relations
	Poor training
Expertise	

Opportunities	Threats
Exploitation of market share	Competitors
Profit potential	Price wars
Acquisitions	European law restrictions
Economies of scale	Imports

Table C6.1 A simple SWOT analysis.

All strategic planning needs to be carefully worked on by management.

A SWOT analysis examines what an organisation is good at, what needs improving, what opportunities there are for developing or growing the organisation and what obstacles or dangers may arise from threats posed by groups of stakeholders such as competitors.

PESTLE analysis

A PESTLE analysis will also assist with the strategic planning process.

A PESTLE analysis examines the internal and external influences placed upon an organisation that may affect its ability to trade successfully if it doesn't react to them. An example is shown in Table C6.2.

The acronym PESTLE stands for:

- Political
- Economic
- Social
- Technological
- Legal
- Environmental.

Economic	Social	Technological
• Interest rates • Inflation • Wage costs • Unemployment • Disposable income • Recession • Consumer confidence	• Attitudes to work and leisure • Lifestyle changes • Social mobility • Population demographics • Levels of education	• Increase in use of internet • Government and industry focus on technology • Government spending on research • ICT developments • New production methodologies
Political	**Legal**	**Environmental**
• Local government rules and regulations • Government funding • Taxation	• Employment law • Health and safety law • Advertising laws • Competition laws • Foreign trade regulations	• Environmental legislation • Environmental impacts • Energy consumption • Reducing waste • Other green issues

Table C6.2 An example of a PESTLE analysis.

Once PESTLE and SWOT analyses have been conducted and the need for change identified, decision making and planning activity to take the organisation into the future will follow.

You need to be aware that large-scale changes may occur in your workplace and, on occasion, change may be necessary in your own area of responsibility. This can sometimes be as a direct result of the large-scale changes taking place in your organisation that has a knock on effect in your department, or a change that has been identified purely within your own department. Either way, it is important for you to be able to implement and manage the change process in a way that will meet with as little resistance as possible.

You need to have sound answers to the following:

- What is to be achieved by making the change?
- Who will be appointed as a change agent?
- What tools and techniques are to be used?
- Who will the change affect?
- How will everyone affected be involved?
- Has a plan been produced that includes deadlines to be met?
- How will reasons and benefits of the change be communicated to everyone affected?
- How regularly will everyone be updated on progress?
- How will the views and opinions of everyone involved be collected?
- What resources will be needed for the change programme?
- What training requirements will be necessary to successfully implement the change?
- How will the change be monitored and evaluated after implementation?

Force Field Analysis

As you work towards the implementation of your change programme, you will need to carefully consider the factors that will help the change process and also those that may hamper the process. A useful tool to help you to identify these factors is Kurt Lewin's Force Field Analysis.

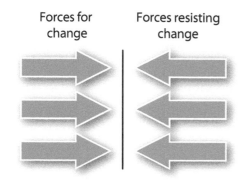

| Forces for change | Forces resisting change |

Figure C6.3 Kurt Lewin's Force Field Analysis

The Force Field Analysis model offers the opportunity to consider factors that will drive the change forward (the driving **forces**) and those that will present potential obstacles (the restraining forces). To use this model effectively, you should list the forces working for and against the change(s) being made as illustrated in Table C6.3.

Driving forces		Restraining forces
• New challenges • Opportunities for self-development • Meeting new people • Increased job satisfaction	C H A N G E	• Loss of status or power • Job insecurity • New managers to work with • Less interesting work

Table C6.3 Forces working for and against change.

The example uses the model to consider the effects of a merger between two organisations.

Some managers score the forces for and against in terms of strength (e.g. 1 = low and 5 = high). This establishes whether there is more emphasis on driving or restraining forces.

The above forces are suggested responses that employees are likely to contribute when asked about their feelings towards a drastic change such as a merger. Of course, in a real workplace situation these lists will probably be considerably longer. The Force Field Analysis can help to alter people's perception of the forces driving change resulting in a fresh attitude and outlook.

Key Term

Force – an influence that results in change.

Remember

Managers sometimes refer to the Force Field Analysis as being the same as the OD model discussed earlier.

Portfolio Task 1 45 minutes

Links to LO1: Assessment criterion 1.1

As discussed above, there are a number of models and methods to assist you in managing change. Write down a brief description of the models, methods and/or tools you use or would use to manage change within your department. Discuss your responses with your assessor.

PLTS

Through evaluating your current tools and techniques used for change management, you will demonstrate your skills as an independent enquirer, analysing and evaluating information, judging its relevance and value (IE).

Activity  45 minutes

Think of something that needs changing or that you would like to change in your own area of reasonability. Produce a Force Field Analysis to identify the factors for and against your proposed change.

Be able to involve and support others through the change process

It's not always easy to convince people that change can also bring benefits. Often employees associate the word 'change' with 'redundancy'. For this reason, managers must emphasise any benefits and explain how the proposed change will benefit individuals, departments or the organisation as a whole. For instance they could show how change could bring increased responsibility for those who want it, improved working conditions, opportunities for self-development and possibly incentives such as salary increases and bonuses. They also need to support staff through these changes, both positive and negative.

Communicating the benefits of change

It is important to communicate the reasons for change to everyone affected well in advance of the changes happening. The earlier everyone is informed of the pending changes, the earlier they may start working with managers rather than against them as the change programme unfolds.

Naturally people will want to know how change will affect them, and it is therefore very important to clearly communicate the benefits that the change may bring. Examples of benefits that could be communicated include:

- reduced costs, leading to greater profits and therefore *enhanced job security*
- increased efficiency, leading to greater customer satisfaction and therefore *enhanced job security*
- expansion of the organisation offering new opportunities, leading to *enhanced morale and motivation* of employees
- introduction of new technologies making the organisation more competitive, therefore *enhancing job security*
- redesigned job description through consultation, leading to *increased morale and motivation*

- improved image and reputation of the organisation, leading to *enhanced job security*.

Initially, responses from employees may be negative and they may show resistance to the changes being made. It is likely that training may be necessary for both existing and new employees to make sure that they will become familiar with the new ways of doing things. However, training is a cost to the organisation and must be factored in to the financial considerations of any change programme.

Portfolio Task 2 ⏱ 60 minutes

Links to LO2: Assessment criteria 2.1, 2.2

Communicating the need for change within your department is vital to ensure the success of the plan.

Provide examples to your assessor of how you communicate a change to your team. This could be in the form of team meeting minutes where it is noted that the benefits and reasons of the change and how the change is related to the overall business objectives have been discussed. A change proposal you have prepared will also cover this criterion.

Discuss the benefits, reasons for the change and how it links in to the business objectives with your assessor.

PLTS

If you present a change proposal you have prepared to your assessor, this document will allow you to demonstrate your self-manager skills, seeking new challenges, setting goals, organising time and resources and managing risks (SM1, 2, 3, 4, 5).

Remember

Not everyone responds to change with negativity. Some people view change as a 'breath of fresh air' and actually welcome new ways of doing things.

Unit C6 Implement change in own area of responsibility

If you present a prepared proposal to your assessor in the above task, this will assist you in developing your Level 2 Functional Skills in English: Writing. You will need to demonstrate that you have presented information/ideas in a logical order, presented complex subjects clearly and concisely, used a range of writing styles and a range of sentence structures within the document. Appropriate punctuation is needed and the written work must be fit for purpose and audience.

Communicating the reasons for change

Whatever the reasons for the changes taking place and whatever the benefits are likely to be, it is important to communicate regularly and effectively with everyone involved, throughout the whole change process. You must think about how you will get the right message to the right people and at the right time. Don't forget that feedback from those people is vital to help you assess how well the change process is being accepted at any given time.

Remember

A change programme will not always bring with it good news. Unfortunately there may on some occasions be negative outcomes, such as redundancies. It is just as important to communicate bad news as it is good news so that everyone knows what to expect, and to support individual employees through any bad outcomes for them.

Activity 30 minutes

Spend some time thinking about why it is important to obtain feedback from people you manage during a change process. How important do you think it is to obtain their views and opinions and why? Write down your responses and discuss them with your assessor.

It is not a good idea to tell colleagues important information one-by-one.

The key to effective communication is to make sure that everyone receives necessary information at the same time. If one sub-group in the team that you manage receives news of the change or an update on developments before another sub-group, then this is likely to lead to:

- suspicion that the change programme is not being managed effectively or properly
- mistrust of you and other managers
- rumours of what the change is and how it will affect everyone
- conflict between sub-groups in your team
- accusations of favouritism towards one sub-group in your team.

You will need to think about the best method to communicate what is being changed and why to everyone concerned at the same time. You may, for example, be able to set up a special team meeting.

The information you give must be accurate and if you don't know something it is better to be honest about it and admit it. You can always promise to find out and then update everyone later, which is far better than pretending you have the answer when you don't.

> **Remember**
>
> Asking for feedback from people affected by the change not only informs you of how they feel, but it also makes them feel involved in the process. Showing you care and value their views helps increase morale and motivation at a time of insecurity.

Brainstorming activity

Once you are ready to communicate the reasons and potential benefits of the proposed change you should arrange a team meeting where you encourage everyone to contribute their views and opinions of the proposed change. At this stage, your team members should be aware of your aim, objective, reasons for change and potential benefits of it.

You could conduct a **brainstorm** activity and use the responses to produce a **fishbone diagram**.

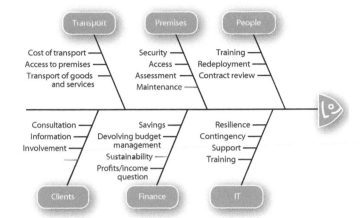

Figure C6.4 A fishbone diagram.

> **Key Terms**
>
> **Brainstorm** – spontaneous group discussion to generate ideas and solve problems.
>
> **Fishbone diagram** – a diagram that identifies possible causes of a problem or reasons for change.

Place the problem or issue that the proposed change will resolve in the head of the 'fish', and the ideas generated from the activity on the 'bones' of the fish, under headings agreed by the team.

This type of activity will raise awareness of why you are proposing the change. Involving your team members from the outset means they are more likely to support the change.

> **Activity** ⏱ 60 minutes
>
> Write down your views in response to the following scenarios and describe how you think you would feel to your assessor.
>
> - Your senior managers call you into a meeting on a Monday morning and inform you that a major change is to take place the next day.
> - Your senior managers call you into a meeting to explain that they are planning a change that will be introduced over the next three months. They explain reasons for the change and its benefits. They ask you to discuss the proposed change with your team to obtain their feedback.

Resistance to change – culture

When implementing a plan to support change, it helps to be aware of the effect the proposed changes may have on the prevailing culture. It may affect the morale and motivation of the people you manage. Remember most people don't like to be taken out of their comfort zone.

Workplace culture can be influenced or developed by:

- policies (statements from top management of what can and cannot be done)
- procedures (step-by-step instructions for everyone to follow)
- routines (regular social activities, such as christmas parties)
- control systems (measuring and monitoring of quality and so on)
- symbols (logos, staff titles)
- rituals (inspections, training programmes).

Workplace culture can be identified as:

- adaptive – adapts well to changes that may be forced upon it
- inert – does not adapt well to changes that are forced upon it.

Implement and agree a plan to support change

To ensure a successful transition period when you have to make changes within an organisation, there must be some sort of a plan. Planning is important so that your organisation can:

- achieve its objectives
- be sure of the direction it wishes to go in
- make informed decisions
- maximise its opportunity to increase profit or acquired funds
- stay ahead of its competitors
- inform everyone of who should do what and when
- budget for staffing levels, equipment and materials.

When planning for change, you must consider:

- your customers' (or service users') needs
- your employees' fears and insecurities
- appraisal for your plan from others (e.g. your senior manager)
- the cost of the change
- the deadlines you wish to meet.

Resources

You must also plan the resources you will need to successfully implement change. Resources include:

- time – amount required/available
- people – who will be involved and in what way
- money – amount available for the change process
- equipment – what is available or needs purchasing
- materials – what is available or needs purchasing.

Other people to involve are:

- finance managers – to discuss budgets and monitoring of spending
- human resource managers – to liaise over training and staff welfare
- health and safety managers – to assess risks and identify potential hazards
- employees – to get their feedback and observations
- stakeholders – to consult over their reactions to the proposed change
- trade union representatives as appropriate – if proposed changes are likely to affect employees' terms and conditions.

Strategic planning and change

You need to be mindful of the strategic planning process for your change programme, namely:

- Where are we now? – What is not working, needs improving or changing?
- Where do we want to be? – What are you trying to achieve by changing something; what is your objective?

- How will we get there? – What is your strategy to achieve your objective?

Where are we now? Organisational objectives

Reasons for change often relate to an organisation's objectives. Take, for example, an organisation with the objective to increase profits by 20 per cent by March 2013.

This objective will require **strategies** to be put in place to make sure it is achieved. An example of a strategy may be to have an intensive marketing campaign.

Key Term

Strategy – plan of action to achieve a specific goal.

Where do we want to be? Aims and objectives of the change

Proposals for change must be backed up with clear aims and objectives. For example, if your aim is to change shift patterns in order to deal with increased customer demand then your objective might be to introduce four days on/four days off shift working for the twelve team members by an agreed date.

With your aims and targets set, you can then seek approval from other managers and obtain the views of the team.

Change programme to change shift patterns in department				
ACTION PLAN				
Responsibilities	By whom	By when	Resources required	Date of completion
e.g. Review current shift patterns	JG	3 Oct	Rota	
Plan produced by: .... Date:.......................... Proposed date for review:				

Figure C6.5 An example action plan for a change programme.

How do we get there? Action plans

The next step is to introduce a timescale and draw up an action plan to move the change programme forward.

The action plan shown in Figure C6.5 on page 205 clearly states who should do what, by when, and what resources will be required for each person to undertake their task. A completion date can be entered into a **master document** (even though everyone involved will have a copy of their own) to help with the review of activities that will follow.

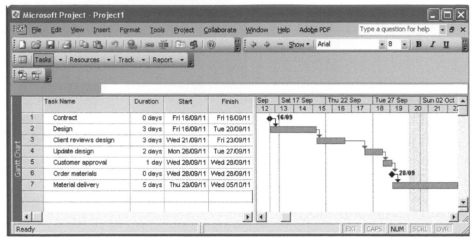

Figure C6.6 Gantt chart

Key Term

Master document – main original document on which all changes are recorded – the document with ultimate authority.

Remember

It is important to obtain approval for your proposed change not only from senior managers but also from peer managers because the changes you propose may have an effect on their team's ability to function effectively.

Gantt charts

Gantt charts are useful visual planning aids that help ensure that activities are completed in the right order and on time, as shown in Figure C6.6.

The Gantt chart should be on show at all times (e.g. on noticeboards/intranet), so everyone can monitor progress towards completion.

Remember

Share your proposed action plan and Gantt chart with everyone involved, to make sure they all approve before they are put into practice as final documents.

Be able to implement and monitor a plan for change in own area of responsibility

Applying SMART objectives to plan for change

If your change process is to be successful, having a clear intention of what exactly needs to be changed is vital from the outset. You can't communicate your goal to others if you are not sure yourself what you are trying to achieve. Start by drawing up SMART objectives.

SMART stands for:

- Specific – the objective should relate clearly to a particular task.
- Measureable – so progress can be checked.
- Achievable – it should be feasible given the existing employees, budget and resources.
- Realistic – unrealistic objectives that are unlikely to be achieved are demoralising.
- Time-bound – there must be a clear date for completion of the task.

An example of a SMART objective would be: To change existing shift patterns to four on/four off rotas for all team members by 31 December 2012.

Activity 45 minutes

Think back to your idea of something you wish to change in your own area of responsibility and devise a SMART objective to drive the change forward. Discuss your objective with your assessor.

The objectives you devise for your change process will take you through similar thought processes applied by your senior managers when they devise the overall business objectives for your organisation. Ideally these should also be SMART objectives. They are sometimes called corporate objectives and may include your organisation's desires to:

- expand its operations
- diversify its product range
- increase profits or funding
- increase its share of the market.

Mission statement

Often, the first stage of planning in an organisation will be its mission statement – a clear setting out of its main aims and purpose. For instance the mission statement of the Royal National Lifeboat Institution (RNLI) is: *To save lives at sea.*

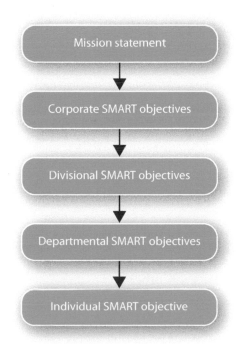

Figure C6.7 The planning process.

Figure C6.7 shows the planning process beginning with a clear mission statement, from which corporate objectives are devised. Each **division** then devises its objectives to work towards the overall corporate objectives. Then, each department formulates its objectives to work towards the divisional objectives. Team members' individual objectives will be discussed in staff appraisals to ensure everyone is being developed to work effectively as part of a team. Your proposed changes must link with the achievements of your corporate objectives!

Key Term

Division – key functional area within an organisation e.g. finance.

You can see the importance of SMART objectives in an organisation and that without giving these careful consideration, an organisation is unlikely to survive. The same can be said about the SMART objectives you must devise for change programmes in your own area of responsibility.

Portfolio Task 3 45 minutes

Links to LO3: Assessment criterion 3.1
Setting SMART objectives with individuals and teams is necessary to ensure a change programme is successful. Provide examples of how you have set individual and team objectives.

This evidence could be in the form of team meeting minutes where change objectives have been discussed and SMART objectives set. One-to-one meeting documentation, such as supervisions or appraisals could demonstrate how you have set individual objectives.

Show your evidence to your assessor and explain the different techniques you use.

Remember

By sharing your proposed SMART objectives for change with everyone concerned before implementing them, you will be giving them opportunity to discuss and suggest alternatives that may be more workable. By listening to others, you will be going a long way to getting them to support the rest of the plans for change.

PLTS

This activity will give you the opportunity to demonstrate your team working skills. Through agreeing objectives with your team you will show you can collaborate with others to work towards common goals and reach agreements (TW 1, 2).

Assessing opportunities and barriers to change

Opportunities for change

There a several different methods to assess the opportunities for change, some of which have been discussed earlier, such as a SWOT analysis, a fishbone diagram and a PESTLE analysis. There is also one other that can be effective.

Cost-benefit analysis

A cost-benefit analysis examines a project's:

- financial costs and benefits
- social costs and benefits.

When planning for change, some managers use a feasibility study, which helps to evaluate whether desired outcomes can be achieved by the planned deadlines using the available resources. A cost-benefit analysis can form part of this.

Your finance manager will be able to help you to estimate the financial costs and benefits of your change programme (i.e. expenditure and income). Social costs and benefits might include such things as more pollution but more jobs.

The rule of thumb is, if the financial and social benefits are greater than the financial and social costs, then this is a good indicator that you should go ahead with your change programme as it is likely to be successful.

Conducting a cost-benefit analysis can help you to address, with your colleagues, whether your SMART objectives for the change programme should be reviewed in any way.

Activity 45 minutes

Think about the social costs and benefits associated with a really large-scale project, such as hosting the Olympics. Write down your responses and show them to your assessor.

Activity 45 minutes

Write down how effective you think the following tools or techniques are in assessing opportunities or barriers to change:

- PESTLE analysis
- SWOT analysis
- fishbone diagram
- cost-benefit analysis.

Discuss your thoughts with your assessor.

Barriers to change

Whatever the reasons for your change, you are likely at some stage to come across barriers to your change opportunities.

Remember

Sometimes change can be of an unplanned nature and you will be expected to react without any notice, for instance you would need to urgently relocate following a serious flood.

Typical barriers to the success of your change programme may be:

- resistance from others
- lack of resources or finance
- conflict between those involved
- inadequate planning
- ineffective communication.

Other barriers you need to be aware of when trying to implement a plan of change might include resistance from:

- local councils – for example denying planning permission for a new warehouse
- local community – disagreement with the new policies and procedures you are considering putting in place
- government – preventing the merger of two multi-national organisations to prevent a **monopoly** situation
- charities – disagreeing with the ethical reasoning behind the change.

You are likely to meet with resistance from others because:

- not everyone will think there is a need to change things
- they feel they haven't received the right information at the right time
- they don't feel they will be able to perform with confidence once the changes are made
- they feel they haven't been listened to when asked to give feedback and offer their views and opinions
- they feel the proposed solution is wrong
- they feel the change will bring with it job insecurity
- they feel their opportunities to develop or achieve promotion will diminish if the change goes ahead
- they feel changes in the past haven't been successful or evaluated effectively.

Remember

People will always question change, so it's useful to prepare yourself with justifiable answers to the question 'Why do we need to change?'

Checklist

To help overcome resistance from others you should make sure you:

- plan well from the outset
- communicate effectively
- involve staff at all levels
- act on feedback from others
- budget carefully for resources and training for the change
- manage your time (and the time of others involved) carefully
- introduce the change agent to all involved as early in the process as possible
- review systems, policies and procedures to support staff involved with the change
- continue to manage existing day-to-day activities while the change programme is rolled out.

Conflict and change

Conflict situations can occur when change programmes are introduced and this can be a major barrier to the change process. It is important for you to watch out for signs that indicate conflict is stirring within your team. For example, people may behave out of character and may:

- show signs of anger or frustration towards others
- lose enthusiasm with their work
- be unco-operative and stop working as part of a team
- not work to their usual standard or quality of output
- take more days off
- stop being punctual
- become aggressive
- become sarcastic.

Change programmes can often create conflict between individuals, which must be managed carefully to stop it from escalating. Sometimes, of course, conflict may arise between you and others, particularly if others are against the change you want to introduce.

Strategies to help you to deal with conflict include the following:

- Avoiding – sometimes letting people calm down may work and this strategy is useful if it is a one-off, trivial situation. This doesn't however always address the root cause of the problem.

- Competing – when unpopular actions have to be introduced this can be useful, as you need to enforce the change and any new rules effectively. This means you are likely to win, but the losing party may resent you and your actions.

- Collaborating – discussions lead to an outcome where you and the other party are both satisfied.

- Compromising – you agree a compromise with the other party. This means you will both be partly satisfied with what you agree on.

- Accommodating – you might consider that the other party's views make sense and you tell them that you recognise this. This strategy helps to maintain effective relationships, but should only be used when you really do think the other party's solution is better than yours.

The Transition Curve

In the late 1990s, John Fisher developed a model of change called the Transition Curve. Fisher suggests that people work through the following stages when dealing with change that affects them.

- Anxiety – feeling unsure about the change and their future and that they have little control over what is happening.

- Happiness – feeling relief that things will no longer continue in the way they did before and that there may be improvement.

- Fear – feeling that there may be an imminent change in their behaviour and this may affect how others view them.

- Threat – feeling unsure about how to react in new circumstances because the old rules will no longer apply.

- Guilt – examining their own past behaviours and beliefs and feeling that they actually didn't live up to them in the past as they once thought they did.

- Depression – becoming demotivated and wondering how they will fit into the new way of doing things.

- Disillusionment – feeling that their own beliefs and goals don't match with those of the organisation. This can lead to demotivation.

- Hostility – reverting back to the old ways of doing things, feeling that they are already a failure and won't fit into the new ways of doing things.

- Denial – refusing to accept change and continue to act as if the change hasn't happened.

You can use Fisher's model to work through the implications of change at each stage of the transition period to manage people through the change process and help you recognise why people might resist the change.

Activity 🕑 45 minutes

Think of a potential conflict situation that may arise as a direct result of the change you wish to make in your own area of responsibility. Analyse each strategy above and decide which one you are most likely to use to resolve the conflict situation you have thought of.

Portfolio Task 4 🕑 45 minutes

Links to LO3: Assessment criterion 3.2

Referring to the change you have discussed in previous portfolio tasks, identify the opportunities and barriers to this change. Discuss these with your assessor.

For example, changing shift patterns may result in a resistance to change and a flexibility of staff.

PLTS

Through identifying the barriers to the change you will be identifying issues of concern. Identifying the opportunities will present a persuasive case for action, which you would put forward to your team (EP1,2).

Reviewing the action plans and activities

With your opportunities and barriers identified, you should think about how you can review your planning activities. You need to be sure about:

- how well your planning activities will help you to achieve the objective for your change opportunity
- how the barriers you have identified can be overcome.

How your planning activities will help to achieve objectives

For example, if your objective is to introduce four days on/four days off shift working patterns for every team member by 31 December 2012, then you need to consider how effective your planning activities will be to help you to make the most of this opportunity for change. You need to think about:

- revisiting your PESTLE and SWOT analysis documents to identify what has been accomplished to date and what further planning and decision-making activity is required as a result of your analyses
- reviewing your action plan to find out what tasks have been successfully completed by the nominated people within the given deadlines and what still needs to be done
- reviewing your fishbone diagram document to establish what aspects of your findings have been addressed to date
- revisiting your Gantt chart to help you to monitor the progress made to date towards the completion of your change programme.

How barriers can be overcome

Most barriers to change can be overcome by communicating effectively with others. For example, if staff members are negative and resisting change, then by holding a meeting and clearly explaining why the change must take place and the benefits it will bring, it is likely that you can change attitudes.

Similarly, if you identify that you won't have enough money to see the change through because

---

Activity ⏱ 30 minutes

With your opportunity for change in mind, think about the barriers you have identified that may get in the way of progress. Using the examples below as a starting point, produce a similar table and list the barriers and that ways in which you think you can overcome them:

Change objective: To
....

Identified barriers	Ways to overcome the barriers
e.g. staff resistance to change	e.g. through face-to-face meetings reassure by communicating reasons and benefits for change

---

you didn't foresee all aspects of the change to budget for, you can approach your finance and line managers to explain the oversight and correct the deficit. Your managers are likely to explain to you that you should learn from this oversight to prevent it from happening again.

One effective way to deal with potential barriers is to think ahead and devise **contingency** plans. For example hospitals have an emergency generator in place which will kick in if there is a power cut.

If a business organisation is affected by a crisis, such as a flood or a workforce strike in a major supplier, then a disaster plan is in place to deal with this. This is a contingency plan.

Key Term

Contingency – a future event or circumstance that might happen but cannot be predicted.

Activity ⏱ 45 minutes

Think about two contingency plans you could put in place for your identified change programme (i.e. plans for something that may or may not happen but if it does it will present a barrier to your change).

Reviewing your change programme

As your change programme progresses, you need to establish whether your goals are being achieved and whether the change is going in the right direction. As part of your reviewing process you can collect information from those affected by the change to obtain their responses and reactions to the change activities to date.

- Stakeholders will be able to supply you with useful information to help you to review how well the process is going.
- Senior managers may offer you feedback on how the change will help to achieve corporate objectives.
- Peer managers may offer feedback on how your changes may affect the day-to-day activities in their own department.
- Your team members will feedback their thoughts and opinions on how they feel the change activities are affecting them.
- Suppliers may feedback how your proposed changes will affect delivery schedules.
- Shareholders (if you trade as a company) may feedback their thoughts on how the change may affect their investment or dividends.
- Customers may feedback how the change affects their customer experience and the service they receive.

Remember

In the public, private and voluntary sectors, service users, shareholders and clients will want to know that money spent on a change programme is necessary and will improve the way things are done to make the organisation more cost-effective.

When reviewing planning activities, you should consider the following:

- What has been achieved to date?
- What has gone well and what hasn't?
- What can be improved?

It often helps to think about the PIE model. PIE stands for Participation, Information and Enthusiasm.

- Participation – getting all those affected by the change involved and participating can help to overcome the barrier of resistance.
- Information – communicating information effectively, clearly and regularly can help to overcome the barrier of uncertainty and fear.
- Enthusiasm – if you're enthusiastic about the change, others are likely to be as well. Be positive throughout the programme and others are more likely to work happily alongside you.

PDSA Cycle

To examine your activities and ideas and to help you to review your plans and activities you should consider using the Plan – Do – Study – Act (PDSA) cycle, as seen in Figure C6.8. It is a very useful tool that can help you to successfully manage your change programme. It was devised by US theorist W.E. Deming and for this reason is sometimes referred to as the Deming Wheel.

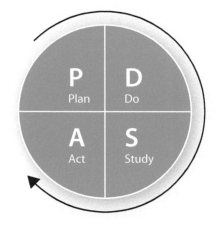

Figure C6.8 PDSA cycle.

The PDSA cycle can be used as a step-by-step model:

Step 1 – Plan: Be sure what your goal is. What are you trying to change and therefore what is your SMART objective and what planning tools, techniques and methods will you use?

Step 2 – Do: Test out how well you think your planning tools are helping you to achieve your objective. Getting feedback from those who will be affected and listening to their views and opinions is so important at this stage. Maybe others have a better or alternative solution to what you are trying to change.

You need to make decisions on how you – and all concerned – can move the change forward in a positive environment.

Step 3 – Study: You review progress to date, summarise what has been learned and keep everyone informed of it. Your cost-benefit analysis will help you to be certain that you should go ahead with the change. What improvements can be made to the way the change programme is being managed and what can be learnt to improve how activities will be undertaken in the future before you fully implement the change?

Step 4 – Act: At this stage you are ready to fully implement your change programme. However, by reviewing your plans and activities in Step 3 and perhaps by listening to feedback from others, you may still revert back to Step 1 to examine the quality and effectiveness of your objectives, techniques tools and methods.

The PDSA tool can be used on a continuous basis working from Step 4, back to Step 1 and then working through the cycle again. This can help you to look for opportunities for improvement if you think the change process is not going as well as you would like it to.

Portfolio Task 5 — 45 minutes

Links to LO3: Assessment criterion 3.3
As stated in Step 3 of the Deming Wheel above, reviewing your actions and activities is an important aspect of change. Therefore, explain to your assessor, showing examples of documentation you use in your workplace if available, how you review your action plans and activities. Discuss with your assessor the importance of reviewing your plans as a result of identifying new opportunities and/or barriers to implementing the change.

PLTS

This activity you will give you the opportunity to reflect upon your progress, identifying your achievements and evaluating your experiences (RL1, 2, 3, 5).

Functional Skills

This portfolio task will give you the opportunity to practise your Level 2 Functional Skills in English: Communication. You should present your information and ideas clearly in your professional discussion with your assessor.

Remember

If your change programme is not monitored, reviewed and evaluated then you'll not know whether it is worth doing.

Team talk

Claire's story

My name is Claire Edwards. I am 48 years old and have worked as a finance assistant for 'Toys are Yours' for four years. I complete the accounts weekly, send the monthly accounts to head office and file the annual accounts at the end of the financial year. I am responsible for the petty cash, departmental budgets and payroll. I have always used a manual accounting system wherever I have worked and I have always met my deadlines working in this way.

This morning, the Finance Director informed all of us in the department that he has made the decision to move over to SAGE accounts from next Monday. The Finance Director is very enthusiastic about this change as he feels it will make the organisation more high tech, and more able to meet our stakeholder's demands. He is determined to remove the need for paper in the office.

This worries me a lot as my IT skills are not that good. I have used a manual system for twenty-five years and never had any problems. I have spoken with my colleagues and they feel the same way as me. I tried to raise my concerns with the Finance Director, but he wasn't listening. He just told me, 'You'll get use to it'.

Top tips

When introducing change of any type into an organisation, regardless of its size and what it does, it is important to involve everyone concerned from the initial planning stages. Claire's Financial Director is clearly failing to do this. The reasons for making the changes should be communicated to everyone well in advance of the change happening so that the benefits to the organisation, its stakeholders and individual members of staff can be emphasised. Failure to do this will breed resentment and fear, leading to demoralised staff. This affects overall performance of the organisation. Staff should be reassured by offering coaching, mentoring and additional training.

Ask the expert	
Q	I have to implement a new computerised accounting system in my department but my team are very unhappy about it, as they are used to a manual system. How do I get them to accept the change?
A	Hold a meeting with all staff in the organisation to inform them that a change will take place in three months time. Remember it's best practice to tell people as soon as you possibly can that a change will be happening. Explain why the change needs to happen and how it will improve performance and customer service. I would also inform the staff who will be using the new system that training will be provided to build their confidence over a period of time.

What your assessor is looking for

In order to demonstrate your competency within this unit, you will need to provide sufficient evidence to your assessor. You will need to provide a short written narrative or personal statement, explaining how you meet the assessment criteria. In addition, your assessor may need to ask you questions to test your knowledge of the topics identified in this unit.

You will demonstrate your skills, knowledge and competence through the three learning outcomes in this unit. Evidence generated in this unit will also cross reference to the other units in this qualification.

Please bear in mind that there are significant cross-referencing opportunities throughout this qualification and you may have already generated some relevant work to meet certain criteria in this unit. Your assessor will provide you with the exact requirements to meet the standards of this unit. However, as a guide it is likely that for this unit you will need to be assessed through the following methods:

- An observation of relevant workplace activities or a witness testimony.

- A written report or reflective account.
- A professional discussion.
- Any relevant work products produced as evidence.

The work products for this unit could include:

- a change proposal
- action plans
- Gantt charts
- fishbone diagram
- team meeting minutes discussing the change
- copies of communications (reports, emails).

Task and page reference	Assessment criteria
1 (page 200)	1.1
2 (page 201)	2.1, 2.2
3 (page 207)	3.1
4 (page 210)	3.2
5 (page 213)	3.3

Unit D2a Develop working relationships with colleagues and stakeholders

In this unit you will examine who your organisation's stakeholders are and investigate how they are linked with your organisation. You will also examine the roles and responsibilities of the different stakeholder groups, as well as investigating the range of possible interests and concerns that they may have.

Working effectively and developing positive ongoing relationships with stakeholders is the best way for a business to conduct its activities. You will investigate ways in which you can create and maintain good working relationships with your colleagues and stakeholders that will bring about a shared understanding of the business and its overall mission. In the final section of this unit you will look into ways of reviewing your stakeholders' needs and motivations, so that the business can acknowledge them and also act on them, where appropriate. You will also examine ways of interacting with colleagues and stakeholders that show respect for the views and actions of others.

What you will learn

- Know how to identify stakeholders and their relevance to an organisation
- Understand how to establish working relationships with colleagues and stakeholders
- Be able to create an environment of trust and mutual respect with colleagues and stakeholders

Links to the Technical Certificate

If you are completing your NVQ as part of an Apprenticeship Framework, you will find the following topic is also covered in your Technical Certificate:

- Benefits of productive working relationships

Know how to identify stakeholders and their relevance to an organisation

Understanding who your stakeholders are and in what way they are important to your organisation is a key consideration underpinning most strategic business decisions. In this section you will identify your own organisation's stakeholders and investigate their relationship with the organisation.

Identifying an organisation's stakeholders

Stakeholders can be defined as those who are affected in some way by, and can themselves affect, the decisions and actions of the organisation.

The main types of stakeholders include:

- customers
- shareholders
- suppliers
- managers
- employees
- the community
- the environment.

The number and type of these stakeholders depends on the size and nature of the organisation. For example, in a local convenience store, the main stakeholders would include:

- employees who work there
- the local community which needs the store, as the nearest supermarket is three miles away, particularly to stock up on basics, such as bread and milk
- suppliers, including the local farmers who supply dairy produce and meat to the store.

By contrast a local charity shop supporting the homeless in the area would have very different stakeholders, including:

- the volunteers who run the shop

- the donors who provide the shop with its stock of clothing and bric-a-brac
- the customers who support the charity by purchasing items from the shop
- the homeless people who receive help from the charity.

Different again are the stakeholders of a local primary school, which include:

- children attending the school
- parents and carers of the children
- teaching and administrative staff who work at the school
- the local council that runs the school
- the local community in which the school is located.

Classifying stakeholders

It can be very useful to look at ways of classifying your organisation's stakeholders as this helps to build up a more detailed image of their characteristics and identify where the key sources of influence, collaboration or even conflict may lie. All of this information is highly valuable in strategic business decision making.

Table D2a.1 gives examples of how stakeholders can be classified.

Stakeholder scorecards

Stakeholder scorecards work by displaying a full list of all of the organisation's stakeholders, along with what they need or receive from the business and what they contribute to it.

Stakeholder scorecards serve to highlight the fact that there are many potential stakeholders linked to an organisation. They also exist to counter the narrow traditional view of the shareholding approach to business, which virtually ignores the other stakeholder groups.

Models such as this work best when they are kept as simple as possible. Only one or two items should be listed against each stakeholder, as shown in Figure D2a.1.

Type of stakeholder categorisation	Examples
Direct and indirect	Direct stakeholders have their own voice and can directly state their stakeholder claim to the organisation (customers, employees and shareholders fall into this category). Indirect stakeholders have no voice and their stake must be relayed via a third party. The environment is a good example of an indirect stakeholder. Environmental issues are often campaigned for by pressure groups, such as Friends of the Earth and Greenpeace.
Internal and external	Internal stakeholders are those inside the organisation, such as employees and managers. External stakeholders include customers and suppliers.
Narrow and wide	Narrow stakeholders are those who are dependent and who are most affected by the organisation, such as employees and shareholders. Wide stakeholders are less dependent and may include the wider community, or suppliers who may also supply many other organisations.
Primary and secondary	Primary stakeholders are essential to the business for its survival, such as customers, employees and shareholders. Secondary stakeholders are non-essential and are usually external to the business, such as the general public or the community.
Active and passive	Active stakeholders choose to take part in stakeholding activities. Passive stakeholders, for whatever reason, choose not to participate. Feelings of powerlessness, or of being a small voice against a huge corporation, often contribute to passivity.

Table D2a.1 Examples of how stakeholders can be categorised.

Activity 20 minutes

1. Using a scorecard similar to the one below, make a list of the main stakeholders of your own organisation. For each stakeholder group, say what it is that they contribute to and receive from the organisation.

2. Give two examples of organisations, other than your current employer, for which you are a stakeholder, and explain why.

PLTS

When you are generating ideas and exploring possibilities you are practising your skills as a creative thinker (CT).

Suppliers	
Contribute	*Receive*
Goods	Income
Services	Ongoing business relationship

Customers	
Contribute	*Receive*
Income	Products and services
Ongoing business loyalty	Value for money

Managers	
Contribute	*Receive*
Leadership	Pay
Management	Career

Employees	
Contribute	*Receive*
Time	Pay
Effort	Benefits

Shareholders	
Contribute	*Receive*
Capital	Dividends

Community	
Contribute	*Receive*
Labour supply	Prosperity

Figure D2a.1 An example stakeholder scorecard.

Evaluating the roles, responsibilities, interests and concerns of stakeholders

Each of the stakeholder groups has certain roles that it performs and responsibilities it must undertake. For example, the managers of a business must ensure that they are honest and transparent in their assessment of the financial performance of an organisation. The different stakeholder groups also have wide-ranging interests and concerns, including pay rates, working conditions, profitability or sustainability, depending on the group which they belong to.

Roles and responsibilities of stakeholders

Employees

Employees have a responsibility to their employer to carry out the tasks and activities related to their position and to show loyalty to the business. They also have a responsibility to their customers and must treat them fairly and with respect. They must act within the policy guidelines set out by the organisation for dealing with customers and for upholding the organisation's customer service standards. Ultimately, employees are responsible for behaving in a way commensurate with their position – accountants are not allowed to go bankrupt, for example, as this shows lack of financial prudence in their personal affairs and will obviously reflect badly on the organisation which employs them. Nurses in the UK are similarly held legally responsible for the standard of care that they provide. Failure to uphold these standards is called professional misconduct. The behaviour of doctors, solicitors, teachers and many other professions is regulated by their respective professional industry bodies, which set out what they must and must not do.

Shareholders

Shareholders' rights, as well as their roles and duties, are set out by legislation in the Companies Act 2006. The main role of shareholders is to attend the company general meetings and to vote on issues, or resolutions. They are also entitled to speak at the general meetings and to review or question the actions and decisions taken by the managers of the business. Ultimately, shareholders have the power to remove directors from the board of a company if they are not satisfied with their conduct in some respect. These are the methods by which they exert their control over the actions of the business.

Managers

Managers are responsible for the smooth running of the business. This involves monitoring and controlling workflow to ensure work targets are achieved, as well as taking appropriate action to make improvements where necessary. Managers also have specific line management responsibilities for the staff who report in to them. This involves ensuring their staff are working to a satisfactory level, providing training and guidance, as well as recruiting and promoting staff, where appropriate. Managers must behave professionally in all of their undertakings and must abide by relevant policies, such as health and safety and employment rights legislation.

> **Activity** 🕐 15 minutes
>
> Outline some of the key roles and responsibilities for three identified stakeholders in your organisation.

Interests and concerns of stakeholders

Each group of stakeholders has its own particular interests in and concerns about the business. Let's take a closer look at what some of these might be.

Customers

Customers generally want good quality products or services at the lowest prices. Where competition is high in a particular market and products from different businesses are similar, customers can easily move to another business to buy their products. Customer service plays a vital role in differentiating a business from its competitors in situations such as this.

Shareholders

Shareholders have a vested interest in the continued profitability of the business, as this is the basis upon which they will receive a financial return on their investment in shares in the business. Shareholders can benefit from an organisation's profitability in two main ways:

- receiving regular dividend payments on their existing shares
- an increase in the value of their shares.

Suppliers

The suppliers to a business depend on continued orders for their own survival and success. They also depend on being paid for these supplies, which means they are interested in the continued **liquidity** of the business, as well as its credit rating.

Managers

Managers are interested in the smooth operation of the business and in producing goods and services at the cheapest cost to the business. They will be keen to keep down costs of raw materials as well as employee pay in order to minimise business costs.

Employees

The main stake employees have in the business they work for is their livelihood. Employees want security of employment and good pay and conditions. They may also want to work for a business with a good reputation in its industry and one which has a good **ethical** policy.

The community

The community can be local, regional, national or even global, depending on the scope of operations of the organisation.

The local community will not want businesses to harm or damage the area, for instance by unacceptable levels of noise, litter, traffic congestion or pollution. Local, regional and national communities want businesses to provide employment, good working conditions and prosperity. Global communities want businesses that respect the laws, surroundings and livelihoods of people in the areas in which they operate.

Respect for the environment is especially important in the extraction industries, such as coal, oil and natural gas.

As you can see, stakeholders have a wide range of interests and concerns. Some of these are **aligned** and others are in conflict with each other.

Key Terms

Accountability – being answerable for actions and decisions.

Aligned – interests that are in agreement across the different stakeholder groups.

Ethical – moral principles on what is right and wrong.

Liquidity – the ability of a business to pay its debts on time.

Social responsibility – contribution to the welfare of the community.

Transparency – openness and honesty.

Aligned stakeholder interests

One of the key interests of all stakeholders includes the desire for the business to continue and to prosper into the long term. Without this, there will be no organisation and therefore no stakeholders.

Beyond this, other aligned interests of the different stakeholders include expectations that the organisation should behave according to the principles of:

- fairness
- **accountability**
- **social responsibility**
- **transparency**.

All stakeholder groups expect these very basic elements of good conduct on the part of a business with which they are linked. They expect the organisation to demonstrate social responsibility, good ethical policies and to take account of the wider environment in which it operates. Customers, employees and the community have increasingly high expectations of organisations in this respect and are likely to voice their objections and even switch to an alternative organisation if they feel that these expectations are not being met.

The Co-operative Group is owned by its customers.

There are many recent examples of companies that have been the subject of customer protests over lack of social responsibility for issues such as oil spills and exploiting factory workers in developing countries.

Activity — 30 minutes

Research the Enron scandal of 2001, which at the time was the largest bankruptcy in American history. Write a brief summary explaining what happened and why Enron failed in its social responsibility. Find out which other major corporation was also brought down by this scandal.

Corporate social responsibility

Many organisations have responded to increased expectations of stakeholders by developing corporate social responsibility statements. These are public statements detailing the ways in which they will work with their stakeholders, including:

- offering the best goods and services to their customers
- offering good terms of employment to their staff
- building good relationships with their suppliers
- helping their local communities
- minimising the impact of their business activities on the environment.

The Co-operative Group is a good example of an organisation that is actively involved in many initiatives with the aim of benefiting its stakeholders, with an emphasis on serving and helping the local communities in which it operates. The Co-operative Group is the UK's largest mutual business, which means it is owned not by shareholders, but by its customers.

While one of the key aims of the Co-operative Group is to be commercially successful, they also emphasise the importance of the socially responsible way in which they want to achieve this. Key commitments they publicise include issues ranging from ethical trading and helping local schools and communities, to campaigning on a number of issues from global poverty to sustainable energy. Among the Co-operative Group's organisational aims are to be an ethical leader and an exemplary employer.

Activity — 20 minutes

Find out what your organisation does as part of its commitment to social responsibility. You can probably find this information on your company's website. Identify which stakeholders are mentioned and what commitments are made by your organisation to each of them. Write a short paragraph summarising the key points.

Remember

Most organisations have some form of social responsibility statement. However, it is what these organisations actually do, not what they say, that determines their true social responsibility.

Conflicting stakeholder interests

Some specific interests of the different stakeholder groups may conflict with each other. Table D2a.2 contains examples of the way some of these conflicts may occur.

Stakeholder group	Key interest	How this interest conflicts with that of another stakeholder
Managers	Cost control via sourcing the lowest priced stock	Customers may want more ethically sourced but more expensive products
Shareholders	Dividends to be paid out of the profits	Employees may want higher pay, which will reduce profits and therefore the amount of dividends to be paid to shareholders
Local community	Reduction in traffic congestion in the area	The managers want as many customers as possible to visit the store, which will mean more traffic congestion as customers travel to and from the store

Table D2a.2 How stakeholder groups may conflict with one another.

Activity

 15 minutes

Consider the possible conflicts of interest that may exist between the different groups of stakeholders in your organisation. List three stakeholders and, for each, explain the nature of a possible conflict with another stakeholder group.

PLTS

When you are identifying questions to answer and problems to resolve, you are practising your skills as an independent enquirer (IE).

The shareholding versus the stakeholding approach

It has been traditionally argued that the only aim of any business should be to maximise profits. This is because profit maximisation provides the highest return to its shareholders – whose money finances the business. This is called the shareholding approach to running a business. It does not take into account any of the needs, concerns or opinions of any of the other stakeholders in the business, such as employees or customers. This approach further argues that seeking to address the concerns of any stakeholders other than the shareholders is in fact a conflict of interest on the part of the shareholders. The reasoning behind this argument is that any money diverted from profits to other areas (such as employees' pay increases or investment in non-polluting production processes) leaves less profit to be distributed to shareholders.

Remember

One of the defining differences between shareholders and other stakeholders is that shareholders want to make money, while the wants of most other stakeholders tend to cost money.

However, it is now becoming more widely accepted that business success can actually be increased by taking into consideration the needs and wants of all the different stakeholder groups. This is called the stakeholding approach. It argues that, by working with – rather than against – its stakeholder groups, and by taking into account its stakeholders' needs in its organisational decision making, a business can achieve greater success. There will therefore be a larger amount of profit generated by this success, which can be used to benefit the different stakeholders, including the shareholders.

Benefits to the business of the stakeholding approach can include:

- better relationships with suppliers
- better pay for employees, leading to increased morale and therefore better work rates
- higher quality products, leading to increased sales therefore increased profits

- a better reputation for the business, which will attract more customers and increase **staff retention**.

The business benefits of adopting the stakeholder approach are compelling. In fact, nowadays stakeholders do expect their views to be taken into account and businesses are increasingly developing channels and forums to allow them to do this. However, from a business's point of view, it is a very difficult task to moderate, or alter, its strategic decisions based on the disparate needs of its many stakeholders. Sometimes, in practice, stakeholder needs and wants cannot be fully accommodated due to either financial, logistical or other constraints on the business. In other situations, companies may look to accommodate these needs and wants in the medium or long term rather than the short term.

Assessing the importance of identified stakeholders

In any organisation, the relative importance of the stakeholders will be different and may change over time. There will be certain stakeholder individuals or groups who are more vocal and more motivated to take action than others. Additionally, some stakeholders may be better placed to influence the actions of the organisation. This can be for a variety of reasons. For example, it may be that they are a large investor or a major supplier to that organisation, or perhaps they represent the views of a large group of consumers.

The most active and influential stakeholders are called **key stakeholders**, as it is these groups that will ultimately have the greatest effect on the actions of the organisation.

> **Key Terms**
>
> **Key stakeholders** – the most influential stakeholders.
>
> **Staff retention** – the proportion of staff who remain within an organisation. Good staff retention suggests that the business is good to work for.

Power and influence

Stakeholders can be analysed in terms of their potential influence on an organisation. This type of analysis generates extremely valuable information for a business in its strategic planning and decision making. It ensures that all relevant stakeholder groups are recognised and that, where possible, their respective needs, wants and opinions can then be factored into the decision-making process in the most appropriate way.

The Mendelow matrix

The Mendelow matrix is a strategic business tool developed in 1991 and used to analyse stakeholders based on their relative positions of influence on the organisation.

The Mendelow matrix works by looking at two key factors that make up total influence – power and interest. Power is the ability of a stakeholder to act and interest is the motivation to do so. Therefore, those with the greatest power, combined with the greatest motivation, will be most likely to exert the greatest influence on an organisation.

The matrix provides general guidance on ways of managing the various categories of stakeholders. Low interest-low power groups require the least intervention, whereas the high power-high interest groups require active and regular communication from the organisation.

> **Remember**
>
> Remember, all stakeholders are not necessarily equal. Those with the greatest power and interest are more likely to have the greatest influence on the organisation.

> **Activity** ⏱ 15 minutes
>
> 1. Find an example of the Mendelow matrix online and print it out.
> 2. Using the list of identified stakeholders for your organisation which you produced for the activity on p219, map them onto the Mendelow matrix to show which are the most influential in your organisation. Use your own judgement to decide in which box of the matrix they should appear.
>
> Show your finished matrix to your assessor to explain your reasoning.

Portfolio Task 1 — 90 minutes

Links to LO1: Assessment criteria 1.1, 1.2, 1.3

1. **(a)** Define what is meant by the term 'stakeholder'.
   (b) Identify at least four of your organisation's stakeholders. State in what way they are linked to the organisation.

2. Evaluate the roles, responsibilities, interests and concerns of each of the four stakeholders identified above.

3. **(a)** Describe the Mendelow matrix and explain how it works.
   (b) Use the Mendelow matrix to assess the importance of the four stakeholders you identified above. You may also wish to apply some of the different types of stakeholder classifications (such as direct or indirect, active or passive) to your answer to show your understanding.

Your assessment could take the form of a written narrative or a professional discussion with your assessor. It could also include the production of workplace evidence, work based observations or the use of witness testimonies, as appropriate.

PLTS

When you are analysing and evaluating information, you are practising your skills as an independent inquirer (IE).

Functional Skills

If you produce a word-processed report as part of the assessment for this learning outcome, you will be practising your Functional Skills in ICT: Using IT systems.

Understand how to establish working relationships with colleagues and stakeholders

Think about how many different people you deal with in a typical day at work. From external customers, suppliers and delivery drivers, to internal superiors, peers and subordinates, it is likely that you will regularly interact with several of these people in order to do your job.

Establishing good working relationships with all of the different groups of people you come into contact with at work is essential. This is for the simple reason that it ensures the smooth running of your team or department. Good working relationships nurture goodwill, enthusiasm and team spirit, all of which are necessary to get things done – and to get people to go that extra mile to help others, especially during challenging situations. In fact, it is the very quality of working relationships that often distinguishes those organisations that achieve great success from those that do not.

Agreeing a common sense of purpose with colleagues and stakeholders

Sense of purpose refers to understanding the reasons why you do what you do at work. This applies along a continuum from daily tasks right the way through to the overall mission of the business. Agreeing a common sense of purpose, therefore, requires engaging in dialogue with colleagues and other stakeholders, both inside and outside the business, to identify and agree common ground, open up discussions and listen to the views of others.

This is an important business activity because it increases stakeholders' understanding of the business activities and explains the reasons why certain actions must be taken by the business, as well as increasing commitment and collaboration.

Unit D2a Develop working relationships with colleagues and stakeholders

Overcoming barriers

There are some barriers that may prevent agreement of a common sense of purpose with stakeholders. These include:

- lack of understanding
- mistrust
- poor communication.

These barriers can all be overcome by implementing an effective communications strategy. This strategy needs to employ the most appropriate methods of communication with the different stakeholder groups, as well as conveying information very clearly.

Communicating with stakeholders

There are several methods that can be used to communicate with stakeholders. The most appropriate methods will depend on the specific nature of the situation and whether it is an exceptional circumstance, such as a business crisis, or whether it is simply a regular scheduled meeting. **Rich communication methods**, such as face-to-face discussions, should be used for exceptional, in-depth or emotive issues, whereas **lean communication methods**, such as emails and newsletters, should be used for routine information circulation.

Meetings

Businesses can hold special meetings with many types of stakeholders, including employees, shareholders, customers and the local community, to share information and to find out what people's issues and concerns are. In fact, organisations are obliged to hold at least one annual meeting with shareholders where the organisation is a public limited company (plc).

Holding regular meetings with stakeholders is a particularly good communication strategy as it is a great forum for two-way discussion. If issues are raised at a meeting, progress can be announced at the next, and so on. This provides a continuity of communication, which increases trust and commitment.

Newsletters

Newsletters for both staff and customers are good for announcing new initiatives and progress and achievements in ongoing stakeholder activities. They can be sent out weekly, monthly or quarterly, to suit the needs of the stakeholders as well as the business and can be a good platform for celebrating successes. External newsletters can also be used to promote the business, to advertise special offers and promotions and to ask for feedback and comments from readers.

Focus groups

Focus groups are useful for holding in-depth discussions on specific topics and are a good way of obtaining detailed thoughts and opinions from stakeholders, such as employees and customers. The type of information obtained from focus groups can lead to significant business improvements to products, prices and even things like the design of retail stores.

Community champions

Tesco has come up with an innovative initiative for further enhancing its presence in, and involvement with, the local communities in which it operates. It employs community champions, who are paid to spend eighteen hours per week working out in the local community. Their role includes finding ways in which Tesco can help the community as well as getting people involved in community activities to help raise money for charity. You can find out more about this and all of Tesco's other community initiatives at www.tescoplc.com and searching for the Our Community Promises page under the Corporate Responsibility section. One of the key benefits of using an approach such as this is that these community champions will pass on their enthusiasm to the local community and help develop links, increase interest and encourage more involvement with the business.

Using communications technology

Businesses have a range of communications technology options available to them for enhancing their communication with all of their stakeholders. For example:

- email
- websites
- social networking.

Email

Email can be used for a wide variety of purposes, from providing information and updates to seeking opinions via online surveys. This method has the advantage that it is cheap and very quick to do. It can also reach a huge number of people at once, conveying a consistent message to all stakeholders who receive it.

Websites

Websites are used by businesses all over the world to publicise their activities and to provide information on how they interact with their stakeholders in different areas. This type of information is often contained within the corporate social responsibility section of the website. The type of information provided about work with stakeholders might include the following:

- working with suppliers to source ethically produced products
- helping employees by introducing flexible working and training
- providing customers with the best quality goods and services at value for money prices
- funding local community initiatives.

Social networking

Social networking sites, such as Facebook and Twitter, among others, are increasingly used by businesses as a means of communication, recruiting customers to their own particular groups on these social networking sites. This is an excellent method of keeping people up-to-date with the company's latest news and achievements as they happen. In addition, these sites offer those who sign up the opportunity to 'like' or 'follow' their businesses. Building up a large network in this way is a very good indication of an organisation's popularity.

> **Remember**
>
> Using communication technology can save your business significant amounts of time and money in communicating with stakeholders.

Creating an environment of trust and mutual respect with colleagues and stakeholders

Creating an environment of trust and mutual respect with colleagues and stakeholders is a very effective way of bringing the best out of people at work, which in turn, makes it possible for the business to perform to the best of its capabilities. However, this is not something that can be achieved overnight. Trust and respect take time and a great deal of effort to become established and require focus and resilience from the managers of the business.

Having a great product range, or the latest high tech production facilities is all well and good, however companies that have a good working environment, actively promoting values such as honesty and respect, are much more likely to be successful. Having an environment in which people are trusted to do a good job and to do whatever it takes to solve a problem, is what really makes the difference. This is because in a good working environment, people will be more willing to work harder and longer when needed and to help out colleagues or customers in order to make them happy – and to get great satisfaction from being helpful to others.

Steps to creating a good working environment

A good working environment requires certain key characteristics including:

- good leadership
- commitment
- diversity
- respect
- effective communications.

Good leadership

The state of any working environment is largely shaped by the quality of its leadership. Top management must lead by example, act in a way that is consistent with the values they promote throughout the business and show integrity, especially during challenging times. These leadership issues apply equally to managing employees as they do to dealing with other stakeholders of the organisation, such as shareholders, customers and the local community.

Commitment

Commitment is the level to which an individual or group feels loyalty to an organisation. Commitment can apply to employees as well as to other stakeholder groups. Suppliers, for example, may be committed to continuing business activities with an organisation. Similarly, the community may equally feel committed to working together with an organisation for the long term. In both of these examples, the stakeholders' loyalty to the organisation is what keeps them working with it. So, enhancing and increasing the commitment of its employees, its customers, the community, and other stakeholders will greatly help the organisation in developing an environment of trust and mutual respect.

Diversity

Central to creating a platform for good communications and dialogue with stakeholders is to actively embrace the diversity which these groups bring.

Diversity means difference, and differences can exist in terms of:

- age
- ethnic background
- skills
- abilities
- experiences and much more.

These differences can bring a wealth of ideas and innovative solutions to problems. The key, however, to getting the most from this diversity is to be receptive and open minded to these different approaches and to evaluate ideas and opinions on their merit. Remember, diversity ultimately brings more possible solutions to the table. It also allows people to learn from one another and creates a broader understanding of the perspectives of different groups. This is all to the benefit of the stakeholder group as a whole.

The following is a particularly good example of how a group of stakeholders came up with an innovative solution to a business problem.

When the Butcher's Arms country pub in Cumbria, which was historically the hub of the community, closed down, its customers rallied round and bought shares in it so that it could be re-opened to serve the needs of the community. Local community members were surveyed to assess their requirements and expectations from the pub and as a result of this feedback, work commenced on improvements and refurbishment and the reopened pub offered a range of high quality food and drink, sourced from local suppliers. Because the pub ended up providing what its stakeholders wanted, it became successful once again.

Respect

Respect means having regard for and positive feelings towards another individual or group. We all learn at an early age to show respect to our parents, teachers and friends. It is this very same principle that should be applied to our working relationships. Respect brings with it certain expected behaviours, such as politeness, fairness and due consideration. Certain other behaviours, such as shouting, bullying and holding others in contempt, denote a total lack of respect and will act to destroy good relationships between colleagues and other stakeholders if they are allowed to continue.

Respect must be demonstrated from the top of the organisation if it is to become the accepted manner of behaviour all the way down throughout the ranks. You can show respect to your colleagues and other stakeholders by demonstrating consideration for their views, even where these may differ from your own. Make sure that your body language and gestures also back up your words to convey a respectful approach. It is no good going to great lengths to verbally show respect to a dissatisfied customer if your body language tells them that you couldn't care less.

Mutual respect means two-way respect between the organisation and its various stakeholders. This is a very important concept, because it forms the basis of all communication and exchanges between stakeholders and the organisation. A lack of mutual respect can mean that dialogue between the organisation and its stakeholders may degenerate into unruly exchanges. For this reason, respectfulness should be the basis upon which all communications occur.

Benefits of productive working relationships

The benefits of being able to create and maintain good and productive working relationships with colleagues and stakeholders include:

- creation of a shared sense of commitment to the organisation
- increased understanding of others' views
- improved decision making based on increased information sharing
- better communications – more listening, more consistent messages and more access to information
- more co-ordinated and timely business activities that take account of a wider range of stakeholder interests and concerns.

Assertiveness

Assertiveness is a method of communicating in which a person has the confidence to speak honestly and openly, to express their opinions and thoughts, while being respectful of the feelings of others. Assertiveness is mid-way between the two extremes of being passive on the one hand and being aggressive on the other, both of which bring with them problems in communication.

People who are passive often do not want to speak up for themselves for fear of rebuke or of engaging in further conflict, which they would prefer to avoid, and therefore often come across as aloof or uninterested. People who are aggressive, on the other hand, get their point across by raising their voice, bullying or using coercion, with no consideration whatsoever for the views or feelings of others. Neither of these approaches is productive in a business situation.

The benefits of being assertive in communication with others are that it will prevent your opinions from being ignored or overruled, whilst also ensuring you make your point clearly, in a way which respects the views and opinions of others.

Assertiveness is a communication skill that can be learned by practice. There are many books, training courses and other resources readily available on the subject. In fact, assertiveness training is a

Activity 🕐 20 minutes

Complete the following assessment form to identify how well your organisation or department is doing in terms of establishing a good working environment.

Characteristic of good working relationships	Score			
	1 Excellent	2 Good	3 Average	4 Unsatis-factory
Good leadership				
Commitment				
Diversity				
Respect				
Effective communications				

PLTS

When you are evaluating experiences and learning to inform future progress, you are practising your skills as a reflective learner (RL).

Unit D2a develop working relationships with colleagues and stakeholders

very common area in business education, as it is recognised that assertiveness skills are of great benefit both to the individuals concerned as well as to the organisation.

Remember

Assertiveness is the ideal approach to take, although many people find it difficult to find this balance in their communication style, tending naturally to behave either passively or aggressively.

Activity ⏱ 10 minutes

Now it's time for you to reflect on your own assertiveness skills. Identify where your natural communication style lies on the continuum below. If your style lies outside of the assertive area, think of three actions you can take to practise making your style more assertive. Over the coming weeks when you are communicating with others, either in meetings, over the phone or in face-to-face discussions, keep in mind your level of assertiveness and make notes on actions you have taken to make changes to your communication style.

Passive — Assertive — Aggressive

Functional Skills

If you produce a written report as part of the assessment for this learning outcome, you will be practising your Functional Skills in English: Writing.

Be able to create an environment of trust and mutual respect with colleagues and stakeholders

It is important for you as a manager, to be keenly aware of the needs and motivations of your colleagues and those of your stakeholders. These needs and motivations can change over time so it is important to keep this knowledge and awareness current. In this section you will examine ways of reviewing and keeping up-to-date with these important issues.

You will also examine different ways of interacting with your colleagues and stakeholders which show respect for others' views and actions.

Reviewing and revising the needs and motivations of colleagues and stakeholders

It is essential for every organisation, whether in the public or private sector, whether for profit or non-profit making, to systematically review the needs and motivations of its stakeholders, including those that are internal to the organisation, such as employees and managers, as well as the many external stakeholders, such as customers, suppliers, shareholders and the community.

The business requires accurate information so that it knows what the key stakeholder issues and

Portfolio Task 2 ⏱ 90 minutes

Links to LO2: Assessment criteria 2.1, 2.2

1. Outline the key things you need to consider in creating a common sense of purpose, with colleagues and stakeholders. Give examples from your own experience if possible. If you do not yet have such experience, you can talk about what you would do, given such a situation.

2. Give examples of some specific actions you and your organisation could, or do, take to enhance trust and mutual respect between colleagues and stakeholders.

Your assessment could take the form of a written narrative or a professional discussion with your assessor. It could also include the production of workplace evidence, work-based observations or the use of witness testimonies, as appropriate.

concerns are. These issues will then inform the strategic decision-making and action planning of the business. Reviewing and revising these on a regular basis is essential to keep the overview of issues and concerns current – as well as to get early warning signals of significant changes or growing unhappiness in a particular area. When stakeholder needs and motivations change, the business needs to be ready to respond to these changes, it may need to adapt its plans accordingly and may also need to take swift action to investigate and find remedies for issues identified.

Needs and motivations of colleagues

How well do you think you know what the needs and motivations of your colleagues are? Are they the same as yours? How do you know?

Needs

At a very basic level, the needs of your colleagues will begin with those for making a living and supporting themselves and their families. This means that they will have a requirement for a certain minimum income that will allow them to achieve this. Beyond this, colleagues' needs may include those for job satisfaction and a rewarding career and career development, with security of employment likely to be a key factor in this too.

Motivations

Motivation is what makes us want to do what we do. If we apply this to our positions in the organisation, there are many possible motivations, and they will differ from person to person, including:

- interesting and varied work
- challenging tasks
- competitiveness
- ability to help others – maybe by teaching, training or even in an advisory or counselling role
- authority over others
- control of resources or departments
- expertise in a particular area such as health and safety, finance or IT.

Having knowledge of other people's motivations can help you to understand their behaviour in certain situations. If someone is naturally competitive, for example, they are likely to be quite vocal and quick to criticise others.

Checklist

Remember, motivation is what drives us. It affects our:

- behaviour
- enthusiasm
- decisions.

Activity 🕐 15 minutes

Review and list your own personal needs and motivations in your current role. Try and think of three or four of each. Read over your list and decide which of these will still be the same twelve months from now. If you foresee any potential changes, write these down.

Needs of stakeholders

The typical needs of stakeholders, for instance customers, suppliers, shareholders and the community, might be as follows.

- Customers generally need to be able to purchase reliable and acceptable-quality goods and services. They may also need instant product availability, fast delivery to their home, payment terms, warranties, good levels of customer service, refunds, exchanges, or even a twenty-four-hour helpline.
- Suppliers generally need regular orders for products, timely payment and continuity of business over the long term.
- Shareholders need a return on their investment by regular dividend payments and a growth in the value of their shares.
- Communities need businesses that provide employment and prosperity in the area. They also need businesses that take responsibility for the consequences of their activities, such as noise, litter and pollution, and are socially responsible in their actions.

Activity 10 minutes

Look back over the list of stakeholder needs above. Can you add any others to the list? Think about the stakeholders of your own organisation and think of one more need for each stakeholder. You could record this information in a table.

Motivations of stakeholders

Examining what it is that motivates your stakeholders is an excellent way of revealing the issues that the business must take on board in its decision making. These are perhaps easily overlooked when the pressure is on and you need to focus on your own departmental goals and objectives. Here are some typical factors that may motivate your stakeholders.

Customer motivations

Customers are motivated primarily by quality, good prices and good service standards. Beyond this are factors such as companies taking social responsibilities seriously.

Supplier motivations

Suppliers need businesses who will keep them in business. This means they will be motivated to supply to stable, established businesses with good reputations. They will be motivated to work with other businesses that provide regular or large orders and who can pay on time.

Shareholder motivations

Shareholder motivations are financial in nature. At a basic level, they are motivated by the opportunity to receive the best return for their investment, which involves consideration of **opportunity cost**. Some shareholders simply want to make the greatest short-term financial gain. Others are happy to receive a moderate return in the short term in return for seeing the value of the business grow over the longer term – and therefore also increasing their share value.

Key Term

Opportunity cost – the return which could have been received by making an alternative investment.

Community motivations

Communities want to have good businesses in their area that provide jobs for local residents and prosperity for the area. They want to have socially responsible businesses that show concern for the community and have an interest in participating in initiatives to help the local community.

Ways of reviewing and revising stakeholder needs and motivations

Now that you have a good understanding of what the needs and motivations of your colleagues and stakeholders might be, you need to be able to outline methods by which you can systematically keep these up-to-date. Last year's customer needs may already be outdated! But you will only find this out by having a strategy of regular information gathering from your customers. This is especially relevant in fast moving markets, such as new technology. Think about the mobile phone industry, for example. Mobile phone technology is developing at such a fast rate that new and better products are coming onto the market every month. People are updating their phones on a regular basis and old models are rapidly becoming obsolete.

To get regular and up-to-date information on your stakeholder needs and motivations, you need to have a communication strategy in place that is capable of acquiring this information in an efficient manner. This can include:

- special meetings
- surveys (especially online surveys)
- suggestion schemes
- incentives.

Meetings with stakeholders

Meetings with stakeholders, especially customers and employees, are an excellent forum for information gathering – if they are handled correctly. This is a very important point because it is very easy for meetings to fall flat and fail in their objectives simply because they are not run properly. They need to be focused on getting the stakeholders to speak up and give an honest and detailed account of their needs and wants. This is the only way you can hope to gather any meaningful information.

This means that the meetings need to be injected with positive energy and vibrancy and an informality that encourages active contributions from those attending. Presentation skills will be central to setting the tone and eliciting a good level of feedback from attendees.

How to handle information received

Here is a brief summary of how to handle information received from meeting participants:

● acknowledge it
● record it, along with the details of the person providing it
● agree to consider it
● thank the person concerned for taking the trouble to participate.

Keeping a detailed log of information and suggestions received allows you to respond at any following meeting and acknowledge the person who offered the information.

Surveys

Regular employee and customer surveys can be issued to gather information on satisfaction levels, as well as on all key areas of interest as seen in Figure D2a.2. Online surveys are a particularly effective method to use, as they have a higher response rate and are extremely quick and easy to administer via email or your company website. In addition, the results are automatically collated for you by the software package.

Suggestion schemes

Suggestion schemes can be run either manually, with comment cards and a box in which to put them, or electronically, with a special email address to which people can send comments. One point to bear in mind with this approach is that you are likely to get the extremes of both positive and negative views and will not be likely to hear from those who are merely quite happy. This is because satisfied customers and employees are not particularly driven to take unprompted action in the same way as those who are either delighted or exasperated might be!

Incentives

One sure-fire way of dramatically increasing the take up rate of your information gathering efforts from stakeholders is to provide incentives for them to give their comments and feedback. Typical incentives might include an automatic entry into a prize draw, a voucher to spend in store, or a large prize to be awarded to a participant selected at random.

Demonstrating interaction with colleagues and stakeholders that allows respect for the views and actions of others

Good communication skills are essential for engaging in interactions with your colleagues and stakeholders in ways that make a good impression and convey the message that you want to get across. They are also essential for conveying empathy and respect for others, even where you may not necessarily agree with them on a particular issue.

Figure D2a.2 A typical online customer survey.

Every interaction, whether it be a quick phone conversation with an individual customer or a formal meeting with senior managers, is an opportunity for you to make a good impression by being professional and business-like and by conveying respect and due regard for others.

Checklist

Ways in which you can show respect to others during face-to-face discussions include:

- making good eye contact
- showing good listening skills
- avoiding interrupting
- having good posture and appearance.

Ways of demonstrating respect

Respect can be demonstrated in the words that we choose to use, the way in which we choose to say them and in our actions and behaviour towards others. It is important to pay attention to being respectful to others at work because it is the basis for developing good quality relationships involving trust and honesty. Good relationships, in turn, are themselves the basis for achieving organisational goals and objectives. There are very few, if any, tasks we can achieve entirely on our own and for this reason, relationship building and network development are essential for goal achievement in our working lives.

Checklist

Remember, non-verbal communication can be more important than your speech. Pay special attention to the messages you give out by your:

- posture
- appearance
- body language
- facial expressions
- eye contact
- proximity to the other person
- gestures
- listening skills
- movements of hands, head, eyes and whole body
- attentiveness.

Active listening

Active listening is a technique that has been developed to help us improve our communication with others at work. Most people, unfortunately, are not naturally good listeners. We only actually hear around half of what is said in many conversations. Distractions, unrelated thoughts and competing noises around us all serve to undermine our focus, attention and therefore our ability to listen.

You can consciously learn to use active listening. It is based on a model of respectful behaviour towards others and is designed to help you to capture and understand more of what is said during conversations and meetings. Failing to pick up on a critical detail discussed in a meeting can cause problems in all working relationships afterwards and these problems could be easily avoided by employing better listening skills. Table D2a.3 shows the process that you should follow.

Pay attention	• Give the other person your full attention • Avoid being distracted by other goings on around you
Show that you are listening	• Nod and smile at certain points during the discussion to show acknowledgement • Use your body language to demonstrate that you are listening
Ask questions	• Use questions such as 'So, it sounds to me that you're saying… is that correct?' • Questions such as these help to ensure key points are fully understood
Give appropriate responses	• Be assertive and respectful when giving your opinions • Avoid put downs or verbal attacks

Table D2a.3 The process of active listening.

Activity — 10 minutes

Rate your active listening skills. For each area below, give yourself a mark out of ten. Then, identify any areas for improvement. You may find it easiest to record this information in a table.

- Paying attention
- Showing that you are listening
- Asking questions
- Giving appropriate responses

PLTS

When you are evaluating your experiences and learning to inform future progress, you are practising your skills as a reflective learner (RL).

Cultural issues concerning respect

It is likely that your colleagues and stakeholders comprise people of varying backgrounds and cultures. This is especially likely to be the case if your organisation trades internationally or even globally. It is important to be aware of cultural differences that may impact on what is considered to be respectful conduct in other cultures or countries. Things that are often taken for granted, such as gesticulating with hands, or even simply making eye contact, can have different connotations in different cultures. For example, eye contact is deemed an indicator of trustworthiness in certain cultures, such as the UK and the USA. However, in other cultures, such as in south Asia, it is deemed rude and disrespectful.

Being aware of the existing norms and customary behaviour of colleagues and stakeholders from other cultures will prevent you from making any potentially damaging culturally disrespectful gestures or actions.

Functional Skills

If you take part in a professional discussion with your assessor as part of the assessment for this learning outcome, you will be practising your Functional Skills in English: Speaking and Listening.

PLTS

Thinking about your actions and behaviours will show that you are a reflective learner (RL).

Portfolio Task 3 ⏱ 60 minutes

Links to LO3: Assessment criteria 3.1, 3.2

1. **(a)** Say why you think it is important to have a systematic process in place for reviewing and revising your colleagues' and stakeholders' needs and motivations, giving examples of potential changes that could occur.

   (b) Give examples of methods you could use for reviewing and revising the needs and motivations of colleagues and stakeholders.

2. Give specific examples of the actions and behaviours that you either have or could demonstrate in order to show respect for the views and actions of others.

Your assessment could take the form of a written narrative or a professional discussion with your assessor. It could also include the production of workplace evidence, work-based observations or the use of witness testimonies, as appropriate.

Team talk

Paul's story

My name is Paul Greening and I am 29 years old. I've been employed as a line manager in a retail electronics store for two months. The company has recently launched a new range of products, which are already selling extremely well, and I have been tasked with gauging customer satisfaction levels with the new range.

I have never had to do anything like this before and I am unsure as to the best methods to adopt. We sell a lot of our products direct to customers from our website, so we have a large database of customer contact details, along with purchase information available. We do not, however, have any contact details for customers who purchase goods in store, so I am unsure of how I could go about getting feedback from this customer group.

I am under pressure to produce a customer satisfaction report for my manager by the end of the month – which also coincides with the end of my probationary period. I need to impress my boss and am getting very concerned that I will not be able to get her the information she requires.

Top tips

You need to go about your information gathering in two stages. First, arrange an email survey campaign that targets all of your online customers who have purchased one of the new products. Remember to include some form of incentive for customers to complete your online survey.

Second, launch an in-store satisfaction survey to target all of those customers who purchase these products from your store. You could do this by collecting telephone and email contact details of customers at the checkout, so that you can follow up with them afterwards, or you could distribute customer satisfaction forms when you issue till receipts. Again, some form of incentive to complete and return the form will increase response rates dramatically.

Ask the expert	
Q	What would be the best methods of gathering customer satisfaction data for our new product range, which comprises both online and in-store customers?
A	You need to tailor your data gathering techniques to target each type of customer, as one single technique will not reach both customer groups. By adopting your data gathering according to customer type, you will be able to compile a report that includes good response rates from both your online and in-store customers.

What your assessor is looking for

You will demonstrate your skills, knowledge and competence through the learning outcomes in this unit. Evidence generated in this unit will also cross reference to the other units in this qualification.

Please bear in mind that there are significant cross-referencing opportunities throughout this qualification and you may have already generated some relevant work to meet certain criteria in this unit. Your assessor will provide you with the exact requirements to meet the standards of this unit. However, as a guide it is likely that for this unit you will need to be assessed through the following methods:

- One observation of relevant workplace activities to cover the whole unit.
- One witness testimony may also be produced.
- A written narrative, reflective account or professional discussion.
- Relevant work products to be produced as evidence.

The work products for this unit could include:

- annual published company reports
- job descriptions
- information and documents relating to any of your organisation's stakeholder initiatives such as customer focus groups, community projects, employee committees or company meetings.

Your assessor will guide you through the assessment process as detailed in the candidate logbook. The detailed assessment criteria are shown in the logbook and by working through these questions, combined with providing the relevant evidence, you will meet the learning outcomes required to complete this unit.

Task and page reference	Assessment criteria
1 (page 225)	1.1, 1.2, 1.3
2 (page 230)	2.1, 2.2
3 (page 235)	3.1, 3.2

Unit D2a Develop working relationships with colleagues and stakeholders

Unit D13 Support individuals to develop and take responsibility for their performance

In this unit you will examine ways in which you can work with individuals in your team to help to identify their development needs based on established standards of performance, as well as giving consideration to individuals' goals and ambitions.

You will also investigate the specific types of support you will need to provide to help individuals create their own personal development plans. Ensuring that individuals' development plans are implemented requires regular monitoring and periodic reviews to make sure everyone is keeping on track. You will examine some useful techniques for keeping on top of your responsibilities in this area and ensuring that the development activities for individuals in your team are undertaken as planned.

In the final section of this unit you will investigate how to provide feedback to employees and look at how it can be implemented to make changes to individuals' development plans.

What you will learn

- Be able to agree their performance development needs with an individual
- Be able to understand how to help an individual create a development plan
- Be able to support an individual in implementing their development plan
- Be able to evaluate an individual's progress against a development plan and provide feedback for continual performance improvement

Links to the Technical Certificate

If you are completing your NVQ as part of an Apprenticeship Framework, you will find the following topics are also covered in your Technical Certificate:

- Providing learning and development objectives for staff
- Evaluating work performance.

Be able to agree performance development needs with an individual

Identifying and agreeing the performance development needs of your team members will be an ongoing and important aspect of your role as a manager. To become successful in this area, you will need to develop skills in **objectively** assessing performance using a variety of techniques and measures. The accuracy of your assessment, combined with discussions with individuals concerning their ambitions and future goals, will provide the basis for the identification of their development needs.

> **Remember**
>
> Development is any experience that helps an individual to grow, gain new insights and learn. It is associated with attitude, rather than skills. So, think creatively about the opportunities you can provide for your staff.

Explaining the standards of performance required for an individual's current or future role

All job roles, from the most senior manager to the most junior apprentice, involve working to certain standards. **Standards of performance** provide ways of measuring work. They allow employees to measure their own performance against defined expectations and they also allow management to measure employees' progress against targets.

> **Key Terms**
>
> **Objectively** – free from bias, prejudice and self-interest.
>
> **Standards of performance** – the precise level of competence required to be proficient in a particular role.

Understanding performance standards

Let's take a look at some performance standards that might apply to a customer service position.

- Achieve target response times in replying to customer queries.
- Keep work area clean and tidy at all times.
- Be positive and professional in all dealings with customers.
- Handle complaints according to company procedures.

These standards of performance tell individuals exactly what is expected of them. They also ensure consistency of work where different people are performing the same role. It is important to remember that standards refer to a *position* and the tasks required of that position, not to the person doing the job. This means that assessment of performance can be fairly and objectively carried out where several people do the same job.

When everyone is working to their expected standards, the organisation will perform well overall. This is because when all of the individual tasks are carried out to the required standard, they feed into and contribute to the achievement of the bigger organisational goals. These larger organisational goals are often expressed in terms of increased profit or revenue.

You can summarise the content of performance standards by breaking them down into their 'what', 'how' and 'when' components. Table D13.1 shows some examples.

Responsibility area	Task to be completed	Manner in which it is to be completed	By when or how often it is to be completed
Office administration	Order office supplies for the team	Efficiently	Every week
Secretarial support	Take minutes of team meetings	Accurately and neatly	Every month
Team working	Help and co-operate with other team members	Politely and in a helpful manner	As required, according to work demands of team

Table D13.1 How performance standards could be summarised.

Performance standards provide an important benchmark of what should be done and how. They also provide the basis for future performance assessment because they state clearly what is expected from a particular role.

Breaking down standards in this way is a good method of demonstrating expectations to employees and helping them to see what they need to be able to do.

Focus of different standards

Examples of standards of performance that might apply to customer service agent roles could include the following:

- answer the telephone within three rings
- respond to all email enquiries within 24 hours
- be polite to customers at all times.

As these examples show, standards can be focused on quality, quantity or time. Quality refers to how well a task must be performed, and this may or may not involve directly measurable criteria. For example, to be polite at all times is a quality standard. However, it is not directly concerned with figures. You could assess the extent to which your team perform to this quality standard by direct observation of them in their role, or by asking for feedback from your customers.

Quantity refers to how many times a certain task must be completed and could be stated in terms such as products produced, calls taken, customers served, or complaints resolved. Time refers to the deadlines imposed on standards. These could be to complete a certain number of tasks per hour, per day, per week or per month.

Activity 15 minutes

Get hold of the performance standards relating to one of your team's roles. Review the standards to identify the key focus of each – quality, quantity or time. Do you think the focus of any of the standards needs improving to make it clearer? Suggest any changes you believe would improve the standards.

PLTS

When you are identifying improvements that would benefit others as well as yourself, you are practising your skills as an effective participator (EP).

Communicating standards

It is your responsibility, as a manager, to ensure that your team are fully aware of their required performance standards. They cannot hope to achieve good levels of performance if they do not know what is expected of them.

Standards need to be clear and concise. They also need to state:

- specific actions required
- conditions attached to the actions (deadlines, number needed, how)
- how performance relating to a particular standard will be monitored and assessed.

Figure D13.1 Communicating required performance standards and assessment methods.

Good methods of communicating standards to individuals in your team include:

- making sure you have a written copy of the standards to give to each of your staff
- setting one-to-one time aside for each staff member to discuss standards
- allowing two-way communication with individuals to let them ask any questions
- being available for ongoing support and guidance, especially where new standards have been introduced or where there are new or inexperienced employees in your team.

The performance standards relevant to an individual position are often stated in the job description. This will be available from your HR department or your line manager.

There may also be team, departmental or even organisational standards that need to be observed. These types of performance standards could be related to industry regulations or codes of practice and will be displayed on staff noticeboards, intranet sites or in company handbooks.

Activity ⏱ 15 minutes

Identify all the relevant performance standards that apply to your own role. State whether these are individual, team-based, organisational or externally set (these could include voluntary codes of practice or regulatory requirements). Ask your line manager or your assessor to help make sure you locate all relevant performance standards.

Producing clear performance standards

Performance standards need to be expressed clearly and succinctly to make sure that they are understood by those needing to work to them. Having clearly expressed performance standards makes it easier for people to perform well, as they will know what is required of them.

In short, performance standards should:

- be brief

- be clear
- set out exact requirements (for example, produce 10 units, answer 30 calls, make 10 sales)
- give a timescale
- give information on the assessment methods which will be used to monitor performance.

Special attention should be paid to the wording used in performance standards. It is also important to periodically review and update them. Standards need to remain current and meaningful, both to you and your team, otherwise they will simply become a form-filling exercise and nothing more. This is a waste of everyone's time. Your team need working standards so that they can do their job effectively.

When reviewing performance standards for clarity, put yourself in the place of the individuals to whom they relate. See whether, based purely on the information given, you would have a good understanding of the job requirements. If not, rewrite the standards to make them clearer.

Knowledge, skills and attitude

Standards can be broken down into the knowledge, skills and attitude that combine to achieve the standard. You should aim to incorporate this level of detail in your team's performance standards where possible to help them understand exactly what is required of them in achieving a specific standard.

For example, suppose a customer service representative had the performance standard of 'Following the customer service policy to deal appropriately with all complaints received within 24 hours'.

The knowledge, skills and attitude needed to be able to fulfil this performance standard might be:

- knowledge of the customer service policy in relation to dealing with customer complaints
- communication skills to respond appropriately to customers, including good verbal and written ability, as well as good interpersonal skills
- attitude – a positive, courteous and professional approach.

Establishing assessment methods for performance standards

Once you have established standards for your team, you must decide on the methods that you will use to assess performance against them. Many standards can be assessed simply by direct observation of the employee doing the job. However, where there are a large number of staff, or where staff are based at different locations, this may be impractical.

Other ways of assessing performance could include:

- measurement of outputs (calls made, units produced, customers served)
- customer feedback (reduction in complaints, satisfaction with customer service levels)
- feedback from colleagues (team working skills, cooperation, interpersonal skills).

It is vitally important that you inform your team about the way in which their performance against standards will be assessed. If you do not do this, and suddenly begin monitoring staff, they will become suspicious of your motives and wonder why you are all of a sudden watching them. So, be sure to inform everyone exactly when and how you will monitor performance against standards. Being clear, open and upfront in this way will increase understanding and trust, which is important in developing good relationships with your team.

Performance standards for current and future roles

Explaining the required performance standards for current roles will ensure that your team are fully proficient in all of their tasks and are operating at satisfactory levels. It is a good method of making sure there are no **performance gaps** in your team.

Telling your employees about performance standards for a future role can also be of benefit in your **succession planning** strategy. It is a good way to prepare employees for the new skills

and responsibilities they will undertake in their next career move. It also minimises problems for the organisation in filling vacant positions in the future, as you will have a supply of suitably prepared candidates ready to move into them.

Identifying and agreeing performance development needs for individuals

Once you have identified and communicated relevant performance standards with individuals within your team, you can use these standards as a basis upon which to agree their individual development needs. The process of individual needs development will consist of a one-to-one meeting between you and each individual within your team. It will be beneficial to both parties if you each prepare your thoughts and reflections ahead of the meeting, make any relevant notes and bring along any relevant supporting materials. This will help make the meeting as productive and positive as possible. The aim of the meeting is to establish agreement between employee goals and employer requirements.

Job analysis

The identification of individual development needs will begin with some type of **job analysis** to establish current performance against existing standards. This will highlight strengths and weaknesses in performance and indicate key areas for intervention, such as training or coaching.

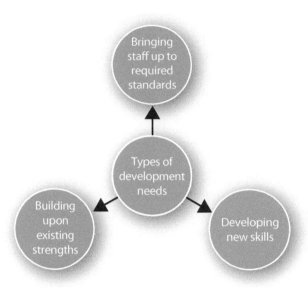

Figure D13.2 Different types of development needs.

Development needs can vary, as shown in Figure D13.2. They can include:

- skills requirements to bring someone up to the existing standards in any areas of their role where they are not already meeting these
- building upon existing strengths and further developing these
- planning ahead for new skills that will be needed in the future, such as in response to the introduction of new technology or new processes.

Individual goals and ambitions

In order to be meaningful, identification of individual development needs must also take into account the future goals and ambitions of the individuals concerned. Remember too that goals and ambitions are very personal in nature and will vary greatly from individual to individual. One team member may be very keen to aspire to a managerial position in the future, whereas another may be more interested in becoming a specialist, maybe in IT or in a technical aspect of their role. Other team members may wish to move to an entirely new area within the company to pursue a change in direction. These are all ambitions that could potentially be accommodated by the organisation and should be taken into

account in planning any future development activities. There are also many employees who are happy to continue in their current role for the foreseeable future. These employees will also have development needs, such as learning new technology, and should not be excluded from the process of needs identification.

Managerial goals

Team members with ambitions to progress to management positions could be given suitable additional responsibilities within the team in order to develop their management skills. For instance, taking on some sort of managing role in suitable upcoming projects or events would be a good introduction to the role of manager. Remember to include some form of mentoring or other support for them as part of this developmental activity, so that they are not simply thrown in at the deep end. Make sure to also include a debrief after the experience to find out how the team member found it, as well as feeding back your assessment of their performance. If the results from this type of intervention prove positive then you can plan further, more challenging experiences for them in the future. This is an excellent method of succession planning – making sure your department has a good supply of future managers with suitable skills and experience to move into such positions when the opportunity arises.

Specialist and technical goals

Individuals with technical or specialist ambitions could be given suitable projects to work on to develop this area of their skills. Someone who is keen to move into web programming, for example, could be given the task of creating an intranet site for the team or department. If there is already an existing intranet, they could redesign it or simply make some basic improvements to the way it works.

Similarly, someone who wishes to develop their IT skills in the future could be given IT helpdesk responsibilities alongside their current job. This would give them the valuable experience of helping employees with a range of IT issues while building their own IT skills at the same time.

Changing career direction

There are different ways in which organisations can accommodate those wishing to change career direction within the company. You should mention any such cases to your own line manager, as they may be able to offer valuable support to you. If somebody wishes to move into a different department, for example, they could be put on an initial placement in that department. If successful, after a trial period, the employee could be permanently transferred.

Accepting that people can have multiple and diverse skills and interests and allowing inter-departmental changes, such as the one discussed in the example above, is good management practice because it:

- satisfies employees' personal ambitions
- keeps valuable skills within the company
- benefits the organisation where employees can bring knowledge and insight from other areas of the business to add value to their new role.

Organisational requirements

The last key consideration in identifying and agreeing performance development needs for individuals is the needs of the organisation in terms of skills and abilities. You need to find out answers to the following questions:

- In what skill areas does the organisation need to focus?
- Can cross-training to create a more multi-skilled workforce be implemented?
- Are there any planned changes to processes or technology that will bring new skills requirements with them?

Organisational needs for skills, both in the short and longer term, will have an effect on the development needs of individuals and will shape the focus of their needs development plan to some extent. These needs, although quite separate from considerations of personal aims and ambitions, are legitimate and indeed critical because they directly address the operational requirements of the business.

As manager, you are responsible for making sure the identification of individual development needs among your team primarily addresses the skills requirements of the organisation.

Portfolio Task 1 90 minutes

Links to LO1: Assessment criteria 1.1, 1.2

1. (a) Define what is meant by performance standards, giving examples to illustrate your answer.

(b) Give reasons to explain why performance standards are important in the workplace. Say in what way they benefit the manager, the employee and the organisation.

(c) Explain the standards of performance required for one of the individuals within your team. These standards could relate either to their current role or to a role that they would like to fulfil in the future.

2. (a) Give some examples of typical performance development needs within your team and say why they exist.

(b) Say what factors you need to consider when identifying performance development needs for your team members.

Your assessment could take the form of a written narrative or a professional discussion with your assessor. It could also include the production of workplace evidence, work-based observations or the use of witness testimonies, as appropriate.

Functional Skills

If you use word processing software to produce a report for the assessment of this learning outcome, you will be practising your Level 2 Functional Skills in ICT: Developing, presenting and communicating information.

Unit D13 support individuals to develop and take responsibility for their performance

Briefly describe the process that exists in your organisation for identifying and agreeing performance development needs with individuals. If you have experience of using this process, say how you went about it and whether, in your opinion, it is effective or where improvements could be made. Get hold of copies of any relevant documents used as part of this process. These will also be very useful in completing the portfolio tasks at the end of this section.

PLTS

When you are evaluating experiences and learning to inform future progress, you are practising your skills as reflective learner (RL).

Be able to understand how to help an individual create a development plan

An individual development plan is a personal roadmap for employees to use to chart their progress and their career development. The plan itself belongs to the employee and documents their personal journey in skills development and performance improvement.

Your role as a manager is to find the best ways to help and guide your staff in taking all available opportunities to develop and enhance their skills. This will involve helping them understand specific actions they need to take to achieve their developmental goals and objectives. You also need to keep the plan focused on relevant issues that are aligned to the needs of the organisation.

Identifying options available to support an individual in meeting desired standards of performance

There are potentially many options available for supporting staff in achieving certain standards of performance. Training and development can be:

- internal or external
- formal or informal
- on-the-job or off-the-job.

However, the support options relevant to you and your team will depend on the particular resources available in your own organisation and the objectives and type of support needed. Table D13.2, below, shows examples of some of the support options that may be suitable for developmental activities.

Staff support options	Features
In-house training	In-house training takes place within the organisation and has the advantage that it is easy to set up and run, as well as being cheaper than external training. In-house training can be exactly tailored to the needs of the trainees as it is run by those experienced in the organisation's current processes and procedures.
External training	External training, such as that provided by professional training organisations, can be expensive and may require lead time to set up. However, it is an excellent training method where, for example, highly complex or in-depth knowledge needs to be learnt. Businesses might typically outsource training in such areas as health and safety, and software and hardware training.
On-the-job training	On-the-job training is training which occurs whilst doing the job and could be termed 'learning by doing'. Benefits of on-the-job training include that it can be carried out as and when needed, it is cheap, flexible and practical. This type of training occurs in the live work environment and is not suitable, therefore, for situations where errors could cause serious harm to others or yourself.
Team training away from the job, such as in a classroom	Training done away from the job has the key advantage that attendees are away from the pressures of their work and are thus able to focus. This type of training is suitable where a group of employees all need to be trained in the same area and where the training is focused on theory or knowledge. It could also be useful for computer-based simulations or for learning how to use new systems in a test environment. The main drawback of this type of training is that an entire group is required to be away from their work at the same time.

Staff support options	Features
Coaching and mentoring	Coaching and mentoring are excellent methods of supporting staff in skills development. They involve one-to-one guidance, usually on the job, where people are shown how to do something and they then have a go themselves. The coach or mentor then provides feedback and any additional help as required. Coaching and mentoring are, however, time consuming methods of training, so consider the existing workloads of any nominated coaches or mentors before committing to this type of support for your staff.
Work shadowing	Work shadowing involves a new or inexperienced employee spending a period of time working alongside a more experienced employee, so that they can see in detail a job being performed along with the skills and knowledge it requires.
Placements and secondments	Placements can involve part- or full-time work experience periods with another department or a partner organisation. They can last from one day to several weeks or even months. Secondments are full-time work experience opportunities and are usually for a longer period – such as one year. Placements and secondments are excellent methods of obtaining real, on-the-job experience and can be of huge benefit to relatively inexperienced employees in advancing their skills.
Attendance at industry events, such as conferences	This is an excellent method of developing industry knowledge and networking with contacts. However, it can be expensive to arrange and requires time away from work.
Distance learning	The key advantage of this type of training is that it can be done at the trainee's own pace. Distance learning can be done in the trainee's own time at home and so does not require time out from the job.

Table D13.2 Types of training and support options.

Activity 15 minutes

Describe two or three development needs that exist in your team. Explain what you consider to be the most suitable type of training or development support to address these needs.

Selecting the most appropriate support for your staff

Some of the key issues you will need to consider in deciding on which are the best support interventions for your staff will include:

- cost
- type of skills
- business priority.

Cost

You will need to have a training and development budget allocated to your team before you can decide on how you will plan specific development activities for them. This will allow you to adequately provide for the development needs of all of your team. Formal training methods such as classroom-based or external training courses are generally far more expensive than in-house and informal methods such as on-the-job training.

You need to keep in mind what it is your staff need to gain from the training (the objective) and if, for example, attending a conference is the best way of achieving this, then that is a legitimate solution. However, remember that there are many ways to achieve development objectives using methods that are in-house, on the job, or that can be carried out in the employee's own time such as distance learning or reading.

Type of skills

The type of skills you are dealing with will have a key influence on the most suitable type of training or development activity to undertake. For example, manual or clerical skills can usually be adequately developed by on-the-job training methods. However, teaching IT programmers a new programming language would require a radically different approach. Classroom-based solutions would probably be the best approach for this type of skill. Teaching customer service skills to restaurant staff might well be dealt with by group training using role-play and simulation.

Business priority

Training and development initiatives must be aligned with the priorities of the business. These priorities may well be determined by **external factors,** such as industry-specific regulatory changes or the introduction of new legislation. Examples of such legislation might include:

- changes to consumer law – requiring staff training in how to deal with new consumer rights
- tightening up of product safety regulations – requiring changes in production techniques and quality control processes.

Internal factors can also have an impact on business priorities. Business decisions on issues such as new products to be launched, new marketing strategies or new pricing guidelines can also have a large impact on the development priorities of employees. In some situations, lower priority development areas may have to be postponed to accommodate key business needs.

Key Terms

External factors – factors that arise from the external environment in which the business operates.

Internal factors – factors that arise from inside the business.

Remember

Remember, when you are deciding on the best approach to implement development activities, you need to consider costs, available budget, skills needed and business priorities.

Activity ⏱ 15 minutes

When you are planning development initiatives for your team, say what your main constraints are from an organisational point of view. These could be things such as pressure to minimise time away from work, cost or limited availability of development resources.

Explain what your key business priorities are for the current year and explain any impact these will have on development initiatives for your team. You can either produce your answer as a brief report or as a professional discussion with your assessor.

Overcoming barriers to learning and development

One of the key areas where you may need to provide support will be where individuals are resistant to taking up development opportunities offered to them. This could be for a number of reasons including:

- lack of confidence
- low morale
- fear of technological change.

Your first task is to find out the cause of the individual's resistance to development. This will require some one-to-one time with the employee and possibly some difficult open and honest discussions with them. Most issues causing such resistance to development can be easily dealt with by adopting a counselling approach. Sell the benefits of the development opportunities to them in terms of the employee's added value to the organisation and this will give them a confidence boost at the same time. Take care to use positive language and offer workable suggestions in these situations.

Other issues causing resistance may require a little ingenuity and problem solving on your part. For example, you could think about offering alternative development opportunities to achieve the desired results. Your key aim is to find ways to win over your employees so that they actively engage with their personal development.

Individual learning preferences

Individuals do not all like to learn new skills in the same manner. Some of us prefer to jump in at the deep end while others prefer to think about things before attempting new tasks. It is important for you to be aware of these differences in learning preferences because these will impact on how well individuals progress with different types of development opportunity.

David Kolb created a learning cycle in 1979 to identify the way people learn. He looked at four points:

- Learning and what was felt during a period of learning.

- Thinking about how useful the period of learning was.
- Looking at ideas and theories related to the learning experience.
- Testing the learning.

Peter Honey and Alan Mumford further developed Kolb's learning cycle to identify four different learning styles or preferences. These styles can be mapped onto the four stages of the learning cycle.

- Activist (maps to the first stage) – prefers to get on with it and experience new challenges immediately.
- Reflector (maps to the second stage) – prefers to think before acting and likes to take a little time to do this.
- Theorist (maps to the third stage) – likes to gather all relevant facts and compile these into a coherent theory. Theorists are rational and objective.
- Pragmatist (maps to the fourth stage) – practical and down to earth. Prefers to be a decision maker and problem solver.

Activity ⊘ 10 minutes

Look back at the different learning styles and decide which type reflects your preferred style of learning. What types of development opportunities do you think best suit your preferred learning style?

Explaining specific actions needed to achieve objectives

When objectives have been set in a development plan, certain actions then need to be carried out to ensure these objectives are achieved. Every objective needs an action plan so that individuals can see exactly what they need to do and by when. Simply being given an objective to achieve can seem daunting and unachievable to many employees, so breaking it down into manageable

steps is an effective way to overcome this issue and to make it understandable. It is also in your own best interests as a manager to make sure your staff achieve their objectives, as this will be reflected in your own performance appraisal.

Your role in explaining the required actions your employee must undertake to achieve their objectives might include:

- helping the employee to break down objectives into separate steps
- allocating times and dates to completion of each step
- providing help and guidance where employees encounter problems in completing steps
- following up at regular intervals to make sure the employee is carrying out the required steps.

Creating action plans for objectives

Creating an action plan for an objective is a very straightforward process, which consists of looking into the details of what needs to be done and how, as in Table D13.3.

Objective: To become an advanced user of Microsoft Word within the next six months.

Action plan:
1. Enrol on the next phase of in-house advanced Word training courses.
2. Select a course start date within the next six months.
3. Fill in a training leave request form from HR, giving at least a month's notice of the course date.
4. Attend the training course and complete all the required training activities.
5. Complete the end of course assessment test.

Table D13.3 Creating an action plan.

As you can see from the above example, the steps in the action plan spell out very clearly exactly what the employee must do by when, to make sure they complete the objective within the given time limit.

Explaining the process of creating a development plan

The process for creating an individual development plan can be easily communicated to your staff by using a simple checklist. Remember that development plans need to be developed by negotiation and agreement between manager and employee. They cannot be effectively developed in isolation by either yourself or your employees. Figure D13.3 is an example of a checklist that you could use to help explain the process of creating a development plan with individuals within your team.

Checklist for creating an individual development plan

1. Carry out a job analysis to identify current strengths and weaknesses in performance.
2. Identify key priority areas for development

depending on the needs of the business and the individual.

3. Set out a plan of action covering the next twelve months, which identifies suitable development activities. These should include short-term and long-term goals.
4. Arrange any required budgets, approvals and other resources needed to implement the development activities.
5. Set up regular follow-up meetings between manager and employee to monitor progress with personal development issues.

Drafting the development plan

Once you and your employee have a rough idea of the development activities that will be set for the period of the plan, the next step is for the employee to complete a draft version of the plan, containing all of the information agreed. They should then give it to you to check, so you can make any necessary additions or changes.

Individual development plan				
Objective	Development opportunity	Deadline	Outcome	Next steps
1.				
2.				
3.				
4.				

Figure D13.3 Template for a development plan.

Remember

Ensure your staff know the development plan is theirs to own. Your role is to help them understand what key actions are needed to achieve developmental objectives and goals.

Functional Skills

If you produce a written report as part of the assessment for this learning outcome, you will be practising your Level 2 Functional Skills in English: Writing.

Portfolio Task 2 ⏱ 90 minutes

Links to LO2: Assessment criteria 2.1, 2.2, 2.3

1. Identify some examples of options available to support an individual in meeting desired standards of performance. It may be helpful to base your answer on one or more individuals for whom you are responsible. State some of the desired standards of performance and match these to suitable development options. Give reasons to explain why you would select the chosen support options.

2. Select three development objectives for members of your team. For each one, explain the specific actions needed to achieve the objective. Remember to also mention in your answer any additional help or resources that may be needed, as well as timelines for completion of each action.

3. (a) State two benefits of individual development plans.

   (b) Explain the process used in your team for an individual to create a development plan.

Your assessment could take the form of a written narrative or a professional discussion with your assessor. It could also include the production of workplace evidence, work-based observations or the use of witness testimonies, as appropriate.

Be able to support an individual in implementing their development plan

The success or failure of an individual's development plans rests on how effectively they are implemented. No matter how meticulous the planning stage, it is the carrying out of the plans that is the key to their success. This is where you have a crucial role to play. You need to establish communication systems allowing frequent updates with your staff. You will need to act quickly in cases where staff have fallen behind or have encountered problems implementing their development plans. You will need the skills to provide support, give practical guidance and to take measures to get things back on track where necessary.

Describing the opportunities provided for an individual to improve performance

Individual development plans contain certain key information for employees including:

- objectives for performance improvement
- development initiatives, such as on-the-job training, attendance on courses of study, industry events or other training and development activities (you looked in detail at some examples of the options available earlier in this unit)
- deadlines for achievement of objectives.

The opportunities provided to individuals are key to their future improved performance and it is important that you give these opportunities due consideration.

Matching development opportunities to desired performance improvements

The development opportunities selected for individuals need to be matched to their performance improvement objectives. This is important because failing to properly address key performance areas by selecting relevant and targeted training means wasted resources on training, wasted time away from work and, ultimately, a lack of desired improvement in performance. So, your first priority is to ascertain that the selected training option will adequately address the desired improvement in performance. This is an assessment of the validity of the training or development. You can do this by examining the learning outcomes of the training opportunities available and cross-matching these to desired performance improvements for your team.

Activity ⏱ 15 minutes

Give three examples of training options that could address desired performance improvements in your team.

PLTS

When you are identifying improvements that would benefit others as well as yourself, you are practising your skills as an effective participator (EP).

Prioritising performance improvement objectives

Central to devising a plan of support opportunities for your team is identifying what is most important both to the individual and to the organisation. There will always be more development opportunities available than it is possible for any individual to possibly undertake, therefore a judicious approach is needed on your part, to distil the critical from the simply nice to have. There is no point sending your team off on a team-building day out, for example, if there are essential skills-development needs to be addressed which are hampering productivity. These should take priority as they are business critical.

Activity ⏱ 20 minutes

Write three headings to show levels of priority of development needs: Business critical, Necessary and Secondary. Now write down as many examples as you can of individual performance improvement objectives for your team under each of the headings.

Matching opportunities provided to individual goals

You should also consider individuals' own career goals and ambitions in relation to offering suitable development and support. This may also involve liaising with other departments in your organisation. For example, if an individual wishes to transfer departments in the future and this is desirable to the organisation, you could work with the other department's manager to provide relevant development opportunities which will make the transfer as smooth as possible.

Where individuals have other clear career goals, such as to specialise in a certain area, you should discuss these with them prior to making decisions on support options. This will ensure that the development options selected will provide the best match to individuals' needs.

Explaining the outcome to an individual for improved performance

Outcomes of development activities are concerned with what difference was made and what benefits were achieved as a result of them from the point of view of both the employee and the organisation. These differences can be quantitative, such as where staff are now working at a higher rate and producing more output per day. They can also be qualitative, such as improvements in employee commitment and motivation. Both types of outcome are highly valuable and are equally useful ways of identifying the benefits of improved performance. Next, we'll examine the importance of communicating these benefits to your staff.

Communicating benefits of performance improvement

In order to really get the most from the opportunities offered by your organisation for development and performance improvement, it is essential that your team have a solid understanding not only of the specific outcomes of a single development activity, but also of the wider benefits of continuously striving to improve their skills and abilities on an ongoing basis. These benefits are shown in Figure D13.4.

Figure D13.4 Outcomes of development activities.

If you can generate such an understanding among your team of the huge benefits of performance improvement, you will go a long way to producing a culture of career commitment and ownership of development. You will also develop a proactive team who take the initiative to seek out opportunities to further their career and progress in their chosen field. This is all part of creating a culture of continuous improvement.

Portfolio Task 3 ⏲ 60 minutes

Links to LO3: Assessment criteria 3.1, 3.2

1. (a) Explain the reasons why it is important to provide development opportunities for your team.

(b) Describe some examples of the opportunities provided within your organisation for an individual to improve performance.

2. Explain some of the specific work-related outcomes, or benefits, of improved performance relating to a selected individual in your own team.

Your assessment could take the form of a written narrative or a professional discussion with your assessor. It could also include the production of workplace evidence, work-based observations or the use of witness testimonies, as appropriate.

Functional Skills

If you use word-processing software to produce a report for the assessment of this learning outcome, you will be practising your Level 2 Functional Skills in ICT: Developing, presenting and communicating information.

Be able to evaluate an individual's progress against a development plan and provide feedback for continual performance improvement

Monitoring and evaluating an individual's progress against the objectives in their development plan allows you to see what is working well and identify key strengths. Importantly, it also allows you to identify areas that are not progressing as planned, and to take appropriate action in either revising the original plans and objectives or in finding another solution to the performance issue. You will look at ways in which you can do this in this section.

Providing feedback is an essential management skill that lets employees know how they are currently progressing and what they need to do next. Providing constructive feedback requires skill and judgement on your part to maintain motivation from staff and to keep them focused on performance improvement. The ultimate aim is to get employees to take responsibility for their own development and to be committed to their careers.

Monitoring and evaluating an individual's progress against their development plan

It is essential that you have a system in place that allows you to regularly monitor and evaluate your team's progress against targets set in their development plans. This will ensure that the whole development process is kept regularly updated and running smoothly. It also allows you to take action earlier rather than later where performance issues need your attention.

Monitoring progress

Monitoring progress is concerned with collecting data on outcomes of training and development events that employees complete. At the most basic level you need to receive confirmation that they have attended planned events. Secondly, you need to be able to gather feedback on actual employee performance and the outcomes of these events to establish whether they were successful or not. There should be systems in place in your organisation to feed back to you on all aspects of employee training and development outcomes. If there are no such systems at present, you could implement one by creating a training and development event form and asking training providers to complete it and return it to you within a few days of the events taking place. It is beneficial to receive this information as soon as possible after an event so that you can address any major issues in a timely manner.

You can corroborate your organisational data by holding periodic, informal progress reviews with your staff in between the main annual review.

These types of meetings are valuable in keeping employees focused on their performance development throughout the year. It should also be motivating if they know that their outcomes are being actively monitored and tracked.

Progress review meetings are also useful for investigating issues of under-performance, in allowing the employee a forum to give their account of the situation before you instigate corrective action. There is a wide range of factors that can contribute to under-performance, from simply having a bad day or not getting on too well with the training provider, to personal issues impacting on work life. Make sure you have collected all the facts before deciding on next actions to deal with under-performance.

Evaluating progress

Evaluating employee development progress is concerned with making judgements on areas where adjustments may be required to an individual's development plan based on results of the data analysis carried out during the monitoring stage.

Persistent under-performance on an advanced IT skills course, for example, may indicate training needs at an intermediate level. This is simple enough to arrange, as long as you are given access to the performance information in the first place.

Becoming skilled in evaluating your staff development needs is something that will occur naturally over time and with increasing experience. Do not be afraid to ask a colleague or your line manager for a second opinion in situations where you are unsure what to do.

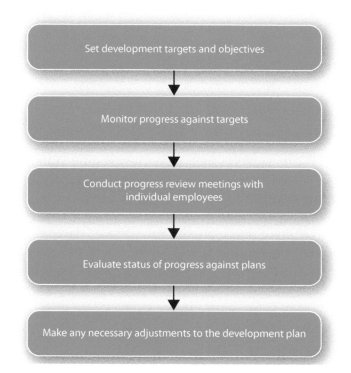

Figure D13.5 A framework for monitoring and evaluating development progress.

Implementing feedback to make development plan revisions

Feedback is essential for informing employees how they are progressing and, in particular, for providing them with a detailed assessment of their current strengths and weaknesses, coupled with guidance for future actions they should undertake to improve performance.

All employees need to receive regular and useful feedback. Without it, they can only guess at how well they are getting on. They may mistakenly believe they are not doing too well and suffer needlessly from a lack of confidence as a result. They may also mistakenly believe they are doing extremely well, when the opposite is in fact the case. Neither of these mistaken beliefs are the fault of the employees, however. It is your responsibility as a manager to find systems for providing regular feedback to your team on their performance. This is especially important where you are managing newly appointed or inexperienced staff, as these groups of employees have the greatest need for performance feedback.

Feedback is essential for employees to revise their development plan.

Constructive feedback

Feedback given to employees should be **constructive** in nature. It should focus on observations, not opinions. It should be given in specific and concrete terms, not in long-winded lectures, so that it is understandable and clear. Never use one hundred words where ten will do! Be open and honest and encourage two-way communication, so that you get to hear what the employee thinks too.

Feedback should be shaped to provide an answer to the question 'How am I getting on?'. If you keep this in mind, it will help you to provide feedback that is clear, brief and helpful to the employee.

There are some key aspects to providing constructive feedback.

- Content – be specific about the point you are making and base it on observations and facts.

- Tone – be careful with the tone you adopt. Avoid sarcasm at all costs. Be sincere and make sure you avoid personal criticisms.

- Method – constructive feedback should be informal, verbal and preferably face-to-face.

- Frequency – constructive feedback needs to be regular and ongoing.

By following the above advice, you will make the process of providing constructive feedback as effective and useful for the recipient as possible.

> **Key Term**
>
> **Constructive feedback** – feedback focused on making improvements.

Giving feedback

You will have to become skilled at conveying both positive and negative feedback to your staff. Positive feedback is, of course, the easier of the two types to deal with – we all enjoy giving and receiving positive feedback. However, when it is necessary to inform someone that their performance is unsatisfactory in some respect, you need to be very careful in the way in which you tell them. Here are some tips for dealing with a negative feedback situation.

- Make sure the meeting is held in private.
- Sandwich the negative content in between two positive comments.
- Keep any negative comments related only to the performance of the job – criticise the work performance, not the person.
- Keep the conversation forward-looking and positive by suggesting ways the employee can improve their performance – agree a plan of action with them to bring about the necessary improvements.
- In cases of persistent poor performance, you will need to get advice from your own line manager and/or your HR department, as this type of situation may become a disciplinary issue. If this is the case, your organisation's disciplinary procedure will need to be invoked.

Remember, the aim of feedback is to provide guidance and to give clarity about performance expectations. This process can increase morale and commitment, as well as improving performance. Effective feedback reduces misunderstandings about what is expected and it can also act as a way of improving interpersonal relationships between managers and their staff.

> **Activity** 🕐 15 minutes
>
> Give an example of how you might provide constructive feedback to one of your team members. Make notes of the things you might say and identify the factors that specifically make your feedback constructive. You can use the guidance provided in the above section to help you.

Making development plan revisions

Development plans are not set in stone. They are working documents and, as such, should be updated and amended when necessary to reflect changes in circumstances. Examples of situations requiring such changes might include where:

- retraining is necessary to bring skills up to the required standard
- an employee develops a new career ambition or even changes job

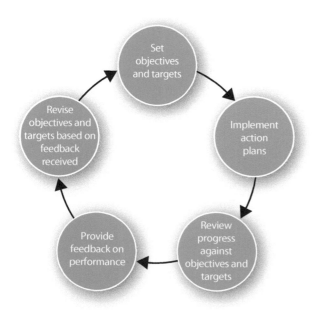

Figure D13.7 Why is feedback important in making development plan revisions?

- there have been changes to processes or technology that have impacted on development needs
- additional development needs have been identified.

There are potentially many situations where changes in development needs or priorities might be required. The key is to be sensitive and responsive to such situations and to proactively address changes in development needs using a carefully executed plan of constructive feedback.

The employee will then be able to implement your feedback into a revised development plan tailored to their new circumstances.

Explaining how to encourage individuals to take responsibility for continuing their performance development

The extent to which employees take ownership and responsibility for their own performance development has a huge impact on the benefits they receive from the process. It also has a potentially huge impact on their future career success. By actively engaging in their own development, employees are more likely to seek out the most appropriate opportunities to benefit their career and they are also more likely to put in the hard work necessary to succeed in doing so.

Performance development requires commitment, hard work and perseverance. It may also require some sacrifices of personal time in order to complete important development activities such as online learning, reading or writing assignments.

With all of this hard work and effort required, how can you hope to convince your team to take responsibility for their own development, rather than simply waiting to be told what training they must undertake? Here are some suggestions.

- Create a culture of career commitment.
- Reward taking responsibility with praise and recognition.
- Create a common understanding among your team of the benefits of being proactive and taking responsibility.

- Build a strong team spirit where employees can help one another and share experiences about self development.

- Take every opportunity to reinforce team values of ownership of development – such as at regular team meetings, in newsletters and in appraisal and development meetings.

You need to bear in mind that making changes to the way people think about their development will take time – so be prepared for this. There is no quick-fix solution to implementing cultural changes to the way people engage with their performance and their work.

If you want your team to buy-in to the idea of taking responsibility for their own performance development you will need to lead by example. This means thinking carefully about the range and type of development opportunities that are offered to your staff, above and beyond the very basics of essential skills acquisition, which is generally dealt with by traditional training methods.

You need to consider how you can provide whole person development opportunities and how you can become a facilitator, rather than imposing required training on staff. You cannot expect them to be motivated to manage their own development where there are no suitable opportunities available. Don't be blinkered by the current offerings of the organisation. You may need to fight for additional development opportunities for your team, where funding or other resources will be needed.

Motivation

Underpinning all of these initiatives is the need to inspire and motivate your team. This is quite simply the most effective method of getting your staff to do anything! Becoming skilled in motivating people is recognised as the single most important management skill and this applies universally, no matter what your line of business.

You have already covered the theories of motivation in other units. Refresh your memory by looking back over these theories and thinking about how they could apply to your team.

Activity — 15 minutes

1. Make a list of at least three things that motivate you and three things that de-motivate you at work.

2. Think creatively of some of the ways in which you could apply the findings from your list to inspire and motivate your team. Put together a mind map showing some examples.

Portfolio Task 4 — 90 minutes

Links to LO4: Assessment criteria 4.1, 4.2, 4.3

1. **(a)** Give reasons to explain why monitoring and evaluating an individual's progress is a vital management activity.

   (b) Demonstrate how you go about monitoring and evaluating an individual's progress against their development plan.

2. Give examples of feedback you have given or might give to an individual and explain the revisions required to an individual's development plan as a result of this.

3. Give examples of ways in which you have encouraged or might go about encouraging individuals to take responsibility for continuing their performance development in your current role.

Your assessment could take the form of a written narrative or a professional discussion with your assessor. It could also include the production of workplace evidence, work-based observations or the use of witness testimonies, as appropriate.

Functional Skills

If you take part in a professional discussion with your assessor as part of the assessment for this learning outcome, you will be practising your Level 2 Functional Skills in English: Speaking and Listening.

Team talk

Kai's story

My name is Kai and I'm 32 years old. I've recently been appointed as a manager in a local merchandising company, where I'm responsible for five staff. One of my first challenges in this new position was to conduct the annual round of staff development meetings with each of my team and to set them some development objectives and activities for the forthcoming twelve-month period.

I found the whole task very difficult indeed. Nobody could help me locate the appropriate staff development files and none of the staff had any development-related documents or information for me to assess. I did eventually manage to find some performance standards documentation for the team. However, when I went through it, I discovered that it was over five years old and had never been updated. I suspected that these standards had simply been filed away and never used.

I found the staff to be completely uninterested and even suspicious about the whole personal development process. I found myself doing most of the talking as nobody wanted to speak up and say how they felt about my suggested development objectives. The whole development process clearly needs an overhaul, but I just don't know where to begin.

Top tips

Developing an effective personal development system includes the production of up-to-date performance standards and the creation of personal development review processes that are regularly referred to, acted upon and updated. The sooner you can establish these standards and processes, the sooner you can start to win over the commitment of your staff to the personal development process.

Instigating a positive change in employee attitudes towards their own personal development will take time, but will have huge benefits both for the individual employees themselves, as well as for the organisation.

Ask the expert	
Q	I've recently taken on a new management position and need to set development targets for my team. However, the current personal development process is almost non-existent. What can I do to create an effective and relevant development system for my staff?
A	The first thing you need to do is to establish some up-to-date performance standards. Without these, your staff cannot hope to know either what they are supposed to be doing or how well they are doing at work. Once you have some standards in place and everyone is aware of them, you can then implement a personal development system tailored to the current tasks and responsibilities required by your team's roles.

What your assessor is looking for

You will demonstrate your skills, knowledge and competence through the learning outcomes in this unit. Evidence generated in this unit will also cross reference to the other units in this qualification.

Please bear in mind that there are significant cross-referencing opportunities throughout this qualification and you may have already generated some relevant work to meet certain criteria in this unit. Your assessor will provide you with the exact requirements to meet the standards of this unit. However, as a guide it is likely that for this unit you will need to be assessed through the following methods:

- One observation of relevant workplace activities to cover the whole unit.
- One witness testimony may also be produced.
- A written narrative, reflective account or professional discussion.
- Relevant work products to be produced as evidence.

The work products for this unit could include:

- job descriptions
- person specifications
- performance appraisal documents
- individual development plans
- your organisation's policies and any related guidance documents on employee training and performance development.

Your assessor will guide you through the assessment process as detailed in the candidate logbook. The detailed assessment criteria are shown in the logbook and by working through these questions, combined with providing the relevant evidence, you will meet the learning outcomes required to complete this unit.

Task and page reference	Assessment criteria
1 (page 245)	1.1, 1.2
2 (page 251)	2.1. 2.2, 2.3
3 (page 253)	3.1, 3.2
4 (page 257)	4.1, 4.2, 4.3

Unit F1 Plan and manage a project

Making changes for the future is vital to ensure the future success of any business. Developing projects to deal with these changes can be very challenging and there are three stages to ensuring that a project will be successful.

The first stage is being able to understand and use the various tools that are available to assist you in managing a project. This unit explores your roles and responsibilities as a project manager and the benefits of using the various principles, processes, tools and techniques that are available.

The second stage is being able to agree the overall scope and objectives of the project with everyone involved.

The final stage is being able to monitor all aspects of the project. For example, as a project manager budgeting is a key responsibility. You will need to set a forecast in place before the project starts and then monitor the budget to make sure you keep on track. There are many reasons why you may not be able to keep to your budget, some of which will be out of your control.

This unit will give you the opportunity to monitor, review and evaluate any project you undertake.

What you will learn

- Understand the principles, processes, tools and techniques of project management
- Be able to agree the scope and objectives of a project
- Be able to identify the budget in order to develop a project plan
- Be able to implement a project plan
- Be able to manage a project to its conclusion

Links to the Technical Certificate

If you are completing your NVQ as part of an Apprenticeship Framework, you will find the following topics are also covered in your Technical Certificate:

- Planning of a project
- Implementing projects
- Managing projects to conclusion

Understand the principles, processes, tools and techniques of project management

Every **project** undertaken needs to be managed effectively if it is to succeed, and while success will require a co-ordinated approach from many different people, someone has to be responsible for overseeing the project from start to finish – the project manager.

Projects vary in size and **complexity** and this will depend upon what is being done within the organisation. As you might imagine, the larger the organisation the more complex a project might be. On the other hand, projects may be isolated to one department or team or be undertaken in a smaller organisation and therefore may not be so complex by nature.

Key Terms

Complexity – how difficult, complicated or involved a project is.

Project – schedule of activities that must have an agreed start date and an agreed completion date.

Remember

Whether a project is of a large or small scale by nature, it still needs to be managed effectively and efficiently.

Examples of projects could include:

- the launch of a new product or service
- the relocation of an organisation to new premises
- a new building in which to house business operations
- installing new information technology
- installing new production technology
- building a new road or bridge
- an intense marketing campaign.

Activity 45 minutes

Talk to as many managers as possible and compile a list of projects that have been undertaken in the last five years at your organisation. Then find out what projects are being undertaken right now.

The roles and responsibilities of the project manager

A project manager must be concerned with the:

- resources needed
- costs involved
- timeframe
- uncertainty attached
- quality levels that must be met.

Ideally a project manager will have expertise or a background of working within the project topic area, will be a good communicator and will be confident in leading people involved in the project, to offer clear direction.

Checklist

A good project manager must be able to:

- plan well
- communicate effectively with stakeholders
- motivate everyone involved
- monitor progress
- learn from mistakes
- work with others to resolve problems.

Activity 30 minutes

You have been given the responsibility of overseeing a project in your organisation. Make a list of the sort of problems you might come across when you are leading your project team.

If you are asked to volunteer as project manager, you should ask yourself the following questions before accepting the responsibility.

- Is the topic area something that you feel passionate about or have an interest in?
- How easy will it be to obtain the data you are going to need?
- Will you feel comfortable leading other people, perhaps from several different departments?
- Are you capable of motivating others?
- Will your line manager be happy to let you devote your time to the needs of the project?

A project is a temporary undertaking, often involving people from different departments or who have expertise in one field or another. Once their role in the project has been completed, these people will go back to their normal day-to-day activities, but as project manager, you will still need to monitor, review and evaluate the success of the project from beginning to end.

Portfolio Task 1 ⏱ 45 minutes

Links to LO1: Assessment criterion 1.1
Prepare a 500-word document outlining your roles and responsibilities as a project manager. Discuss your findings with your assessor.

PLTS

In completing this portfolio task, you will demonstrate your skills as a creative thinker, generating ideas and exploring possibilities with your assessor on the roles and responsibilities of a project manager (CT1).

Functional Skills

Preparing a word-processed 500-word document for the above task will give you the opportunity to practise your Level 2 Functional Skills in ICT. Also, you will be practising your ability to communicate information, ideas and opinions effectively and persuasively, which forms part of the Level 2 Functional Skills in English.

How to apply principles, processes, tools and techniques of project management

A project proposal is a first step in project management and makes it clear to everyone what the purpose of the project is. It could be a new idea you have had, or something you have been asked to do.

To ensure success from start to finish there a number of tools and techniques you can use. These include:

- **scheduling**
- work breakdown structure (WBS)
- Gantt charts
- critical path analysis (CPA)
- flow diagrams
- business process models.

Key Terms

Feasible – achievable.

Scheduling – a plan of procedures put in place to achieve a specific goal or objective.

Anyone who has an interest in your project can be classified as a project stakeholder. Your project stakeholders may be interested in the:

- research, planning and investigation of your project idea
- implementation of your project idea
- evaluation of the success of your project idea.

You must consider the best way to execute your project successfully and how you will keep your stakeholders updated during the project. Regular progress reporting also gives you the opportunity to obtain feedback on how people are feeling the project is going and what might need to be changed as it develops.

Remember, things both within your organisation or in the external environment might change as your project develops altering the focus of your project, so always be flexible and aware that change might be required. This is one good reason to report progress to stakeholders regularly so that the feedback they give you in return will keep you informed of any such change.

> **Remember**
>
> Some of your project stakeholders may have conflicting views of how the project should be introduced, developed and implemented. Wherever possible, listen to everyone's views and acknowledge and address any concerns they have. This will go some way to getting their support!

Terms of reference

Ideally your objective will form part of the **terms of reference** for your project. These terms need to be agreed with your project stakeholders and should clearly outline:

- what the project is about and hopes to achieve (based upon your SMART objective)
- whether the project is necessary and worthwhile
- what the current situation is (in relation to what is being reviewed by the project)
- how the project will be delivered
- how feasible the project is
- suggested changes, alternatives or improvements to the current situation
- the implications of going ahead with the project
- the consequences if the project is not undertaken.

> **Key Term**
>
> **Terms of reference** – purpose and structure of a project.

You could list your terms of reference numerically as seen in Figure F1.1.

Feasibility of the project

To find out whether your project idea is intrinsically feasible, you must assess how easy or difficult it is going to be to implement. You will need to be sure that you have:

- people with the right skills to work on the project and its implementation
- enough money available to see the project through to its end result
- enough time available to carry out all aspects of the project.

You can use techniques such as Force Field analysis to test the feasibility of your project plans. See Unit C6 for more information on this.

Tools and techniques to enhance the success of your project

There are a range of project tools and techniques that you can use in the organisation and planning of your project. Some of these are discussed below.

Cost-benefit analysis

This can help you identify your:

- financial costs – the actual costs of planning, implementing and evaluating the project
- financial benefits – the additional revenue received if the project is successful
- social costs – increased pollution and noise if the idea goes ahead
- social benefits – good for the local economy and creation of new jobs.

Using the sub-headings, you simply list your responses in terms of your identified costs and benefits. The general rule of thumb is if the financial and social benefits outweigh the financial and social costs, then this serves as a good indication that the project should go ahead.

> **Activity** ⏱ 30 minutes
>
> Draw up a list of financial and social costs and benefits for the project idea you identified earlier. Discuss your responses with your assessor.

There is a certain amount of risk attached to a project of any size, including:

- the potential to spend too much money and go over-budget
- strong levels of resistance from your project stakeholders

Terms of reference

SMART objective: To introduce four hours on/four hours off shift-working pattern for all team members by 31 December.

The purpose of this project is to investigate the introduction of a new shift-working pattern to meet extra customer demand for our products. The estimated deadline for introduction of the new shift pattern is 31 December.

1. This project will investigate how a new shift-working pattern will help the organisation meet additional customer demand for our products (see SMART objective above).

2. The introduction of a new shift-working pattern is necessary as the organisation has recently won a new contract for the supply of its products.

3. Currently, the existing shift patterns of 8am–5pm daily will not create sufficient volume of production to meet existing and new customer demand.

4. The project will be delivered through a sequence of activities to research, investigate, plan and review the effectiveness, feasibility and performance levels associated with the introduction of the new system.

5. A feasibility study will be conducted to assess whether the new system can be introduced within the boundaries of cost, capacity and human resource availability.

6. By changing from a 8am–5pm daily shift pattern to a new system of four days on/four days off, and then four nights on/four nights off shift working patterns, flexibility of staff, maintenance of equipment and the meeting of targets can be better planned and improved.

7. The implications of going ahead with the project will be the costs of the investigation, health and safety risk assessment and legal advice and the effect upon the morale of staff, which links to performance and target measurement. Stakeholder approval will need to be sought, but customer expectations should more easily be met.

8. The consequences if no action is taken will be that new customer demand will not be met, impacting upon the organisation's wish to expand and grow. Stakeholders will be unimpressed and customers may switch to our major competitors, adversely affecting our opportunity to increase our profit margin.

Figure F1.1 An example of terms of reference for a project.

- health and safety concerns relating to the new way of doing things
- the quality of the product or service you provide may be affected
- the process may take longer than estimated
- insufficient resources are available to help you to drive the project forward.

By identifying and listing your potential risks, you will be better placed to deal with them should any of them rise. You can devise a **contingency plan** for each risk, so that you have a 'Plan B', should anything go wrong.

Key Term

Contingency plan – a plan put in place in case the original plan does not work out.

Work breakdown structure (WBS)

This document, as shown in Table F1.1, below, will enable you to examine your SMART objective for your project and work out how you can break it down into smaller and more manageable tasks which are then allocated to the appropriate project team member.

Critical path analysis (CPA)

This tool will help you to breakdown the tasks involved in your project, allowing you to place them in a sequence of activities. You can then estimate how long each activity will take. You need to be aware that some activities will be critical to the success of your project, and if they are delayed, it will take you longer to complete your project and obtain your desired result. Your aim is to find the shortest time to complete your project and this will very much depend on the sequence of activities on the critical path you have identified. An example of a critical path analysis diagram is shown in Figure F1.2 on the following page.

Project objective:
To introduce a 4 on/4 off pattern for all team members by 31 December

Date produced: 29 September

Produced by: BB

1 Project start-up	2 Data gathering	3 Data analysis and development of options	4 Preparation and presentation of report of final outcomes	5 Monitoring and evaluation
e.g. Meeting to agree SMART objectives with stakeholders	Collect feedback from stakeholders (meeting) **Competitor Analysis**	Analyse and process data into useful information (e.g. graphs and tables)	Produce draft report Prepare a visual presentation of facts and figures to support change	Decide on monitoring techniques

Table F1.1 Work breakdown structure sheet.

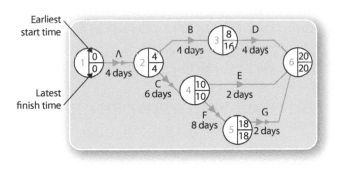

Figure F1.2 An example critical path analysis diagram.

Flow diagrams or charts

Flow diagrams or charts allow you to map out the activities needed to complete your project. This is a visual technique that will show how one activity may depend upon the outcome of the previous one, if the project is going to be successfully completed on time. An example is shown in Figure F1.3.

Project life cycle

By categorising each phase of your project, you are more likely to gain the commitment of your project team, as they will understand the sequence of events attached to the project.

You can think about the **project life cycle** as the following sequence:

1. Initiating
2. Planning
3. Implementation
4. Monitoring
5. Evaluation.

Each phase is equally important as they are dependent upon each other and must all be completed if the project is to be successful.

Key Term

Project life cycle – the stages a project will go through.

Unit F1 · **Plan and manage a project**

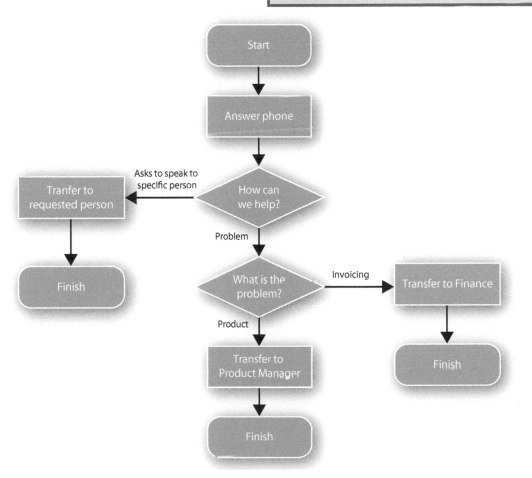

Figure F1.3 An example of a flow diagram.

Phase 1 – Initiating

- Agree your project SMART objective with stakeholders.
- Carry out a Force Field analysis.
- Decide on the scope of your project.
- Agree with your stakeholders what the potential risks might be.

Phase 2 – Planning

- Decide who is needed from other departments to bring necessary expertise to the project.
- Agree which planning techniques you will use.
- Agree how you will document your planning and progression.
- Agree how you will launch the project.

Phase 3 – Implementation

- Be clear about your planning and monitoring activities.
- Know exactly what communication methods you will use with all of your project stakeholders.
- Decide how, as project manager, you will keep everyone on your project team motivated.

Phase 4 – Monitoring

- Agree how you will monitor progress – which monitoring tools and techniques you will use.
- Plan in your milestones.
- Decide on how regularly you will hold review meetings with project stakeholders.
- Decide how often you and your project team will produce progress reports for stakeholders.
- Be prepared to adjust, amend or update your plan if need be, to keep your project on track.

Phase 5 – Evaluation

- Use a checklist to help you to evaluate.
- Has your project objective been achieved?
- What has gone well?
- What hasn't gone well and why?
- What could have been done differently?
- Are the perceived benefits of going ahead with the project realised?

- What is the feedback from stakeholders (especially staff directly involved and customers)?
- How effective was the process you used to get feedback?
- Did you stay within budget/manage to reduce estimated costs?

Portfolio Task 2 — 45 minutes

Links to LO1: Assessment criterion 1.2

Using a table like the one below, identify the principles, processes, tools and techniques you currently use to manage your project. An example has been given to help you. Explain the benefits of using these to your assessor.

	Example and explanation of its use
Principles	
Processes	
Tools	e.g. Action plans are used to allocate responsibilities to team and to monitor progress of the project
Techniques	

Remember

Monitoring and evaluating activities need to continue long time after the project is fully implemented.

Be able to agree the scope and objectives of a project

Your project stakeholders will play an important part in every stage of your project, from planning, to completion and evaluation. For this reason, they must be kept informed of your intentions at all times but, perhaps more importantly, they must be involved in all your planning activities. This includes agreeing with them:

- your SMART objectives for the project
- the scope of your project.

Your project sponsor

Your project sponsor is the person who will have overall control and authority over the project. As project manager, you will need to consult with your sponsor from the initial planning stage and update them regularly afterwards. They should be involved in the initiation, planning and implementation phases of your project. Your project sponsor must be consulted over major decisions at any stage of the project and should make sure that they are available to advise as and when required.

Your project sponsor is likely to be your line manager or perhaps a senior manager in your organisation, depending upon the size and nature of your project. On occasion, there may be more than one project sponsor who will share the authority and control and must all be reported to in the same way.

Discuss your limits of authority as a project manager with your project sponsor so that you agree from the outset what decision making authority you have. Try to get this documented in your plans, so everyone is fully aware of how much responsibility and authority you hold throughout the duration of the project.

Using SMART objectives

Your project aim should be developed further into SMART objectives that you can communicate to everyone involved. Your project objectives should:

- let everyone know what the project is trying to achieve
- inform everyone what the expected outcome will be and by when (i.e. estimated end date)
- make everyone aware of how the success of the project will be measured (e.g. to introduce and have a new system fully operational by 30 December).

Your project SMART objectives must be agreed with your project team and project sponsor at the initiation phase of your project life cycle. Any other project stakeholders (such as managers from other department who your project will effect) should also be invited to your meeting to agree your objective.

SMART objectives should be:

- Specific – the objective shouldn't be woolly and should relate to a particular task.
- Measureable – it should be measurable in some way, so progress can be checked.
- Achievable – it should be within reach of being achieved, given the capacity that exists, money available and the existing number of employees.
- Realistic – if the objective is not realistic and can't be achieved this will only serve to demoralise everyone.
- Time-bound – there must be a clear date for completion of the task.

Managers often refer to the breaking down of project objectives as shown in Figure F1.4.

Project SMART objective: To introduce a four days on/four days off working pattern for all team workers by 31 December		
Purpose of project	**Proposed result**	**Success criteria**

Figure F1.4 How project objectives can be broken down.

Breaking the project objective down helps everyone involved to fully understand the aim, nature and purpose of the project.

When you devise your SMART objective with your project sponsor and project stakeholders, you must all agree that it will, in some way, assess how successful the project has been when it reaches its 'end state'.

Another way of looking at this is to say that your agreed SMART objective must allow everyone to easily:

- measure the success of the project in a quantifiable way (i.e. using numbers in some way)
- recognise the project's purpose (so that all projects stakeholders are committed to the same goal)
- understand the success criteria applied to the project (e.g. total budget allowed and must be completed by 31 December, for the new system to go live on 2 January.

When you hold your project initiation meeting with your project sponsor and project stakeholders, you must make sure everyone is given the opportunity to contribute their views, opinions and ideas. As part of your meeting activity you could brainstorm ideas to devise several versions of a project objective, until you all finally agree on the one you should use.

Activity 45 minutes

Think of an idea for a project that you could manage and devise a SMART objective for it. Then produce a table similar to the one in Figure F1.4, to decide the purpose, proposed result and success criteria of your project. Discuss your findings with your assessor.

Remember

When large scale projects are undertaken, a series of smaller objectives might be set which will all be related to the main project SMART objective. For complex and large projects, managers sometimes break down the project into a set of smaller sub-projects each with their own objectives but which will all contribute to the objective of the main project, helping it to reach its end state.

Scoping the project

Having agreed upon your SMART objective and arrived at a conclusion of how feasible the project is (perhaps by using a Force Field analysis) you will now be ready to agree with your project sponsor and project stakeholders, the scope of the project. You will need to consider and agree:

- what each stage of the project will involve
- the responsibilities of everyone involved in the project
- who the department/teams are that the content of the project (and its outcome) will affect
- the estimated timescales attached to each stage up to completion
- what resources (people, time, money and equipment) will be needed
- who must be communicated with regularly (project sponsor, project stakeholders, finance for budget and cost information, human resources for staffing issues and so on).

The scope of your project, once agreed, should be documented. The scope should clearly state what the focus of the project is, but it should also identify what can be left alone and doesn't need to be done.

No one wants to spend too long sitting around a meeting table, but by allocating sufficient time to be able to agree the scope of your project, you will benefit long term by gaining the commitment of everyone involved, who will all have contributed their views and opinions.

Activity 45 minutes

Carefully examine each of the bullet points listed above and then draw up a list of questions that you should ask of your project team (at your project initiation meeting) as you seek agreement from everyone. Discuss your list of questions with your assessor.

Links to LO2 and LO3: Assessment criteria 2.1, 3.2

Provide examples for your assessor of documents you currently use to agree SMART objectives and scope of the project with your project sponsor and stakeholders. These documents could include a project proposal you have been involved in preparing, action plans noting the objectives and scope of the project and/or minutes of meetings from meetings with sponsor and stakeholders. Give a brief explanation of how you set and agreed these objectives to your assessor.

PLTS

Being involved in the preparation of the project proposal for this task, you will put forward a persuasive case for action and propose practical ways forward in completing the project, showing you to be an effective participator (EP 2, 3).

Functional Skills

By reading and selecting information from your project proposal and presenting the information to your assessor, you will have the opportunity to practise your summarising techniques as part of the Level 2 Functional Skills in English: Reading and Writing.

Be able to identify the budget in order to develop a project plan

After discussion with your project sponsor and project stakeholders, you should have negotiated a realistic **budget** that will give you enough capital to see your project through to completion. The amount you have agreed will need to be authorised and released by your finance manager.

As your project develops you will need to monitor your expenditure carefully. Your project stakeholders, senior managers and certainly your finance manager will want to see that you have stayed within budget! It is important that you keep records of all expenditure, no matter how small,

and if you purchase any items for your project, receipts must be stored safely and securely.

Identifying budget and timescales in order to develop the project plan with stakeholders

Organisations usually use two types of budget:

- Capital – money is allocated for spending on machinery and equipment often referred to as assets.
- Operational – money is allocated for spending on consumables, such as ink cartridges and other stationery.

Operational budgets are sometimes called revenue budgets and will forecast the expected income and expenditure of a business activity over a period of time. It is likely that you will use an operational budget for your project, although if you need to purchase new equipment or machinery then you will also have a capital budget.

Key Terms

Budget – an estimate of expenditure (and in some cases income) over a given period of time.

Seconded – when a worker is moved from their post to a different department or job role for a period of time.

Remember

You will need to justify that the money being spent on your project will ultimately help your organisation to achieve its objectives.

Project stakeholders

The stakeholders in your project will be dependent on the size of the undertaking, its nature and complexity, but they might include any or all of the following:

- Finance manager – concerned with how much money you will spend and the additional revenue that will be received.
- Human resource manager – concerned with staff being **seconded** from their day-to-day roles to assist with the project and how those roles will be filled temporarily.

- Peer managers – concerned about how the outcome of your project will affect the work of their teams. They may need to change how they do things as a consequence.

- Line manager – concerned with your workload and supporting you in your role as project manager, while overseeing your usual day-to-day tasks and making sure these are not neglected.

- Shareholders – will want to know how the outcome of your project will affect the profitability of your organisation and whether it will affect their value of their shareholdings.

- Project sponsor – will require regular updates of development and progress and is the person who has ultimate control and authority over the project.

- Suppliers – concerned with whether your project will require any change in their delivery patterns to you.

- Customers – who may be affected by changes in the product, service, quality or delivery schedules you provide as a result of your project.

- Local community – concerned about the effect of your project on things such as the introduction of new jobs or causing heavy traffic or pollution.

- The staff within your organisation – who will want to know to what extent your project may change their job, company culture etc.

At the beginning of your project you should identify what the needs or interests of your different stakeholders are.

Negotiating a paper-based or software-based approach with your stakeholders

You need to make it clear to your stakeholders whether you and your team intend to use a paper-based, software-based or integrated (a combination of both) approach to your project. This needs to be negotiated carefully with your stakeholders, as everyone involved needs to be comfortable with the techniques and reporting systems being used for the planning, reviewing, monitoring and evaluation of your project. You and your stakeholders might agree to use:

- a paper-based approach – hard copy documents will be produced that will inform stakeholders at every stage of the project from the definition stage through to the completion and evaluation stage.

- a software-based approach – software packages such as Microsoft Project® that offer a computerised approach to your project management. These types of packages have a solution that manages the whole process from start to finish. For example, Microsoft Project will offer a different way to manage projects as the software reminds you of critical deadlines, assisting in selecting the right resources and helping you manage your team.

Your timescale

Time is a very important resource, and you should consider how best to use it. You can discuss this at your early project stakeholder meetings. Managers and stakeholders will share a concern that the longer the project takes to complete, the bigger the draw on costs and other resources. Some of the tools already discussed, such as scheduling, will help you track progress against timescales so you can report your progress to your project stakeholders regularly.

Activity ⏱ 30 minutes

Using the table below as a template, list all the stakeholders that have an interest in your project idea and what that interest may be.

Project stakeholder	Their needs or interest
e.g. The organisation's employees	Job security and pay reward

You need to identify:

- how long each part of the project will take
- how long the project will take to complete in its entirely.

Of course, your responses to the above will be what you identify, estimate and agree with your project stakeholders.

To help breakdown the scheduling of your project further, and identify whether you are on track to meet your completion target date, you could introduce a series of **milestones**. At various stages of your project schedule you should simply insert 'milestone 1, milestone 2, milestone 3' and so on, alongside appropriate dates in the schedule. Each milestone will prompt you to evaluate progress to date enabling you to keep your project stakeholders fully informed.

Key Terms

Milestones – markers on your schedule to remind you and your team to evaluate whether you are on target or not as you work towards completion of your project.

Variance – a difference.

Remember

Poor time management can result in you and your team rushing to get parts of your project completed on time, which can lead to costly mistakes.

Portfolio Task 4 90 minutes

Links to LO3: Assessment criterion 3.1

Setting budgets and timescales are vitally important to ensure the success of any project.

Provide examples to your assessor of how you set budgets and timescales with your stakeholders for your project. These examples could include project plans, project proposals, and minutes of meeting or action plans. Explain to your assessor the process you went through and the difficulties you experienced with setting the budget and timescales with your stakeholders. Your assessor will record your discussion to generate evidence for your portfolio.

PLTS

This activity will give you the opportunity to reflect on how you agreed budgets and timescales with your stakeholders (RL 3, 5, 6).

Your project stakeholders will need to see that you have given a lot of thought to the costs that your project might incur. When you hold a meeting with your stakeholders to discuss the project's budget, you should aim to clarify and agree:

- the purpose of the budget (what you must spend it on)
- how expected income (after completion of the project) will outweigh costs: refer back to your cost/benefit analysis
- how research has been undertaken/will continue in order to examine the costs associated with the project
- how costs have been broken down, so nothing has been left to chance
- timescales to achieve the project.

Before your meeting is concluded you should agree upon a budget which may be drawn up in a format similar to that seen in Table F1.2 on page 274.

Table F1.2 is an example of how you could arrange your project budget into the items you need to purchase and the estimated costs you have attached to them. As you actually make the purchases, you will fill in the 'actual costs' column. If there is a **variance** between your estimated and actual costs, this will be recorded in the final column. Of course, you won't be able to fill in the 'actual' and 'variance' columns until you have actually purchased the items you require or received actual costing (e.g. staffing).

Shift pattern review project – September 2012			
BUDGET			
Item	Estimated costs	Actual costs	Variance
Staffing (secondments/time etc)	22,500	24,500	−2,000
Equipment	89,000	102,000	−13,000
Materials	6,000	5,400	+600
Consulting fees	20,000	20,000	Nil
Research fees	8,000	8,700	−700
Software	2,800	2,800	Nil
Totals	148,300	163,400	−15,100

Produced by: Signature: Date:

Stakeholder approval date:

Authorised Finance manager
Name: Signature: Date:

Table F1.2 How a budget could be drawn up.

Activity ⏱ 45 minutes

Using a template similar to the one above, draw up a budget for your own project idea. If you don't have established figures to work with, you could make up figures to practise. Fill in the 'estimated', 'actual' and 'variance' columns for the 'items' you have identified and then total your figures up. Discuss your findings with your assessor.

Consult with stakeholders to negotiate the project plan

Communication is key to successful project outcomes as you negotiate your project plan with stakeholders.

Stakeholders must be consulted over and be clear about:

- any factors *inside* the organisation that may influence the success of the project (e.g. lack of expertise, low budgets, objections from some stakeholders)

- any factors *outside* the organisation that may influence the success of the project (e.g. objections from some stakeholders – perhaps the local community – new laws regarding disposal of waste and so on)

- the project title and its main SMART objective

- the timescales involved with the project

- how often you will review progress and inform stakeholders accordingly

- the resources that will be needed to make sure the project is successful

- the budget requirement and how it has been arrived at

- how you and your project team will research information you need for your project

- how the project will be monitored and evaluated.

Remember

In your planning meeting with your stakeholders ensure you agree the projects terms of reference with them and introduce them to the tools you will use, such as your cost-benefit analysis.

Activity — 45 minutes

Think back to your own project idea and your identified project stakeholders. Write down how you intend to negotiate your project plan with them. You should consider:

- the best way/format to discuss the plan with them
- which topic areas of the project you should discuss with them
- which planning tools and techniques you need to agree should be used, if your project is to be successful.

Show your responses to your assessor.

Activity — 30 minutes

Think back to the project idea you identified and list the stakeholders you think will be involved and in what capacity they will have an interest in your project. Discuss your responses with your assessor.

As your project develops, some of your stakeholders will be supportive while others may not be, or support may vary for different aspects of the project. For example, your finance manager might object to the way you have sourced quotes for new equipment you need and suggest you look elsewhere to minimise costs. On the other hand, your finance manager may support your project in terms of the additional revenue it will bring into the organisation if it is successful.

Remember

Your project team itself is an important group of stakeholders, as naturally each team member has an interest in the project, its outcome and its success!

Identifying potential risks and contingencies

When managing your project, you must be aware of potential **risks** that could hamper the progress you make towards a successful outcome. It is best practice to have contingency plans in place to deal with unforeseen events.

Key Term

Risk – something that could happen in future to jeopardise or change your project objectives or outcome.

Activity — 35 minutes

With your project idea in mind, and by referring back to your identified stakeholders, identify which of them are likely to support or oppose what you are trying to achieve with your project. An example has been given below.

Stakeholder	Interest in project	Supporter or opponent
E.g. local community	Environmental impact	Supporter if appropriate environmental policies are in place

Checklist

Identifying potential risks will help you to:

- change the way you and your team work
- make informed decisions about your future actions
- instil confidence in your project stakeholders that a successful outcome will be achieved
- act on any threats against your project's objectives.

Remember

You must communicate effectively with all of your project stakeholders about any potential risks and how you and your team intend to address them.

Risks might include:

- insufficient money to complete your project if your budget isn't monitored carefully
- strikes or supply problems preventing equipment and materials you need getting to you on time
- objections to all or part of your project from some groups of your stakeholders (e.g. the local community)
- legal and regulatory problems (for example, difficulties obtaining planning permission)
- key members of the project team leaving the organisation – taking their knowledge and expertise with them

- the project falling behind schedule which could result in frustrated stakeholders and those team member who are seconded, being delayed from returning to their normal roles, causing problems for the organisation
- the project team underperforming (e.g. due to conflict between team members).

Of course, there are many other risks that could occur depending upon the size and nature of the project you are working on.

> **Activity** 🕐 45 minutes
>
> Think back to your own project idea and list as many potential risks associated with it as you can.
>
> Talk through your responses with your assessor.

> **Checklist**
>
> There are four key steps to help you to manage risk. You should
> - identify the potential risks to your project
> - assess how damaging those risks could be to your project
> - plan how you will address these risks to your project
> - implement your plans to address the risk you have identified.

When you have identified potential risks, addressing them must become one of your main priorities. You should record any identified potential risks and your plans to address them as the information should appear in your project documentation and reports. Not only will this keep your project stakeholders fully informed, but it can be used as reference material for future projects.

Contingency planning

Contingency planning is the process of putting carefully considered plans in place just in case something unexpected happens. Sometimes contingency plans are referred to as a back up plans, 'what if' scenarios or having a 'Plan B'.

In March 2006, it was announced that the £757 million project to build the new Wembley National Football Stadium in London had fallen

Wembley Stadium, opened in 2007.

behind schedule, and although the first planned match was due to be in May 2006, it would not happen until 2007. This created a debate about the reasons for the delay and who was at fault. At the time, many reasons were suggested, including inefficient working by planners and contractors, and problematic relationships with suppliers. If the alleged reasons for delay are accurate, then risks would have been identified and contingency planning would have been a discussion point at project stakeholder meetings.

> **Remember**
>
> Your local hospital is likely to have a contingency plan in place to deal with disruption to its power supply. If the electric should go off, an emergency generator will automatically switch on to restore temporary power.

If sufficient attention isn't given to the identification of risks and the concept of contingency planning, then your project and its success may be affected by:

- additional expenditure (perhaps taking you over budget)
- delays towards completion
- lowered levels of quality
- dissatisfied project stakeholders
- overall organisational problems (e.g. on its profit margin).

When consulting with your project stakeholders, especially your project team, it is important to encourage commitment right from the planning stage. You could do this by:

- treating everyone equally and fairly
- listening well to what they say and responding speedily to their requests
- showing that you encourage a team effort towards problem solving
- praising others when appropriate for good work and contribution of ideas
- communicating effectively and making sure everyone knows what channels of communication will be used for the project team
- finding time to talk to everyone and being approachable, even when you're busy
- making sure everyone knows what their and everyone else's project responsibilities are
- making sure everyone is given the opportunity to contribute during meetings
- making sure everyone receives regular project related updates.

Portfolio Task 5 (45 minutes)

Links to LO3: Assessment criterion 3.3

Using a table similar to the one below, identify potential risks and contingencies of your project.

Project X	
Associated risks	**Contingencies put in place**
E.g. material cost increases	E.g. a sum of your budgeted amount of money put aside to deal with unexpected costs

Explain these to your assessor. Your assessor will record this discussion to generate evidence for your portfolio.

Establishing criteria and processes for evaluating the project on completion

You should establish through agreement with your project stakeholders the criteria you will use for your evaluation process. You could for example, consider the following:

- Have the SMART project objectives been met?
- Were all of the project's milestones met?
- Was the project completed by its agreed deadlines?
- Was the project completed within budget?
- Did you have sufficient resources?
- Has anything *not* been achieved?
- Were any contingency plans used?
- What has been learnt and documented for future use?

The above list can be used as a basis for you to establish:

- what went well
- what didn't go well
- what you would do differently next time.

Portfolio Task 6 45 minutes

Links to LO3: Assessment criterion 3.4

Prepare a brief document outlining the criteria and processes you are using to evaluate the success of your project upon completion.

Discuss this document with your assessor. The document will serve as product evidence for your portfolio.

Functional Skills

By completing this activity using a computer, you will be practising your Level 2 Functional Skills in ICT and English.

Be able to implement a project plan

When you are managing your project, there are three key factors that you must think about.

1. What is the project's overall objective? (i.e. the end state that will be achieved if the project is successful).

2. What is the scope of the project? (i.e. what exactly must be done? What tasks must be carried out by whom, in what time frame and with which identified resources?).

3. What are the project's strategies? (i.e. exactly how will the project's objectives be met? What milestones will be set?).

To help to address these points, it is useful to design a document that can be shared with everyone involved – all of your stakeholders – from the outset. The document should set out clearly what you have agreed with your stakeholders and will identify:

- exactly what the project intends to do
- why the change, improvement or introduction of something new needs to happen
- what the benefits will be if the project is successful
- the risks attached to the project if it isn't implemented
- the responsibilities of the project team, project manager and project sponsor
- an overview of the project schedule
- how the project will be evaluated.

Scheduling and allocating roles and responsibilities

You could consider producing a project action plan that serves as a timetable of activities and milestones as you work through your project timeframe. This will highlight roles and responsibilities that each member of your project team will need to undertake. Simple headings can be used as shown in Table F1.3, below.

It will be necessary to ensure that each team member allocated to a specific role has the appropriate level of knowledge and sufficient skills to carry out the task effectively. A skills audit could be carried out for this purpose.

Any additional training and development activity would have to be agreed with the human resources department and this will incur extra project costs.

Project title:			
Project activity	**By whom**	**Estimated completion date**	**Actual completion date**
e.g. Agree terms of reference with project stakeholders	Mary Smith	25 August 2012	20 August 2012

Table F1.3 An example project action plan.

You might agree with your project sponsor, peer managers and other managers (such as your human resource manager) that each person in your selected project team will only be taken away from their normal day-to-day activities for a maximum of four days at any one time during the duration of the project.

Provide project resources

The resources that you may need for your project include:

- time (selected members of staff assisting will be allocated time, taking them away from their normal jobs)
- money (you will have a budget for equipment, training programmes etc)
- people (staff with expertise will be selected to work on the project you manage)
- equipment (you may need to replace, repair or modify equipment at some stage of your projects timescale)
- materials (you may need a selection of materials at your planning, implementation and evaluation stages).

This activity will give you the opportunity to respond positively to new priorities, whilst organising resources and prioritising actions (SM3, 5).

Briefing project team members on their roles and responsibilities

Your project team members must understand why they have been allocated specific roles and responsibilities. To help with this process, you should initially make sure that they are briefed about:

- the project's SMART objectives
- the project's terms of reference
- the resources that will be used
- who the project stakeholders are
- any risks associated with the project.

Face-to-face meetings are likely to be the best way to brief your team members as this gives everyone the opportunity to contribute and share their views. Should any team member not be happy with their roles and responsibilities they can make this known and discussions can take place to allocate the right person to the right role.

It is important that meetings are held regularly to monitor and review the project plan.

Implementing your project plan

You can design your project implementation document in various ways but a good example is shown on the following page.

Portfolio Task 7 — 45 minutes

Links to LO4: Assessment criteria 4.1, 4.2, 4.3

Think back to your project idea from your previous activity and list the resources you will need to investigate, implement and evaluate your idea successfully. Then produce a table or chart that identifies the roles and responsibilities of each of your team members for each stage of your project, and the resources they will need.

Discuss this document with your assessor and explain how you brief your team on the content of this document. Your assessor will record the discussion to generate evidence for your portfolio.

Portfolio Task 8 — 45 minutes

Links to LO4: Assessment criterion 4.4

Using the headings of the project implementation plan on the next page, draw up your own template for your identified project idea and then take steps to fill in each section. Alternatively, provide evidence to your assessor how you will monitor the implementation of your project (e.g. project proposal or objectives).

Discuss your response with your assessor.

Name of project:
Project SMART objective: *Write here what you expect to achieve by the end of the project.*
Department: **Produced by:** **Date:**
Stage 1 – Finance, budgets and costing: *Write here your estimated additional revenue or expected savings if the project is successful. Also give an estimated overview of what the project will cost (ie cost of resources used) and the budget for spending agreed with your Finance manager.*
Stage 2 – The project team: *Write here the names of those selected to assist with the project and in what capacity they will help (e.g. Mary Smith from accounts will oversee project financials). Also state who you are as project manager and who your project sponsor is.*
Stage 3 – Project definition: *Give an overview of what has been agreed must be done and why it needs to be done. Briefly describe the benefits (e.g. happier staff, happier customers and more profit) and what the risks to the department or perhaps customer loyalty might be in the future if the project isn't undertaken.*
Stage 4 – Aim of the project: *Repeat your SMART project objective here and your identified milestones, scheduled into your planning activity every so often so you and your stakeholders can take stock and measure your progress to date.*
Stage 5 – Scope of the project: *Write in here what the project will investigate and what it won't investigate.*
Stage 6 – Start and end dates and evaluation: *Write in your estimated start and end dates of your project. Then briefly explain how the project will be evaluated after its implementation.*
Signed: _____ **Position:** _____ **Date:** _____
Authorised by: Name: _____ Position: _____ Date: _____ Signatures: _____

Figure F1.5 Project implementation plan.

Be able to manage a project to its conclusion

Apply a range of project management tools and techniques to monitor, control and review progress

There is a range of project monitoring tools you can use to monitor, control and review the progress of your project as you work towards its conclusion. Using appropriate tools and techniques can help you to identify when you might need to take corrective action to make sure you reach successful outcomes. Some of the tools and techniques you could use are discussed below.

Gantt charts

Invented by Henry Gantt in late 1800s, this chart offers a visual overview of the tasks that need to be carried out, and by when. This means you can schedule tasks by attaching dates to them so at a glance everyone knows what needs to be done by when. Examine the example shown in Unit C6.

Variance analysis

If there is a difference between what was expected to happen in terms of money spent and time taken and what actually happened, then an investigation should be carried out. This type of investigation is known as a **variance analysis**, and your stakeholders will want to know what the findings are. Finding out why there is a difference between expected values and actual values (whether of a positive or negative nature) can help you to plan and make decisions in the future that will improve the way you do things.

The difference between the sets of figures should be broken down and analysed very carefully. If there is a **negative variance** and more than expected has been spent, reasons why should be established to minimise the risk of it happening again. If there is a **positive variance** and less than expected has been spent then reasons for this should also be investigated so that lessons can be learnt and shared with others as best practice.

Key Terms

Negative variance – more than expected has been spent.

Positive variance – less than expected has been spent.

Variance analysis – a statistical tool to help identify the difference between budgeted and actual figures.

Earned-value control (EVC)

The concept of earned-value control (EVC) enables analysis of the performance of the project in terms of costs and time. This means that at any one time, the cost of the project to date can be examined to establish to what degree activities have been completed. For example:

- Total value of the project = £148,300.00
- Value of activities completed (when progress measured) = £75,000.00

This indicates that the project is approximately half way towards its completion stage. This is known as a measurement of progress of a project using an earned-value concept.

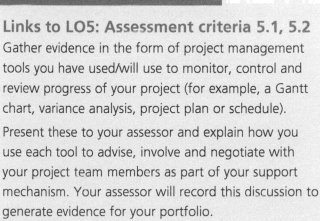

Portfolio Task 9 — 45 minutes

Links to LO5: Assessment criteria 5.1, 5.2

Gather evidence in the form of project management tools you have used/will use to monitor, control and review progress of your project (for example, a Gantt chart, variance analysis, project plan or schedule).

Present these to your assessor and explain how you use each tool to advise, involve and negotiate with your project team members as part of your support mechanism. Your assessor will record this discussion to generate evidence for your portfolio.

Providing support to project team members

Most project managers will realise that if a project is to be successful, then they must be willing to listen to others in the selected project team and discuss any ideas they put forward.

Ideally, throughout the duration of the project you will have held regular meetings with your project stakeholders but in particular with your project team members. Regardless of the size or nature of a project, it is important that team members feel fully supported at all times. This will enhance morale and motivation and help you to gain their commitment.

It's often useful to produce a step-by-step process as you will have done with your project life cycle to ensure that team members know exactly what will need to be done throughout the duration of the project. In your meetings, you could discuss and negotiate how you intend to work through the following stages of the project.

Through effective communication, you can make sure that every member of your project team knows exactly what is expected of them and you should make it clear how you intend to offer support. For example, you could issue a meeting schedule and offer an **open door policy** to deal with any queries team members may have.

You must make sure that you gain commitment from your project team members by supporting them and showing them respect. To help you to do this you should:

- explain how you value their views opinions and expertise
- show that you are really listening to their views, and supporting when they have concerns

Figure F1.6 Project stages chart

- treat everyone with respect and fairness
- challenge a view or opinion with **tact** and **diplomacy**
- explain you will keep them updated of any problems that arise during the project's time frame
- explain how you will keep them regularly updated (e.g. by email or through meetings)
- agree how regularly you should hold project team meetings.

Key Terms

Diplomacy – negotiating and handling difficult situations.

Open door policy – where a manager offers support to staff by making it clear that they can be contacted at any time to discuss concerns openly.

Tact – avoiding saying something offensive.

Remember

As project manager you need to understand that your project's objective must not be too ambitious. In other words, how certain are you that your desired outcome can be achieved – and what will the consequences be if your project fails?

Team talk

Jordan's story

My name is Jordan and I have been working for CTP Healthcare Products as an operations manager for two years. I love my job as I get to work with a wide range of people and every day is different. CTP Healthcare Products launches new products into the market each year and part of my responsibility is to work with other managers to ensure new products are launched successfully.

Before joining CTP Healthcare Products I was an operations manager for an organisation where I had less responsibility. For example, there was a separate finance officer who was in charge of monitoring the budget and therefore I didn't have to worry about this. However, at CTP I have been given responsibility to trial and launch a new skin-care product and I have been told I have full responsibility to involve a project team in the planning, monitoring and evaluation of the launch through to its completion.

I'm worried about failing my project team, my managers and the organisation if I don't manage to plan and monitor the project properly. I have been told by my project sponsor that under no circumstances must I allow the project to overrun or go over budget.

Top tips

Jordan must start the project off by identifying the stakeholders and negotiating the project objective and terms of reference with them. This will be based on the project proposal or aim of the project. Careful consideration must be given to planning, implementation and monitoring of the project and the use of appropriate tools and techniques is vital to make sure the project is successful. Jordan must take steps to communicate effectively with the project team members, project sponsor and other project stakeholders.

To alleviate worries and concerns, Jordan must regularly review the project schedule and milestones and the budgeted amount that has been agreed for the project. Tools, such as a variance analysis and earned value control will assist with this process.

Ask the expert	
Q	How do I make sure I don't go over budget with the launch of this product?
A	A budget can be drawn up which identifies: ■ estimated costs of the project components and resources ■ actual costs of the project components and resources ■ the differences (variance) between the estimated and actual costs. By carefully monitoring the estimated allowance for each component, steps can be taken to reduce the risk of overspend. However, should the actual amount spent be more than the estimated amount, at least you can examine why there is a difference (variance) and will be able to minimise the risk of this happening again in the future.

What your assessor is looking for

In order to demonstrate your competency within this unit, you must provide sufficient evidence to your assessor. You will need to provide a short written narrative or personal statement, explaining how you meet the assessment criteria. In addition, your assessor may need to ask questions to test your knowledge of the topics identified in this unit.

You will demonstrate your skills, knowledge and competence through the three learning outcomes in this unit. Evidence generated in this unit will also cross reference to the other units in this qualification.

Please bear in mind that there are significant cross-referencing opportunities throughout this qualification and you may have already generated some relevant work to meet certain criteria in this unit. Your assessor will provide you with the exact requirements to meet the standards of this unit. However, as a guide it is likely that for this unit you will need to be assessed through the following methods:

- An observation of relevant workplace activities or a witness testimony.
- A written report or reflective account.
- A professional discussion.
- Any relevant work products produced as evidence.

The work products for this unit could include:

- project proposal
- terms of reference

- SMART objectives
- minutes of meeting
- project implementation plan
- project schedule
- Gantt chart
- budgets
- variance analysis
- emails communicating with stakeholders and project sponsor
- force field analysis
- final project report.

Task and page reference	Assessment criteria
1 (page 263)	1.1
2 (page 268)	1.2
3 (page 271)	2.1, 3.2
4 (page 273)	3.1
5 (page 277)	3.3
6 (page 278)	3.4
7 (page 279)	4.1, 4.2, 4.3
8 (page 279)	4.4
9 (page 281)	5.1, 5.2

Glossary

Absenteeism – a member of staff away from work sometimes long term, usually on sick leave.

ACAS – Advisory, Conciliation and Arbitration Service – a statutory, independent body that offers advice to employers and employees on many workplace matters including grievances and disputes.

Accountability – being answerable for actions and decisions.

Aligned – interests that are in agreement across the different stakeholder groups.

Assertive – speaking up for yourself and stating your opinions firmly but not aggressively.

Assimilate – to take in and understand fully.

Asynchronous – where the sending and receiving of information do not happen at the same time, such as with a posted letter.

Attributes – the qualities you have, e.g. hard working.

Authoritarian – strict and controlling.

Authority – the power or right to make a decision.

Bottlenecks – areas where progress slows or stops due to one part of a process becoming overloaded.

Brainstorm – spontaneous group discussion to generate ideas and solve problems.

Budget – an estimate of expenditure (and in some cases income) over a given period of time.

Capabilities – skills and abilities.

Capacity – availability to take on further tasks.

Chain of command – the line of authority.

Chairperson – the person leading the meeting.

Change agent – someone appointed to oversee the process of change from start to finish and to work with everyone involved in the process, offering constructive advice to overcome any problems.

Characteristics – your character, e.g. good humoured.

Comfort zone – where people feel at home and like to exist in the general conducting of their daily lives, carrying out tasks in a familiar, non-threatening way.

Commission – a monetary reward, often a set percentage of the value involved, paid to an agent in a commercial transaction.

Complexity – how difficult, complicated or involved a project is.

Confidential – kept secret, or shared only among a limited number of people on a need-to-know basis.

Consequence – the effect or result of something taking place.

Constraint – something that gets in the way of what you are trying to achieve (i.e. your objective).

Constructive feedback – feedback focused on making improvements.

Consultative – discussing issues with those affected before making a decision.

Contingency – a future event or circumstance that might happen but cannot be predicted.

Contingency plan – a plan put in place in case the original plan does not work out.

Continuous professional development – when employees are given opportunity to gain new skills and knowledge through work-related training.

Continuous improvement strategy – policy to improve the overall quality of the organisational process, for example, total quality management.

COSHH – Control of Substances Hazardous to Health – regulations that apply to certain products and chemicals. COSHH data sheets will be provided by the supplier or manufacturer for substances covered by these regulations. This will detail the contents of the product and its potential to cause harm and how it should be stored.

Critical path – shows the sequence of tasks through a project that must all be conducted on time for the project to complete on time.

Culture – written or unwritten code of an organisation that influences the staff attitudes, management decision-making and style. How things are done in an organisation.

Data Protection Act (DPA) 1998 – an act that specifies how personal information should be gathered, used, stored and shared.

Delegation – assigning tasks or responsibilities to someone else to complete.

Diplomacy – negotiating and handling difficult situations.

Division – key functional area within an organisation, e.g. finance.

Downtime – time lost at work due to machinery or system failure or personnel problems.

Duty of care – a general legal duty on all individuals and organisations to avoid carelessly causing injury to other persons.

Empowered – when an individual or a team is given the authority to do something, such as make their own decisions.

Ethical – moral principles on what is right and wrong.

External factors – factors that arise from the external environment in which the business operates.

Fishbone diagram – a diagram that can be used to help with brainstorming to identify possible causes of a problem or reasons for change.

Force – an influence that results in change.

Grievance – a cause for complaint, which can be the result of a wrongdoing or a hardship suffered.

Gross misconduct – serious act by an employee, such as theft or fraud, leading to instant dismissal.

Hazard – anything that may cause harm, such as chemicals, electricity, working from ladders or a trailing cable.

Health and safety committee – a regular meeting to discuss health and safety issues attended by all relevant staff, including the director responsible for health and safety, the health and safety adviser, relevant team leaders, managers and supervisors and union representatives.

Holistic – looking at all parts of the team's efforts so that individuals work closely together to achieve the same overall goals of the team.

Housekeeping – making sure the meeting room is safe and tidy, all the equipment is working and in place and that the refreshments have been ordered.

Implementation – putting your plan into practice and making it happen.

Incentives – any items (monetary or otherwise) that motivate a particular action.

Internal factors – factors that arise from inside the business.

Job analysis – a method of determining strengths and weaknesses in a current role.

Job satisfaction – enjoying your job on a day-to-day basis.

Key stakeholders – the most influential stakeholders.

Laissez-faire – a hands-off approach, leaving actions and responsibility to others.

Lean communication methods – communication methods requiring little time or focus.

Lean system – ways of working that simplify processes and organise the working environment to minimise waste, and keep people and equipment working adequately to meet demands.

Liquidity – the ability of a business to pay its debts on time.

Master document – main original document on which all changes are recorded; the document with ultimate authority.

Mediation – help from an independent third party in reaching agreement between opposing individuals or groups.

Meeting agenda – a list of the main points to be discussed in a meeting.

Micro-managing – closely monitoring and controlling the work activities of others.

Milestones – key stages within a project.

Monopoly – when one organisation has exclusive control over the selling of products or service.

Negative variance – more than expected has been spent.

Norm – the standards set within the organisation that everybody follows.

Objective – what you want to achieve.

Objectivity – based on facts; neutral and unbiased.

Objectively – free from bias, prejudice and self-interest.

On-the-job – taking place while doing the job, i.e. not away from the workplace, for instance in college.

Open-door policy – where a manager offers support to staff by making it clear that they can be contacted at any time to discuss concerns openly.

Opportunity cost – the return which could have been received by making an alternative investment.

Originator – the person who has decided the meeting is necessary (this may be you).

Outcomes – the things that have been achieved or decided.

Participation – actively taking part.

Performance gap – a gap between the current and the required performance standards.

Performance indicators – measures that show the achievement of objectives.

Performance standards – minimum targets in the workplace that need to be met by you and your team.

Personal protective equipment (PPE) – clothing and equipment used by workers to reduce risk and ensure their safety when going about their daily tasks, for instance goggles, hard hats and harnesses. In terms of a hazard's potential to cause harm, PPE is the last line of defence.

Person specification – a document that identifies the essential and desirable skills and knowledge to complete a job role.

Piece rate – a payment system where workers are paid per unit produced or per sale made.

Policies – written statements set by managers that everybody must follow e.g. No smoking policy.

Positive variance – less than expected has been spent.

Proactive – thinking ahead and initiating events rather than waiting for things to happen.

Procedures – ways of doing something e.g. a filing procedure will outline how to store and organise documents correctly.

Process – a series of actions to achieve a desired objective.

Processed – inputs are changed or altered in some way resulting in outputs.

Project – schedule of activities that must have an agreed start date and an agreed completion date.

Project life cycle – the stages a project will go through.

Rich communication methods – in-depth communication methods requiring a high degree of focus and participation.

RIDDOR – Reporting of Injuries, Diseases and Dangerous Occurrences Regulations 1995. This act places a responsibility on organisations and employers to report all relevant accidents to the HSE within specific timeframes.

Risk – something that could happen in future to jeopardise or change your project objectives or outcome.

Rivalry – competition between individuals or teams.

Scheduling – a plan of procedures put in place to achieve a specific goal or objective.

Scientific management – a theory of management that used science to improve work efficiency.

Seconded – when a worker is moved from their post to a different department or job role for a period of time.

Self-actualisation – achieving your highest career potential.

Self-motivated – in work terms, coming into work each day in a positive frame of mind and you are able to complete the tasks by taking ownership of your job.

Skills audit – reviewing of existing skills against the skills needed to complete a task.

Social responsibility – contribution to the welfare of the community.

Stakeholders – any individual or group of individuals who has an interest in what the organisation is doing.

Staff handbook – information pack for employees containing the organisation's policies and procedures.

Staff retention – the proportion of staff who remain within an organisation. Good staff retention suggests that the business is good to work for.

Standards – rules used as a basis for comparison or judgement.

Standards of performance – the precise level of competence required to be proficient in a particular role.

Stand-up meeting – where a group of people meet to discuss issues standing up. Useful for short meetings and can often focus people's attention better than a meeting where people sit down around a table.

Strategies – Tools and processes used to achieve objectives.

Succession planning – planning to maintain consistency in a role, so that when one employee moves on, there is someone suitably qualified and with the requisite knowledge to replace them.

Synchronous – happening at the same time.

Tact – avoiding saying something offensive.

Team identity – commitment to shared values, behaviours and goals.

Terms of reference – purpose and structure of a project.

Timely – something which occurs exactly when it is needed.

Transparency – openness and honesty.

Values – standards or principles of individuals or organisations.

Variance – a difference.

Variance analysis – a statistical tool to help identify the difference between budgeted and actual figures.

Versatile – capable of carrying out a variety of different tasks.

Index